QUESTIONS IN THE HOUSE

QUESTIONS

IN

THE HOUSE

THE HISTORY OF A UNIQUE
BRITISH INSTITUTION

PATRICK
HOWARTH

THE BODLEY HEAD

First Published 1956

Made and printed in Great Britain by
WILLIAM CLOWES AND SONS LTD, LONDON AND BECCLES
for JOHN LANE THE BODLEY HEAD LTD
28, Little Russell Street, London, W.C.1

Preface

THE PEOPLE of Britain may be said to have created the greatest Parliament in the modern world, but they have failed to record much of the evidence for that belief in any form except the verbatim records of *Hansard*. Hundreds of books have been written about Parliament's procedure, its growth, and different aspects of its business. Yet one of the greatest institutions in our political life, the asking of questions in Parliament, remains virtually unanalysed, and its history almost unrecorded.

In an official exhibition on Parliament staged in 1951, in connection with the Festival of Britain, the fact that questions could be asked was shown, but no indication was given of how and when the practice arose; yet the exhibition was designed largely as a historical survey. Nearly all authoritative writers on Parliament have commented, in passing, on the importance of questions, but however thorough their researches may have been into other forms of procedure, when dealing with questions they have mostly done little more than reiterate the brief remarks of their predecessors. In the latest edition of Erskine May's *Parliamentary Practice*, the acknowledged standard work, some ten pages out of a total of more than a thousand are devoted to questions, and there are some valuable notes on procedure. But the growth of the practice is left largely to conjecture. Even Lord Campion in his masterly short survey,[1] quite the best of its kind, pays little heed to the history of the parliamentary question.

In England a parliamentary question is recorded as having been asked in 1721; the first time a question was asked in the United States House of Representatives was in 1950. That fact alone may cause surprise at our failure to recognize the growth of this unique native institution; and there is the accompanying circumstance that for 235 years the history of the parliamentary question, however it may be treated, must be a reflection of most of the absorbing and fascinating issues in British public life.

In writing this book, I have tried to extract from the pages of *Hansard* and the earlier records the story of how the custom of asking questions in Parliament began, how it developed, and where it has led. I have also had another purpose beside the telling of a story.

As an institution, the parliamentary question has never, perhaps, been more important than it is today. Our modern form of government is a bureaucracy. This has been the startling, but probably inevitable, outcome of the continual extensions of the electoral franchise. The greater the number of people who have had claims on the Government, the more demands they or their representatives have made, and the more powers Governments have been given to meet those demands. Relatively few of these powers are exercised by the Ministers who face the glare of publicity; most of them in practice rest with bureaucrats who belong to the comparatively new class of professional administrators. Government by regulation, administrative tribunals, and decisions, of which a Minister has never heard, taken in his name are common features of our lives today. More than a quarter of a century ago a Lord Chief Justice described the modern form of government in a book which he entitled *The New Despotism*, and the characteristics which he then exposed are much more widely apparent today.

Whether the new bureaucracy is really a new despotism is arguable. My own view is that the twentieth century bureaucracy is a comparatively benevolent organism, with a tendency for the benevolence to decline. That it is benevolent at all is principally due to two factors. One is a tradition of integrity, which has deeper roots in an ethical tradition. The other is the bureaucrat's knowledge that he may at any time be called upon to account for his actions.

Neither of these safeguards is adequate without the other. If the tradition of integrity is lost, there will be little more effective benevolence in bureaucracy. And if the danger of exposure becomes remote, the tradition will not be enough for any except the strongest vessels.

A number of years spent in the Civil Service has brought me to the conviction that of all the checks on a bureaucrat's actions none is so effective as the parliamentary question. In many cases the real check is provided not by the question which is asked, but by the question which may be asked. In the Ministry of Housing and Local Government, for instance, a new file is opened for every parliamentary question, and on the covers of these files are to be found the words: 'To be dealt with IMMEDIATELY and not placed with other papers.' That is symptomatic of an attitude of mind.

The general public are often poor judges of political issues. But they are quick to relish an administrative scandal, and they know when an injustice has been committed. The knowledge that at any moment unjust treatment of an individual or an administrative blunder may, by means of a parliamentary question, be exposed to public indignation and to that intolerance, which, as George Orwell pointed out, is so often characteristic of public opinion, is the supreme check on the rectitude and industry of public servants. The fact that parliamentary questions may be asked does not make the tasks of civil servants easier. It tends, inevitably, to strengthen inclinations towards excessive caution, excessive use of paper and even excessive expenditure. But these do not seem to me high prices to pay for the safeguard the system affords.

In writing this book, I have tried to show what an important part the parliamentary question has played in our history. It is my firm belief that if ever a serious attack is made on the question as an institution, our dearest liberties will be in danger. At the same time my hope is that the more that is known about the parliamentary question, the more it will be cherished as a now indispensable part of our constitution.

I owe a great deal to Mr. J. S. Watson, Fellow of Christ Church, Oxford, for the most valuable advice and guidance he gave me while I was writing this book. I am also very grateful to Sir Frederic Metcalfe, formerly Clerk of the House of Commons, for kindly reading the typescript and for his encouraging reassurances.

CONTENTS

I

The Whig Supremacy (1721–1760)

IN JANUARY 1720 Charles Spencer, third Earl of Sunderland and First Lord of the Treasury, accepted a plan which aimed at the immediate elimination of a large part of the national debt. During the first half of the eighteenth century a number of proposals for freeing the Government of debt were considered seriously, and it was only after successive wars had made their demands that a state of permanent indebtedness was accepted as inevitable. The scheme put forward in 1720 had the backing of a great trading company, which had been formed nine years earlier, and Parliament approved the company's proposals when they were first advanced.

The company was known as the South Sea Company. It was granted a monopoly of trade with the ports of South America, and the essence of the new scheme was the incorporation of public debts and annuities in the company's capital stock. The company expected to benefit from immediate and substantial rises in the value of its shares, and the trade with South America was presented to the public as a source of limitless wealth.

When the House of Lords in April 1720 debated the Bill which had been introduced to enable the South Sea Company to increase its capital stock, a few peers opposed the whole measure. Among them was Earl Cowper, who had had the distinction, following the Act of Union with Scotland, of being the first man to fill the office of Lord High Chancellor of Great Britain, and who had also achieved some notoriety by writing a treatise in favour of polygamy. Cowper declared: 'In all public business it is incumbent on those who are entrusted with the administration to take care that the same be more advantageous to the State than to private persons. . . . None but a few persons, who were in the secret and early bought shares at a low rate, will in the end be gainers by this project.'[2] To this the Earl of Sunderland replied that it was 'but reasonable that the South Sea Company should enjoy the profit procured to it by the wise management and industry of its directors.'[3]

In spite of Earl Cowper's warning, the Lords passed the Bill, and a wave of gambling in shares and of company promotion, such as had never before been known, began. Soon after the South Sea Bill was passed the company's shares rather surprisingly fell, but then a rumour was spread that Gibraltar was to be exchanged for Peru, whereby the company's trade would be secured. As a result there was a new rush of buying.

The immediate apparent success of the South Sea Company's venture became infectious, and hosts of new companies were formed to serve an astonishing variety of purposes. Among them were projects for trading in hair and for making a wheel for perpetual motion, and one company was even advertised as being 'for carrying on an undertaking of great advantage, but nobody to know what it is.'

These newly launched companies soon came to be known by the name of 'bubbles.' Certain people, of course, made money quickly, but a reckoning had to come. It came when it was realized that the biggest bubble of all was that of the South Sea Company.

By the end of August 1720 the level of the company's stocks was falling fast. At one time the level had been above 1000, but by Michaelmas Day it was down to 150. Towards the close of the year there was no further doubt that many speculators were ruined irretrievably, and in December the House of Commons ordered 'that the Directors of the South Sea Company do forthwith lay before this House an account of all their proceedings whatsoever.'[4]

A tremendous public outcry against everyone concerned with the promotion of the scheme followed. Streams of petitions poured into Parliament, the people of Buckinghamshire declaring that they had seen their country, 'which, about one year since, was in as flourishing a condition as possible, especially in respect of trade, manufactures and the public credit, reduced in little more than half that time to the lowest degree of misery and distress occasioned by the avarice, fraud and corruption of the South Sea Company.'[5]

The storm was such that the Earl of Sunderland had to resign. Sir John Aislabie, the Chancellor of the Exchequer, who, together

with the Duchess of Kendal, King George I's mistress, was considered to be among the chief villians, suffered worse, and was
expelled from the House of Commons. A new administration, faced
with the tasks of settling the affairs of the South Sea Company and
conducting a satisfactory enquiry, came into being. This new
administration was headed by Sir Robert Walpole.

One of the immediate consequences of the South Sea Bubble was
therefore to bring into power the man who, during an occupation of
office of some twenty years, enjoyed, as perhaps nobody had done
before him, many of the powers of a Prime Minister in the sense in
which that term is now understood. Walpole gradually ousted from
office those who would not accept his leadership; he presided at
Cabinet meetings; and he depended for his support on a majority in
the House of Commons. It was on these grounds that he has sometimes been considered the first holder of an office which had not yet
received legislative sanction or other formal recognition.

The bringing into power of Walpole was not the only by-product
of the South Sea Bubble of major constitutional importance. There
was another, whose significance was recognized more slowly. This
other development was the direct consequence of the criminal
activities of an absconding cashier.

A parliamentary Committee of Secrecy had been set up to investigate the South Sea affair, and it duly discovered what it described as
'a scene of iniquity and corruption, the discovery of which your
Committee conceived to be of the highest importance to the
honour of Parliaments and the security of His Majesty's Government.'[6] One of the people whom the Committee examined most
closely was, naturally enough, Robert Knight, chief cashier of the
company.

Parliament had decided to restrain the directors of the South Sea
Company from leaving the country while their affairs were being
examined. But one day a report was received from the Committee of
Secrecy that Knight 'had withdrawn himself from his habitation and
had not been heard of since by his family.'[7]

Knight's action was understandable. The Committee was to discover 'endless frauds, false entries, blanks, erasures and alterations,'[8]
and a week-end happened to intervene in the course of Knight's
examination, during which he was allowed to collect some papers
before being re-examined on a Monday morning. On the Saturday

night he boarded a ship to Calais, taking with him, as he explained
in a letter to the company, 'but little more than a sufficiency to maintain myself.'[9] He added that 'the effects left will more than answer
for all deficiencies.'[10]

Knight fled from England in January 1721, but soon afterwards
he was arrested in Brussels, and on 9th February Earl Cowper, who
by then enjoyed the prestige of one who had not been taken in by
the South Sea Company's scheme, decided to press the matter
further in the House of Lords. In the words of the *Parliamentary
History* he 'took notice to the House of the report of Mr. Knight's
being taken and in custody, which being a matter in which the
public was highly concerned, he desired those in the administration to acquaint the House whether there was any ground for that
report.'[11]

The recorded reply was that 'the Earl of Sunderland having upon
this informed the House in what manner Mr. Knight had been
apprehended and secured, a motion was made to address His
Majesty to order his ministers abroad to use the most effectual
instances to have him delivered up and sent over.'[12]

This was not easily done, because the request to have him sent to
England had to be made to the Emperor in Vienna, and the Emperor,
in spite of his authority over the Low Countries, had first to consult
the States of Brabant.

This enquiry of Earl Cowper's on the subject of Robert Knight
was the first recorded parliamentary question. It cannot be stated
with certainty that it was the first parliamentary question, in the
sense in which that term is now understood, ever to be asked.
Parliamentary records are too incomplete to warrant any such
definite assertion. But Cowper was asking the Government for
information, and he was not himself speaking to a motion. To that
extent he made a significant and, apparently, an unprecedented
departure from normal practice.

The method of asking parliamentary questions initiated by Cowper was not readily accepted as a proper parliamentary procedure.
Indeed, during the period of Whig supremacy, which extended until
the accession of King George III in 1760, little progress in the
elaboration of the method was made.

There were many reasons why parliamentary questions were
seldom asked for forty years after Cowper had made his departure

from regularity in 1721. One of the chief of these was the very fact that the procedure was a novelty.

Parliament in the eighteenth century, as in the twentieth, was governed by forms which were both elaborate and generally observed. A number of these forms have been retained with little variation down to the present day. It was, for instance, already the practice to give three readings to bills. In 1734 the Speaker stated that 'it has always been taken for granted that the Speeches from the Throne are the compositions of ministers of State.'[13] Six years later Lord Carteret gave a reminder that 'it is well known that His Majesty's name ought never to be brought into any of our debates;'[14] and the custom of addressing the Speaker in the House of Commons, and of referring to any other Member by a description and not by a name, was already an accepted convention.

One of the most important of the parliamentary rules then in force was that it was normally permissible only to speak to a motion —or, as the confusing but commonly accepted terminology had it, to 'speak to a question.' In 1754 William Murray, at that time the Attorney-General and later, as Lord Mansfield, to become Lord Chief Justice and perhaps the greatest authority of his time on the laws and constitution of the country, made a speech on procedure in the House of Commons for the benefit of new members. 'It is,' he said, 'and always has been the rule of Parliament that no gentleman should rise up to speak unless there be a proper question before the House. When a gentleman makes a motion to the House, he is to be sure to explain the meaning and the intention of the motion he has to make.' Any other manner of speaking would, Murray declared, be 'taking up the time of the House to no manner of purpose.'[15]

In the face of a rule of this nature in a Parliament strongly governed by forms the precedent of a single question unrelated to a motion asked in the House of Lords, which then as always was less rigid than the Commons in its adherence to forms, would not in itself have been enough to justify a new kind of procedure. Parliamentary questions could be admitted only when the need for them was clearly felt, and for many years Members of Parliament found other forms of procedure adequate for their purposes.

The traditional method of airing grievances was the presentation of petitions. Two famous resolutions of the seventeenth century had

established the indisputable right of every commoner in England to
present a petition to the House of Commons, and of the House to
determine how far such petitions were fit to be received. The
petitioning of Parliament in its judicial, as opposed to its legislative,
capacity is, as a practice, almost as old as Parliament itself, and the
eighteenth-century Parliaments spent much of their time considering petitions concerned with the troubles of private individuals. As
late as the year 1775 the Archbishop of Canterbury was one of the
principal speakers in the House of Lords in the hearing of an appeal
following a tithe dispute between a man named Charles Chaplin
and one of his neighbours, and it was not until the next century
that the hearing of appeals came to be left exclusively to the law
lords.

The Commons too not only debated the subjects of petitions, but
frequently heard petitioners at the Bar of the House. In many cases
petitioners were represented at the Bar by counsel, and in 1738 the
Speaker had to point out that the House could not hear both the
petitioner and his counsel, but only one of the two. Speeches made
at the Bar were frequently of great length, and on one occasion a
lawyer named Glover, acting as counsel for a group of petitioning
West Indian planters, opened his peroration with the words: 'I
begin with investigating the general system of the British
Empire.'[16]

Another liberty, now no longer enjoyed, which the lack of congestion of parliamentary business permitted, was the right of any
Member to make a motion when he chose and without notice. This
commonly served the purpose for which many questions today are
designed, for the normal method of demanding information, as
opposed to airing a grievance, in the first half of the eighteenth
century was to move for papers on a certain subject. The motion for
papers permitted, as it still does today in the House of Lords, a
general debate on the subject raised.

Before papers demanded could be produced it was, of course,
necessary for the motion to be carried, and the practice grew up in
the eighteenth century on the part of successive Governments of
opposing motions of this nature. In 1740 a motion for papers
revealing the instructions given to Admiral Vernon in the course of
the war with Spain was defeated in the House of Lords, and a protest
was thereupon entered in the Journals by some dissident peers, who

asserted: 'We do not find any negative put upon motions for instructions before the year 1721.'[17]

The practice of moving for papers, and carrying the motion to a division, had therefore both advantages and disadvantages, as was shown during a debate in the Commons in 1739. A motion had been made for the production of papers on relations with Spain, which at the time were strained, but which had not yet led to war. Henry Pelham opposed the motion. A petition to the King, he said, for the production of papers was advisable when the actions of the administration were considered defective, but when this was not so, any such petition would suggest that Parliament was 'resolved to fish for faults.'[18] This somewhat specious argument was attacked by Sir William Wyndham, one of the more outspoken Jacobite sympathizers, who declared that there could be no encroachment on the Royal Prerogative in a motion for papers, for in any case it would be the conduct, not of the King, but of his ministers which Parliament would examine. He went on to express the hope that 'the House will never know any difficulty on this head.'[19]

The irregularity of using the King's name, and the action of the Government in justifying a refusal of information on the grounds that there might be an implied attack on the royal person, were then scathingly commented on by Sir William Pulteney, the future Earl of Bath, who declared: 'I hope we shall continue to follow the ancient maxim of this House, which has always been to call for such papers as we think may contribute towards giving us a full and perfect knowledge of the affair we are to enquire into.'[20]

Apart from the procedural reasons, there were also reasons of a political or a constitutional nature why the custom of asking parliamentary questions developed slowly.

The range of matters for which the Government could be held responsible and on which it could be challenged in Parliament was much less extensive than in all succeeding periods of our history. Local government was relatively more important than it is in England today and than it was in other comparable European countries at the time. The Crown too had enormous powers, both through the financial control afforded by the Civil List and in its exercise of many functions which were free of detailed control by Parliament. Even the elder Pitt, the greatest popular champion of his time, opposed a suggestion that certain Army officers should be examined at the Bar of the House of Commons. The task of Parliament, he insisted, was to consider the number of forces necessary and to vote money accordingly; the conduct of the Army was the business of the King.

Much of the business of the nation indeed lay outside the scope of effective parliamentary enquiry, and there was no systematically organized Civil Service which could supply information on demand, and whose actions could have been subject to perpetual scrutiny. In the latter half of the eighteenth century demands came to be made for sweeping administrative reforms, and then the inadequacy of the Civil Service on which earlier Governments had had to depend was publicly exposed.

In 1780 Burke could declare that 'neither the present nor any other First Lord of the Treasury has ever been able to make a survey, or even a tolerable guess, of the expenses of Government of any one year.' About the same time the Commissioners on Public Accounts found it necessary to make such recommendations as that 'every office should have a useful duty annexed to it,' and that 'every officer should execute himself the duty of his office.' The need for this last recommendation was illustrated by the practice of even the charwomen in public offices of appointing others to carry out their duties while they themselves drew the pay.

Astonishingly little information on the life of the country was at the disposal of Governments in the first half of the eighteenth century, and public opinion was slow to demand that the extent of this information should be increased. In 1753 Thomas Potter, who had been secretary to Frederick, Prince of Wales, introduced a Bill to provide for the taking of a census of the people, and the outcry against this demand for statistics was violent. On the first reading of the Bill, William Thornton declared: 'I did not believe that there was any set of men, or indeed any individual of the human species, so presumptuous and so abandoned as to make the proposal we have just heard.' Later he added: 'We are to entrust petty tyrants with the power of oppression in confidence that this power shall not be executed; to subject every house to a search; to register every name, age, sex and state upon oath; record the pox as a national distemper; and spend annually £50,000 of the public money—for what? To decide a wager at White's.'[21] The Bill was defeated in the

House of Lords, and the institution of a census was postponed for nearly half a century.

The conservatism of procedure, the existence of alternative methods of airing grievances, Parliament's lack of control over many aspects of administration, and the knowledge that the Government had not the means to provide much in the way of information, all served to check the growth of the parliamentary question. But these causes would probably not have been enough in themselves to prevent its development in the first half of the eighteenth century, had it not been for two other important factors. These were the relative calm of the political scene and the lack of publicity given to proceedings in Parliament. Both factors ceased to prevail soon after the accession of King George III.

To describe the political scene between 1721 and the accession of King George III as calm is to use a relative term. In 1745 the whole system of government came near to being overthrown, when Prince Charles Edward was able to hold court in Edinburgh, and when his rebel army exacted tribute from Manchester and reached Derby. Britain was also during these forty years engaged in two lengthy world wars, and political feeling at times rose to such a pitch that when Walpole eventually fell from power there was a strong movement in favour of impeaching him.

But between 1721 and 1760 there was no great party struggle. One effect of the 1715 rebellion had been to spread the belief that the Tories could not form a loyal opposition, and that the only people who could provide a respectable alternative Government to those of Walpole and the Pelhams were other Whigs. Walpole had vociferous opponents in Parliament, but Henry Pelham managed the House of Commons with singularly little difficulty, and the greatest period of the elder Pitt's power was as a wartime Minister with unusual popular support. The great party struggle of the eighteenth century, that between the Ministers chosen by the King and a variety of groups of Whigs, did not occur until some years after King George III had come to the throne.

Until 1770, too, parliamentary proceedings had little publicity value. Before that time it was a tradition of long standing that the public had no right to know what went on in Parliament. Secrecy was rarely maintained, and Queen Elizabeth, for instance, had had occasion to complain that she heard 'how parliament matters was the common table-talk at ordinaries, which was a thing against the dignity of the House.' Already in her day Members of Parliament copied out their speeches and distributed them as examples of oratory, and this practice was continued for some centuries. In the eighteenth century accounts of parliamentary proceedings, often with the use of fictitious names, even appeared regularly in the newspapers. These reports were by no means accurate transcripts, as was shown by Dr. Johnson's famous explanation of how he carried out the duties of a parliamentary reporter. 'Sir,' he declared, 'I wrote it in Exeter Street. I never had been in the gallery of the House of Commons but once. Cave had interest with the door-keepers. He, and the persons employed under him, gained admit-tance; they brought away the subject of discussion, the names of the speakers, the side they took, and the order in which they rose, together with notes of the arguments advanced in the course of the debate. The whole was afterwards communicated to me, and I com-posed the speeches in the form which they now have in the parlia-mentary debates . . . I took care to see that the Whig dogs should not have the best of it.'

Nevertheless, publication of the proceedings of Parliament still constituted a breach of privilege, and it was liable at times to lead to severe punishments until the personal popularity and courage of John Wilkes and Lord Mayor Crosby showed that after 1770 such punishments could no longer be successfully inflicted.

In the nineteenth century a belief grew up that the eighteenth-century Parliaments were the products of little else but corruption, and that they were grotesquely unrepresentative of the people whose interests they were supposed to maintain. Macaulay declared that after the revolution of 1688 Parliament revealed some of the worst symptoms of irresponsible autocracy, and Disraeli wrote in *Sybil* of M.P.s 'who were appointed by an extremely limited and exclusive class, who had no responsibility to the country, who debated and voted in secret, and who were regularly paid by the small knot of great families that by this machinery had secured the permanent possession of the King's Treasury.' From this state of affairs he drew the conclusion that 'Whiggery was putrescent in the nostrils of the nation.'

On the strength of these descriptions it might be argued that in addition to the causes already listed, one reason why the practice of asking questions in Parliament developed slowly was that Members were not concerned with representing the interests of the constituencies which returned them. But such an argument does not stand up to serious scrutiny, for the Disraeli-Macaulay picture is really little better than a caricature. Perhaps the most remarkable feature of the eighteenth-century Parliament was that it succeeded in being at the same time both a representative and a controlling body. That was one of the main reasons why the British constitution made so deep an impression on critics such as Voltaire and Montesquieu, and why in later times the British constitutional achievement served as a model to so many other nations.

The eighteenth-century House of Commons was certainly elected through an extraordinarily complicated system of franchise, the variations being greatest in the boroughs. Some boroughs returned their M.P.s through the votes of a handful of members of the governing body of the borough. In others, the so-called potwalloper boroughs, a vote was relatively easily come by, since the qualification was that a man should be in a position to boil his own pot or, in other words, not be dependent on someone else for his meals. Constituencies also bore little evident relation to population, and the disparity became more and more preposterous as the industrial towns of the north and midlands grew in size. Cornwall, for instance, was notoriously full of rotten boroughs, and the Scottish Members for many years were regarded as little more than hirelings of the Crown.

Bribery and personal influence also played a large part in the return of Members, as they were bound to do before the secret ballot was adopted. The Members themselves, too, though they might be thought to represent the common people, could not belong to them, for entry to Parliament was restricted to the ruling classes. The law required that Members for counties must derive an income from land of at least £600 a year, and Members for boroughs an income from land of at least £300, exceptions to the general rules being made in the cases of Scottish and University Members. These property qualifications, which were often met fictitiously, were designed to ensure independence and freedom from corruption. The House of Lords, too, enjoyed one of its periods of exceptional power during most of the eighteenth century. It was certainly less powerful than the Commons, for the Commons retained control of finance, but the Lords could still reject Bills passed by the Commons with impunity.

In short, the eighteenth-century Parliaments were not, and were never intended to be, institutions of a democracy. But it is equally true that Members regarded themselves as representatives of the people, and were considered as such not only by their electors but by many of the disfranchised. Public opinion played a large part in deciding both elections and policies, and the popular form of the Government was even held to influence the nature of the people, as contemporary generalizations about the national character showed. In a debate in the Commons in 1745 on the powers of the aldermen of the City of London, Sir William Yonge declared: 'Among foreigners we have long had the character of being a turbulent, inconstant and unsteady people.' The chief cause, he argued, was 'the nature of our Government, for under a popular Government the people will always be turbulent, inconstant and unsteady.' He went on to point the contrasts with the calm which prevailed in Venice under the oligarchic rule of the Council of Ten, and the anarchy of Poland, a country enjoying the power of the individual veto, where 'there has never been any steadiness in their councils, order in their assemblies, or tranquillity among the people.'[22]

When Burke in 1774 declared that Members of Parliament could not receive mandates or authoritative instructions from their constituents, he was not enunciating a truism, but arguing what was considered a debatable proposition. Earlier in the eighteenth century Members commonly spoke, when presenting petitions, of the instructions they had received from their constituents, and the old tradition that a Member was the servant of the body of electors who returned him had not died out, although the custom of paying such servants had come to an end in the seventeenth century. Pepys had been among those who regretted this change, for he noted in 1668 that 'all concluded that the bane of the Parliament hath been the leaving off the old custom of the places allowing wages to those that served them in Parliament, by which they chose men that understood their business and would attend it.'

Not only did eighteenth-century Members often feel they had to carry out instructions; many also took considerable trouble at

election times to woo their constituents. A ballad from the year 1727
contains the lines:

'Away to the tavern they quickly retire,
The ploughman "hail-fellow-well-met" with the squire
... But as soon as the day of election is over,
His woeful mistake he begins to discover;
The squire is a Member—the rustic who chose him
Is now quite neglected—he no longer knows him.'

The ballad was written to show the fickleness of Members of Parliament. It indicates equally clearly that the good-will even of plough-
men was sought at election times.

The most telling proof that Parliament had, by its very nature, to
conform to the wishes of the people lies in the outcome of the chief
contentious political issues which occurred before the accession of
King George III. In the 1730s there was a tremendous outcry
against Walpole's proposal to extend the excise duties to beer and
tobacco. Even though it was expected that the duties to be levied
would lead to the elimination of the land tax, popular pressure was
such that Walpole's Bill had to be withdrawn after its second reading.
Twenty years later the voice of the people gained an even more
striking triumph, when an Act which had received the Royal Assent
the year before, and which allowed Jews to petition for naturaliza-
tion without denying their religion, actually had to be repealed
because of popular clamour. In 1739 too Britain was drawn into a
war with Spain which the public demanded, but which Walpole, as
Prime Minister, wanted to avoid; and public opinion was perhaps
the most important factor in giving Britain in the person of the
elder Pitt one of her two greatest wartime Prime Ministers.

Whether the popular view on all these issues was the right one is
questionable. Indeed, except for the choice of Pitt, where the people
were demanding a man not a measure, it is much easier in every
case to argue that the public were wrong. What is certain is that the
Parliaments in the reigns of the first two Hanoverian Kings had to
respond to and reflect public opinion.

In doing so they did evolve, to a limited extent, the practice of
putting questions to the Government and demanding, in one form
or another, satisfactory answers. There were many reasons why the
method of the parliamentary question developed slowly in the first

seventy years of the eighteenth century. The main reason why it developed at all was probably the very fact that Parliament was a representative, outspoken and, in more than one sense of the word, responsible body.

After the first recorded question had been asked in 1721, Members of Parliament continued to demand information from successive Governments on many of the most important political issues of the times. But they did so by a variety of methods, and the success they attained also varied.

In 1722 a lawyer of the name of Christopher Layer was tried for treason. Layer was a Jacobite, who believed he would become Lord Chancellor after a Stuart restoration, but he made the mistake of leaving highly compromising papers with a brothel-keeper. His conspiracy involved among others the learned Bishop of Rochester, the Duke of Norfolk, and a gang of roughs whose tasks included the seizure of the Tower of London, the Bank of England, and the Royal Exchange. Early in the next year the Earl of Anglesea stated in the House of Lords that it was 'somewhat strange that no particulars relating to the said conspiracy have yet been communicated to this House.'[23] He therefore moved that an account of Layer's trial should be published after being first perused by King's Counsel. Lord Carteret, the Secretary of State, pointed out that the motion was unnecessary, as an account of the trial would certainly be published.

On this occasion the information demanded was made public, but other enquiries pursued by Members were less fruitful. In 1726 a motion made by William Pulteney for the appointment of a committee to provide information on public debts was defeated after Walpole had declared that such an enquiry would be 'unseasonable and preposterous.'[24]

The next year too a motion for an address to the King praying that he would lay before the House documents concerning Spanish designs on Gibraltar was defeated, Walpole enunciating the doctrine that the private letters of princes were 'almost as sacred as their very persons.'[25] In 1727 too the Commons succeeded in carrying a motion asking for details of the expenditure of a sum of £125,000. But after the lapse of a week Sir Paul Methuen, the man whom Horace Walpole described as 'dull, formal, romantic braggadoccio,' informed the House that he had been commanded by the King to state that 'the sum of money mentioned . . . has been issued and disbursed, pursuant to the power given to His Majesty by Parliament, for necessary services and engagements of the utmost importance to the trade and navigation of this kingdom and the tranquillity of Europe, which require the greatest secrecy; and therefore a particular and distinct account of the distribution of it cannot be given without manifest prejudice to the public.'[26] A motion expressing dissatisfaction with this somewhat bleak answer was defeated.

On each of these occasions the amount of information which Parliament succeeded in extracting by means of regular motions was limited, but a rather different result followed when the method of asking a direct question was once again resorted to in 1739.

In January of that year the Duke of Newcastle laid before the House of Lords a copy of a convention which had been concluded between Great Britain and Spain. Some three weeks later Lord Carteret, who was then in opposition to the Government, asked whether there were any supplementary papers which had emanated from the Spanish side, adding: 'I dare say the noble Duke, and those who have had the honour to be in the secret of this transaction, will be extremely glad to have this opportunity of vindicating their own characters by letting this House and all the world see that they have entered into no scandalous, no clandestine measures.' The answer came from the Earl of Cholmondeley, who said: 'I must beg leave to put your Lordships and the noble Lord in mind that the forms of this House are not to be dispensed with on this or any other occasion. . . . I think the noble Lord's question extremely improper to be answered here.'

He also suggested that Carteret was acting in bad faith, since he must have got his information from a Privy Councillor sworn to secrecy. As a further reason for not laying all the relevant papers before the House, he pleaded the extra work which the administrative machine would have to perform. The papers, he said, 'have been so many that the very copying them must employ all the clerks in the Secretaries' office for some days, if not weeks.'

Carteret was not altogether satisfied. He was, he said, 'much for keeping to our forms,' but added: 'I am far from thinking them equally essential on all occasions. . . . I am very sensible, my Lords, that we have no right to require the noble Duke to give a full and explicit answer to this, but if His Grace does, it will save the House a great deal of time.' At this point the Duke of Newcastle, who was a brilliant political organizer but a much less skilful parliamentarian, interposed. 'The noble Lord who spoke last,' he said, 'has put it upon me to answer a question, which I conceive the noble Lord, as a Member of this House, has no right to ask, and I, as a Minister, am under no obligation to answer.'

This was a clear enunciation of the rules of the House, which the question asked by Earl Cowper eighteen years earlier had failed to modify. But in spite of his views on procedure, Newcastle went on to give an answer of a kind. 'The papers,' he said, 'now laid before you are the only papers that have been subscribed by our Ministers at the Court of Spain relating to the conclusion of the convention . . . I hope this answer will be satisfactory to the House.'[27]

By implication Carteret's right to ask a question had been admitted, and he was quick to take advantage of the concession by reverting to his original point. Were there, he asked, any papers 'signed on the part of Spain and transmitted to our Court'? Newcastle was drawn, as Carteret had evidently hoped he would be. He admitted that a paper had been given to the British Ministers by the Spanish negotiators. This, he said, referred to the private affairs of the South Sea Company.

A fortnight later he laid a copy of the paper before the House of Lords. The paper did indeed refer to the private affairs of the South Sea Company, but it also served to inform the Lords that Spanish claims were by no means satisfied by the convention signed in January.

The points of dispute between Britain and Spain at the time were numerous. One of them was Gibraltar. Another was the monopoly of the slave trade with the Spanish West Indies enjoyed by the South Sea Company, a monopoly rendered possible by the Spaniards' lack of access to the raw materials of the slave trade. A third was the right given to the South Sea Company under the Treaty of Utrecht to send one ship a year to the great trade fairs at Vera Cruz, in Mexico, and Cartagena, a right which was consistently either abused on one side or disallowed on the other. A fourth was the manner in which the Spaniards carried out their search of other British ships. This amounted in many cases to little more than piracy, and even led to the famous incident in which Captain Jenkins had his ear cut off.

The 1739 convention offered no real solution of these differences, and the paper which was brought to the attention of Parliament by Carteret's questioning contained a declaration that unless the South Sea Company agreed to pay within a short time £68,000, which was said to be owing for duties payable on negroes, the King of Spain reserved the right to suspend the slave trade monopoly and to withdraw from the terms of the convention. This sum of £68,000 would have served substantially to reduce another sum of £95,000, which the Spaniards had agreed in one of the clauses of the convention to pay.

Such satisfaction as the convention had given in English political circles was largely destroyed by the sudden revelation of the Spanish attitude to it afforded by the paper Newcastle had laid before Parliament. In March 1739 a spirited debate took place in the Lords on a motion for an address approving the terms of the convention. The motion was carried by only 13 votes, the Prince of Wales voting with the minority. A protest was then entered in the Journals, in which the Spanish claim for £68,000 was stigmatized as 'a dishonourable conclusion, hurtful to public credit.'[28] A week later a similar motion for an address was barely carried in the Commons, although the seconder of the motion had pointed out, rightly enough, that 'the necessary consequence of our not agreeing to it would be an immediate war.'[29]

In May Newcastle informed the Lords that Spain had not paid the sum of £95,000, and shortly afterwards Carteret initiated a further debate, in which he declared: 'We must, therefore, my Lords, now have recourse to arms, and I believe I need not suggest that the sea is the only element where our quarrel can be decided, as it is the element on which it began.'[30]

Four months later Britain declared war. Bells were pealed to greet its outbreak; the Prince of Wales joined in a procession through London, stopping at the Rose Tavern at Temple Bar to drink to success; Walpole's pleas for peace were disregarded; and the dispute which had begun as the War of Jenkins's Ear developed into a lengthy world war of a most inconclusive nature. Its conduct was not confined to the 'element on which it began,' the sea, a high proportion of the major battles being fought in Central Europe.

Britain's continental entanglements provided the subject of another important question, which was asked in 1744, this time in the course of a debate on a motion in the House of Commons. The subject of the debate was the estimate for the maintenance of 16,000 Hanoverian troops at British expense and largely for the benefit of Maria Theresa, Queen of Hungary. Horatio Walpole, Sir Robert's younger brother and the uncle of the diarist, who for a number of years had been simultaneously a Member of Parliament and British Ambassador in Paris, explained that the Queen had had a number of recent successes in the country now called Czechoslovakia. Thereupon Sir John Strange, a former Solicitor-General, rose and said:

'Sir, there is one question very material in this debate, which I should be glad to have answered and fully explained before I give my vote upon the motion now under our consideration, and as no gentleman is more capable than the hon. gentleman that spoke last, I hope he will rise again and give us his opinion. The question I mean is whether the alliance with the Queen of Hungary is an offensive or only a defensive alliance.'[31]

The method adopted by Strange was not, of course, that of asking a parliamentary question in the sense in which the term is now understood, and there is no record that he received a direct answer. But there is evidence that his curiosity must have been satisfied by some means.

Rather more than a year later the Commons debated in Committee of Supply a resolution for a direct grant to the Queen of Hungary of £500,000. This sum was intended to compensate her for the fact that she had dismissed from her service the Hanoverian troops paid by Britain. Two Members of Parliament, Thomas Carew and Sir Thomas Winnington, asked during the debate for assurances on the nature of the alliance with the Queen, and Strange stated emphatically: 'We are obliged to assist her in the defence of her dominions and no further.'[32] This unequivocal statement was not contradicted.

From the day on which war had been declared against Spain in 1739 Britain continued in a state of warfare for nearly a quarter of a century, with the exception of a comparatively brief interlude which followed the inconclusive Peace of Aix-la-Chapelle in 1748. Although the impact of war on the conduct of parliamentary business was barely comparable with that which it was to have in the twentieth century, the constant preoccupation with hostilities certainly had the effect of limiting the amount of information which Members demanded of Governments, and which Governments were prepared to supply.

In 1749, for instance, a motion was made for papers relating to a treaty which had been concluded six years earlier, and during the debate Henry Pelham declared: 'A parliamentary enquiry, Sir, must always be attended with many and great inconveniences. In the first place, it must always raise a ferment in the nation, and when it relates to foreign affairs, it generally disobliges some of our allies. . . . In the next place, it possesses the thoughts of our Ministers so much, as every enquiry must relate to some part of their conduct, that they have no time to mind anything else.'

Horatio Walpole came to his support and added: 'All parliamentary enquiries into the conduct of Ministers which I have either heard or read of have either produced no effect or a very bad one.'[33] Sir John Strange, who was less easily satisfied than most Members, cited rather aptly the enquiry into the affairs of the South Sea Company to refute this contention. Even so the motion for papers was defeated.

Records of parliamentary proceedings during the last years of the reign of King George II and the first years of those of his grandson are scantier than for any other period of modern history. The enforcement of the laws against the publication of debates and the rigid application in certain sessions, as for instance in 1768, of the Standing Order of the House of Commons for the exclusion of strangers, meant that by far the greater part of what was actually said in Parliament remains unrecorded.

The available evidence, however, suggests that it was not until the parliamentary struggle between those who were prepared to do King George III's bidding and those who were not reached its greatest intensity that any further significant developments in the methods of asking questions in Parliament occurred. When this struggle reached its height, a number of the factors which had served to restrict the asking of questions ceased to operate any longer.

II

The Great Parliamentary Struggle (1760–1784)

THE great parliamentary struggle which took place over the period of nearly a quarter of a century between the accession of King George III in 1760 and the choice, for the first time, of the younger Pitt as Prime Minister was, in its most simplified form, a contest between the King and the Opposition. When Charles James Fox described the administration of Lord North as 'His Majesty's Ministers supported by the influence of the Crown against all Britain,' he was greatly overstating his case. The outstanding achievement of King George III was to revive the Tory party and to give it a new focus of loyalty and a new familiarity with power. In this respect he may be compared with Disraeli in the nineteenth century and Stanley Baldwin in the twentieth.

It was not true, as Barré, Savile, and others insisted, that the parliamentary struggle was simply between corruption and the will of the people. The voice of Dr. Johnson thundering through time is clear enough proof that a sincere, intelligent, and respected man could also be a convinced Tory. But one effect of King George's policy, and of his personal limitations, was to intensify the vehemence of parliamentary opposition.

In opposition the Whigs, notably Burke, evolved new political theories. They also found a steady supply of major issues on which to attack the Government, one of these being the liberty of the press, which included, of course, the liberty to make parliamentary proceedings known to the public. For these reasons, between 1763, the year in which John Wilkes published his famous number 45 of the *North Briton*, and 1784, the year in which the younger Pitt became Prime Minister, great changes occurred in the practice of questioning the Government in Parliament.

The Whigs in opposition were far from united. They consisted of a number of separate groups, the most effective of which was probably that led by the Marquis of Rockingham, whose secretary was Edmund Burke. There were also a number of political figures outstanding for their individual achievements rather than the strength of their party allegiance. The greatest of these was the elder Pitt, still a powerful force for a number of years after the accession of King George III and after his own elevation to the peerage as the Earl of Chatham, although tending to become more and more crippled with gout, and presenting a grotesque appearance as he hobbled into the House of Lords wrapped in bandages.

A figure who was to become even more disturbing to King George's ambitions to exercise the powers of a patriot King entered Parliament when Charles James Fox was returned as Member for Midhurst at the age of nineteen. A Whig magnate of the wenching, horse-racing kind in the Duke of Grafton, a relatively austere man of learning in the Earl of Shelburne, and the brilliant radical, John Wilkes, helped to make up the diversity of the Opposition, a diversity which only occasionally became a community of interests.

In comparison with figures such as these the King's supporters were a poor lot. For a few years the King relied on the Earl of Bute, who had barely any qualification for office other than the King's esteem. Bute was a Scotsman, and following him came a crowd of Scots, who were wholeheartedly King's men, and who began to gain as rewards profitable posts concerned with Indian and colonial administration, which were dispensed by the Lord Advocate. It was a Scottish M.P. who later in the century declared: 'The Government ought always to select a tall man to fill the office of Lord Advocate. We Scotch Members always vote with the Lord Advocate, and we therefore require to see him in a division. Now I can see Mr. Pitt, and I can see Mr. Addington, but I cannot see the Lord Advocate.' The venality and unpopularity of these Scottish politicians was such that they provided Wilkes with a ready-made title for his anti-Government periodical, and induced even the Tory Dr. Johnson to decide, on rather flimsy evidence, that he could not abide their race.

In addition to the Scotsmen there were Charles Jenkinson, whom Horace Walpole described as 'the sole confidant of the King'; the Earl of Sandwich, who, the King—perhaps unkindly—declared, was 'no use in his department'; and Lord George Germaine, who in the reign of the last King had suffered a peculiarly humiliating punishment for disgraceful conduct on the battlefield. Almost the only politician of distinction among the King's regular servants was Lord North, a man of both charm and wit, whom it must have been difficult not to like. North was a brilliant parliamentary debater, but he was also a calamitously unsuccessful statesman, chiefly because he frequently disbelieved in the policies which he remained in office to execute.

In the parliamentary struggle over a number of years the articulate forces consisted largely of Lord North on one side and many of the outstanding minds of the age on the other. Intellectually it was not an equal contest, but the weight of numbers was with Lord North, and perhaps for that reason a new violence came into parliamentary language, and the Opposition carried out the task of questioning what the Government did with a new determination.

In a debate which took place in 1770, for instance, Burke rose as soon as North had sat down, and said: 'The noble Lord who spoke last, after extending his right leg a full yard from his left, rolling his flaming eyes, and moving his ponderous frame, has at length opened his mouth.'[1] In the same debate Fox declared that the licence in the language used that day indicated that 'the old decent freedom of debate is at an end.'

On another occasion in the House of Commons Colonel Luttrell described Wilkes as 'an infernal parricide,' and in April 1780 Lord George Gordon, who was, it is true, somewhat mentally deranged, declared that the Ministers of the Crown wanted to 'make pimps and panders of the Members, to convert the Speaker into an old bawd, and perhaps, for aught I know, to introduce the whore of Babylon.'[2]

This vigour of parliamentary language is almost without parallel in earlier reports of debates. How far this was due to the greater accuracy in reporting which occurred after 1770 is questionable. The unfailing dignity of the utterances of the age of Sir Robert Walpole, as they have reached us, may well be suspect, especially when one recalls Walpole's admission to Boswell that 'he always talked bawdy at table, for in that all could join'; or the judgment on Walpole and his sexual exploits passed by his nineteenth-century biographer, John Morley: 'He boasted of his successes with a coarseness that would now cause instant expulsion from the mess of any garrison or any circuit in Great Britain.'

But there is no doubt that tempers ran much higher and Governments were attacked with much greater energy in the Parliaments of King George III than in those of his predecessors. By March 1780 matters had reached such a point that Sir James Lowther had to call attention to the growing practice of settling parliamentary disputes by duels, and to point out that if it increased, 'Parliament would resemble a Polish diet.'[3]

This emotional violence reached its greatest heights in the conflicts of which Wilkes was the centre. Burke declared that the climate of the House of Commons changed as soon as the name of Wilkes was mentioned. This was not surprising, for Wilkes brought to a head more than one major issue of parliamentary liberty, and Parliament has at all times shown its greatest vigour in the defence of its own rights.

The main facts of Wilkes's struggle are well known. In number 45 of the *North Briton* he described passages in the Speech from the Throne in 1763 as untrue. Parliament thereupon declared number 45 'a false, scandalous and seditious libel.' After having him arrested, in spite of his privilege as a Member of Parliament, on a general warrant, an action which was found to be illegal, the Government trumped up a charge against him on the grounds of an obscene poem, which he had not even had printed. 'Wilkes and Liberty' became the most popular political cry of the day, and the numerals '45' were forcibly implanted in the most surprising places, including the soles of the Austrian Ambassador's shoes. After spending some years in Paris, Wilkes returned to England, and from 1768 onwards the county of Middlesex, which enjoyed a wide franchise, returned him with regularity to a Parliament which, as long as it could manage to do so, voted him not elected.

Wilkes's greatest triumph occurred in 1771, when the Government ordered the arrest of a man of the name of Miller, who had committed the offence of printing reports of parliamentary debates, but who had the good fortune to live east of Temple Bar. An officer sent by the Speaker of the House of Commons tried to arrest Miller, who retaliated by giving the Speaker's officer in charge for assault. The Speaker's officer duly appeared before a bench on which sat the Lord Mayor Crosby and Aldermen Oliver and Wilkes.

3

Parliament made one last attempt to assert what were claimed to be its rights: Crosby and Oliver were sentenced to six weeks in the Tower, but Wilkes was felt to be too dangerous a man to meddle with again. The immediate consequences of this were that Miller escaped with impunity, and the publication of parliamentary debates was tacitly accepted as inevitable. The further consequences were of the greatest importance to all forms of parliamentary procedure.

Once Wilkes had gained his victory, the attitude of Parliament towards the subject of publicity altered appreciably. The House of Lords was the first to admit strangers freely, but references to the presence of strangers during debates in the Commons became relatively frequent in the 1770s. In 1777 North actually expressed the hope that strangers in the gallery would not misunderstand facts which had been mentioned in a debate on Spain; and in the same year Temple Luttrell, M.P. for Milborne Port in Somerset, put forward a proposal that every M.P. should be allowed to introduce before 4 p.m. one person to the gallery below the Bar, after first submitting the name of his guest to the Speaker. Fox and Wilkes spoke in support of the motion, but it was defeated, the principal argument advanced against it being that expressed by a Member named Rigby, who declared: 'What good can result from strangers being in the gallery? Only to print speeches in newspapers of all sorts.'[4]

Yet three years later the Speaker, when called upon to enforce the Standing Order for the removal of strangers, said he had not acted earlier, because he had taken it to be 'the sense of the House that they should be admitted.'[5] A year after this Horace Walpole expressed his decision not to record any more parliamentary debates in his journal, because they could now be read freely in a variety of publications. Already Parliament was conducting its business with the realization that what was debated and asked and answered would reach a wide public.

Two changes of major importance in the development of the parliamentary question therefore occurred some time after 1760. One was that parliamentary proceedings became public knowledge. The other was that a new intensity came into the conflict between the Government and the Opposition.

Many issues were found on which Lord North's administration could be attacked with energy, one of the most frequently recurring being its reluctance to provide information. In 1772, for instance, after North had moved the appointment of a secret Commons committee to enquire into the state of the East India Company, a Member named Hussey declared: 'It has been a uniform complaint against Ministers that they at all times labour as much as possible to keep concealed matters of national concern from the public eye.'[6] Five years later, during a debate on a motion advocating the ending of hostilities in America, the Duke of Grafton said of the Government: 'If called upon in Parliament for information which every Member in either House has a right to expect, they either give no reply or evade the question.'[7]

The methods by which the Opposition tried to break down this barrier of silence continued to be varied and extemporized. The parliamentary question was one of them, but a clear procedural pattern was evolved only slowly, and a number of years were still to pass before a Speaker's ruling on the subject of questioning Ministers was made.

In January 1769, for instance, Sir George Savile, one of the more outspoken of Lord North's critics, presented a petition from Boston, Massachusetts. In this the hope was expressed that the House of Commons would not agree to a series of resolutions which had been passed by the House of Lords in December 1768.

One of the Lords' resolutions, to which the Whigs took exception, had declared the proceedings of the House of Representatives in Boston 'illegal, unconstitutional and derogatory of the Crown and Parliament of Great Britain.'[8] This declaration had been made on the grounds that the Boston Assembly had questioned the authority of the King to make, with the advice and consent of Parliament, laws to 'bind the colonies and people of America, subjects of the Crown of Great Britain, in all cases whatsoever.'[9]

In the Commons debate which followed the presentation of the petition, Thomas Pownall, who had himself been Governor of Massachusetts, insisted that the resolution of the House of Lords had been based on a false report of the Massachusetts proceedings, and in order that this point might be cleared up, the Ministers were asked to state correctly what had been resolved in Boston. There were loud cries of 'read! read!' but unfortunately the Boston resolutions could not be found, and in the words of the sober record of the *Parliamentary History*, 'this threw the whole bench of ministers and clerks into a most ridiculous confusion.'[10]

The Government won on the divisions on this occasion, the Lords' resolutions, somewhat amended, being carried at 4 a.m. A fortnight later the King returned an answer to the addresses he had received from Parliament on the subject of Massachusetts, in which he stated he would not fail to give instructions for bringing 'the authors of the late unhappy disorders in that province to condign punishment.'[11] But the general ministerial ignorance of what was happening in America at the time had been effectively revealed.

Another searching question relating to the dangers of war was asked in the course of a debate the next year by Colonel Isaac Barré, a tall, impressive figure with one eye, whom King George III hated almost as much as he hated Wilkes. Pointing to Sir Edward Hawke, the First Lord of the Admiralty, Barré said: 'I call upon that gentleman . . . to declare to this House the real state of the dispute which is at this time subsisting between the Courts of Great Britain and France.' This drew from Hawke an admission that there was indeed a subject of dispute, for, following a disagreement about naval courtesies, a British lieutenant had fired at a French frigate.

Barré pressed for further information on the Government's policy, and North answered him with the words: 'We have at this instant no particular contest about which there is a probability of going suddenly to war with France. Is that fair?'[12] It was fair, for in spite of the action of the naval lieutenant, the answer proved to be a correct one.

A method of questioning the Government much more nearly resembling the modern procedure was adopted in the House of Lords in 1770. On 10th January Lord Mansfield, who was then Lord Chancellor, let it be known in a manner which aroused interested expectation that he had a communication to make to the Lords. He then laid a paper with the Clerk of the House, but no motion was made, and Lord Camden pointed out that in the absence of a motion there was no means of satisfying the general curiosity. The next day, therefore, Camden put six questions to Lord Mansfield.

The paper laid by Mansfield had contained the judgement in the celebrated case *Rex v. Woodfall*. Henry Woodfall was the printer and publisher of the *Public Advertiser*, a periodical in which there appeared from time to time the famous letters of *Junius*, many of which contained withering attacks on the Government. The verdict returned against Woodfall had been a special one of 'guilty of printing and publishing only.'

Although this special verdict amounted to a virtual acquittal, there were good reasons for uneasiness over the whole problem, and it was this uneasiness which Camden's questions reflected. The first of the questions was: 'Does the opinion mean to declare that upon the general issue of Not Guilty, the jury have no right by law to examine the innocence or criminality of the paper, if they think fit, and to form their verdict upon that examination?' His other questions also related to a doctrine enunciated by Mansfield in directing juries in more than one case. This doctrine was that where the jury were satisfied of the fact of publication, they should return a verdict for the Crown, the question of whether the publication contained a libel not being one for the jury to decide.

Mansfield had clearly not expected that Camden would resort to the method of asking questions, and the showing he made was a poor one. He complained that this method of putting questions had taken him by surprise, that it was unfair, and that he would 'not answer interrogatories.' After some hesitation he agreed that the matter could be discussed. This led the Duke of Richmond to congratulate the House on the fact that Mansfield had pledged himself to discussion, whereupon Mansfield denied that he had done anything more than agree to give his opinion later, and when asked to appoint a day for discussion, he refused to do so.[13]

The exercise showed clearly how effective the direct question could be in discomfiting a man who normally commanded both fear and respect. Mansfield was not only the outstanding lawyer of his time, but Horace Walpole ranked him alone with the Earl of Chatham in his ability normally to command attention in an otherwise noisy assembly.

Another effective question asked immediately after papers had been laid was put in the House of Commons in November 1775. Lord Barrington, the Secretary of War, had laid the Army estimates before the House, and Colonel Barré took the opportunity to ask 'the number, state and disposition of troops in America, according to the latest returns.' Barrington admitted that he could not answer at once, but undertook to consult some papers, which would enable him 'to answer as much of these particulars as is prudent to be disclosed.'

As the battle of Lexington had been fought more than six months before the question was asked, and as the American colonists were already in a state of open warfare with the troops whose numbers were demanded, this answer might have been considered reasonable. But Barré was not satisfied. He moved for a proper account to be laid before the House, and this drew from Barrington an admission that according to the latest return, which was some four months old, the number of troops in Boston, excluding three regiments which were going over to join them, was 8,550, of which 1,482 were sick and wounded, and 354 missing.

The obvious objection on grounds of security to giving further details was made, whereupon Burke declared: 'So, Sir, it is now laid down as a maxim not only to refuse the information, but to take care that such information shall never be given—and this is to be the case because Parliament, instead of calling for information, should give confidence to Ministers. . . . This is a mode of reasoning I never heard of before.'[14]

Barré's motion was defeated, but it had a remarkable consequence. One week later Barrington gave the House the fullest details of the strengths of the garrisons in Gibraltar and Minorca, and then went on to say that in America there were 34 battalions of 811 men each, including two regiments of light horse. The total force he estimated at rather more than 25,000 men. As Barré openly sided with the colonists, whom he had described as 'sons of liberty,' the manner in which his demands were met must be considered generous.

The war in America and its consequences provided the Opposition with a number of opportunities to ask questions which served to embarrass the Government. Lord John Cavendish elicited by means of a question the news that the brothers General and Admiral Howe had made an offer of peace to the colonists in 1776, and that an authentic copy of their proclamation had appeared in the newspapers before the Government had published it. The reason advanced for the Government's slowness to act was that the official copy of the Howes' proclamation had been 'left at Falmouth with other matters,' and had come 'up to town in the ordinary way.'[15]

Barré also forced from the Government admissions about payments made to the Duke of Brunswick and the Landgrave of Hesse for the hire of their mercenaries to fight against the colonists; and in 1777 he extracted the answer that the number of troops serving in America had risen in two years from some 25,000 to a figure 'on paper' of more than 55,000.

But the most damaging questions were asked early in 1778, and they were the outcome of tactics skilfully preconcerted by the Opposition. Fox had heard through private sources of a treaty signed between France and the American colonies, which by then had already declared their independence. Instead of communicating his knowledge to the Government, he asked for confirmation of the report during a debate in February. In the words of Horace Walpole, who had himself played a large part in staging the intrigue with Fox, and who recorded the scene in his journal, 'Lord North was thunderstruck, and would not rise.' In the end North did rise and admitted that what Fox had alleged was 'possible, nay too probable, but not authenticated by the Ambassador.'[16]

That was as far as he was prepared to go, but the Opposition did not let the matter drop. On 5th March the Duke of Grafton rose before the Order of the Day was read in the House of Lords, and said he had 'a question to put to the Lords in office, which it is their duty to reply to without reserve.' It was the question which Fox had already asked during the Commons debate.

After putting his question, Grafton went on to say that if the Ministers admitted the truth of the report, they were 'culpable in the highest degree in concealing intelligence of so important a nature from Parliament.' If they did not, it would be evident that they lacked information, which it was 'the duty of their stations to procure.'

Viscount Weymouth, one of the Secretaries of State, then made an admission, which was of some importance in the development of the parliamentary question. He said it was his duty to give 'every possible satisfaction respecting all sorts of questions in my power to answer and fit to be answered.' But he denied any knowledge of the treaty between the United States and France. Grafton duly pointed out that as Fox had raised the matter more than a fortnight before, the administration had had plenty of time to find out.[17]

Over the treaty between France and the United States the Opposition did in fact win a major tactical triumph. On 16th March a vigorous debate took place in the Commons, in which Fox gained most of the honours, and North actually declared his willingness to resign, if this would help the nation out of its difficulties; although he went on to say 'it would be cowardly to give up in the hour of danger.'[18] The next day it was announced that the British Ambassador had been withdrawn from Paris, and a week later the militia was called out. But even these last-minute suggestions of vigour did not revive the Government's credit.

The Opposition's attack continued throughout the year, and in December the Duke of Grafton declared that 'the last concurrent great cause of all our misfortunes was our not having timely notice of the treaty entered into with France by the Congress delegates.'[19] In the same debate he drew from Lord Stormont, who had been British Ambassador at the time the treaty was concluded, an assertion that he had both known of the treaty and communicated his knowledge to the Ministry.

This was an unfortunate admission, and Weymouth made the Government's case worse by recalling the question asked by Grafton on 5th March, and saying that if asked again, he believed he would give the same answer. This attempt at self-defence was scathingly described by Shelburne as 'indeed novel.'[20]

Whether the Government, by acting earlier on information received, could in 1777 or 1778 have prevented the alliance between France and the United States is questionable. How far Fox was exploiting the nation's misfortunes for limited party ends is also a debatable problem of political ethics. What is certain is that the Government could hardly have entered into a war in a more thoroughly discredited state, and its immediate loss of prestige was largely due to the use of the parliamentary question which Fox and Grafton made.

The embarrassment which Governments were being caused by the increased use of the direct question was again shown in a debate which took place in the House of Lords in April 1780. Lord Stormont, who had not made a good showing when the Ministry had been attacked some eighteen months earlier on the subject of his Embassy in Paris, complained of what he called 'a greater degree of intercourse and communication between this country and France' than he wished to see.

Civilian intercourse between two countries at war was common enough in the eighteenth century, but Stormont was referring to something much more serious, namely personal attacks, amounting to charges of treason, which were being made in the press against one of the leading Whig politicians, the Duke of Richmond. Shelburne thereupon asked Stormont whether, in his former post as Ambassador or his present one as Secretary of State, he had 'information amounting to a charge of treasonable correspondence against any one Member of either House.'

Stormont defended himself by an appeal to the House, in which he asked whether he was bound 'upon the requisition of any one Lord to answer to matters of state, the knowledge of which could only have been gained through the channel of office.' Shelburne admitted that an answer was not obligatory, but maintained that questions put by an individual peer 'might become questions of the House . . . to which it would become incumbent on any noble Lord to give a direct answer.'

The impasse reached showed the need for established precedents on the subject of questions, and the fourth Duke of Manchester, who was himself to be named Ambassador in Paris three years later, tried to solve the difficulty by suggesting a new formula. He made a motion 'that notice having been given of some words spoken by Lord Viscount Stormont . . . and thought to allude to certain noble Lords; and the question being thereupon put to him, but the said Viscount declining to give any answer—resolved that he be requested to answer on his legs.' But the Lord Chancellor said he had found nothing offensive in Stormont's words, as he had not particularized, and the Duke of Manchester withdrew his motion. The problem of procedure remained unsolved.[21]

In spite of the inconclusive nature of this debate in the Lords, significant advances in the elaboration of the methods of asking questions were made in the next three years. During this period questions were asked which were designed to serve many of the principal purposes for which questions are put today.

In June 1780, for instance, Shelburne used the question as a means of bringing reassurance to the public on a matter of general concern. This matter was the appalling rioting to which the anti-Catholic hysteria voiced by Lord George Gordon had led, and which in the next century was to be described so memorably in the pages of

Barnaby Rudge. Shelburne asked what steps were being taken to quell the riots.[22]

In January 1782 the Duke of Richmond asked a question in order to call attention to what appeared to be a case of extreme injustice towards an individual. His question was based on newspaper reports that an American, Colonel Isaac Hayne, had been executed without trial. On this occasion Stormont once again took refuge in a complaint against the impropriety of asking questions. 'The established order of parliamentary proceedings,' he said, 'ought on all occasions to be strictly adhered to.' He then added: 'I shall best show my respect to the House in not prematurely discussing a business which is not regularly before your Lordships.'[23]

Fox asked a question in the same year which enabled the Government to make a statement on a major matter of policy. His question was whether the provisional treaty, in which the independence of the former American colonies was recognized, was conditional on a successful outcome of negotiations with France. The younger Pitt, who was then Chancellor of the Exchequer, answered with an assurance that 'the clear, indisputable meaning of the provisional agreements made with the American commissioners is the unqualified recognition of their independence.'[24] This was as important a statement of Government policy as had yet been made in this form of parliamentary procedure, and in March 1783 Pitt took the surprising course of using an answer to a question as a means of announcing his resignation.[25]

The method of asking a question in order to bring into the open what was believed to be a grave public scandal was adopted by John Rolle, Member for Devonshire, on 21st May 1783. His question was put to Edmund Burke, who was then enjoying one of his brief periods of office as Paymaster-General, and it referred to the affairs of the Pay Office. This particular question had an outcome of exceptional importance in the history of parliamentary procedure.

Rolle asked Burke whether he intended to retain two Pay Office officials named Powell and Bembridge in their posts. Powell and Bembridge had helped Burke to effect certain economies during his first period in office as Paymaster, but when the Rockingham Ministry fell, they had been dismissed for 'gross misbehaviour.' There is little doubt that both were guilty of peculation. Powell subsequently went out of his mind when full details of the affair

were made public, and Bembridge, who was found guilty of con-
niving at the concealment of a sum of more than £48,000, was
sentenced to six months in prison and a fine of £2,600.

Burke regarded any attack on Powell and Bembridge as an attack
upon himself. In an earlier debate on the subject he had had to be
forcibly restrained by Sheridan from rising in a fit of rage, and on
another occasion he insisted that Powell and Bembridge were in the
habit of working from 8 a.m. until midnight. When Rolle asked his
question, therefore, Burke began a long speech in defence of his
actions, explaining how he had spent sleepless nights considering the
affair. Speeches expressing strong feeling were made on both sides
of the House, and Pitt then suggested that the 'conversation' should
be shortened.

At this point the Speaker, Charles Cornwall, who was notorious
even in that age for his habit of keeping a flagon of porter beside the
Chair, and who had an unfortunate tendency to fall asleep during
debates, intervened. 'I have often repeated,' he said, 'that conversations are disorderly, but any Member has, in my opinion a right
to put a question to a Minister or person in office, and that person
has a right to answer or not to answer as he thinks proper; and if he
pleases, to explain and enter into a justification of his conduct and
give his reasons before he gives his answer to the question.'[26]

A fortnight later Speaker Cornwall elaborated on the ruling he
had already given. 'When an hon. Member puts a question to a
Minister,' he said, 'the Minister ought to be heard in reply, or in
assigning his reasons why he chooses to decline giving any direct
answer. Such a deviation from the strictness of the general rule of
order has been at all times allowed as a means of obtaining the House
information, which may, as it has in many instances, throw light on
the business before them, and serve to guide their judgement as to
their future proceedings. This deviation from the general rule,
however, ought to be adopted with great care, sobriety and
prudence, because otherwise it might put the House out of temper
and prove a source of much inconvenience.'[27]

Once these rulings had been given, there could be no further
doubt of the propriety of asking questions. After a period of uncertainty lasting more than sixty years, questions had become a
fully recognized form of parliamentary procedure.

III

The Age of Oratory (1784–1803)

THE political atmosphere in the early months of the year 1784 was
one of excitement and expectancy. It was difficult for anyone to
believe the Government could last long, and the Whigs had good
grounds for supposing that the line of Ministers who were willing to
carry out King George III's wishes compliantly had at last come to
an end. The humiliation of the American war was complete, and for
Prime Minister the only choice left to the King had been that of
William Pitt, who was then aged twenty-four. This arrangement
could hardly be regarded as anything but a makeshift, for Pitt had
had the greatest difficulty in forming a Government at all, and he
could not command a majority in the House of Commons. Heavy
bets were laid in White's on the number of days the Government
could survive.

It was a question asked in the Commons on 23rd January 1784
which brought to a head the indignation felt by the Opposition at
Pitt's efforts to cling to office. Pitt had been defeated in the Commons over his Bill for the better management of the affairs of the
East India Company, and before moving for leave to bring in
another Bill, Fox asked the question to which everyone present was
waiting for an answer. The question was whether Parliament was to
be dissolved.

Somewhat surprisingly Pitt refused to answer, a refusal which led
Fox to declare that it was impossible for him 'to speak of the sulky
silence of the right hon. gentleman in any other terms than those of
indignation.' General Conway, a former Secretary of State, who
had opposed the continuance of the war with the American colonies,
supported Fox. He repeated the term, 'sulky silence,' and went on:
'The present Ministry, originating in darkness, maintain themselves

44

by artifice. . . . They exist by corruption, and they are now about to dissolve Parliament, after sending their agents about the country to bribe men.'[1]

It was a formidable attack on a man of twenty-four, even though Conway had revealed the Opposition's fear of a dissolution and preference for a new Government formed by themselves with the existing Parliament. Pitt answered with extraordinary self-assurance. He had, he said, been accustomed to the 'violence and harsh language' of the House long enough to be upset by 'neither un-supported slander nor intemperate invective.' He stubbornly refused to answer what he called 'interrogatories which I do not think gentlemen entitled to put to me.' At 2 a.m. Fox moved an adjourn-ment until noon that day, a Saturday, to allow Pitt 'to think of his situation for some time.' When the House reassembled, a Member named Powys asked whether on the following Monday the House would meet again. This time Pitt gave an answer. He had, he said, made a rule not to pledge himself that he would not in any circum-stances advise the King to dissolve Parliament, but he would do nothing to prevent its meeting on the next Monday.[2]

The answer given by Pitt to Powys's question indicated the line he was to follow for the next two months. During that period he was defeated in division after division, and government came nearly to a standstill. Fox demanded an explanation of Pitt's determination to stay in office not as 'the constitutional Minister of the people' but as 'the unconstitutional Minister of the Crown.' Pitt admitted the novelty of his situation, but said there was 'nothing illegal in a Minister's remaining in office after the House has declared against him.'[3]

A motion declaring that the continuance of the Ministers in office was an obstacle to the formation of an administration which would enjoy the confidence of the House was carried, but more than a fortnight afterwards Pitt announced that the King had 'not yet, in compliance with the resolutions of the House, thought proper to dismiss his Ministers.'[4]

The Opposition then went further. They carried a motion for postponing consideration of the Mutiny Bill, and another for representing to the King that his action was 'injurious to the true interests of the Crown.'[5] But it was not until 24th March 1784 that Parliament was dissolved.

The election which followed vindicated Pitt's extraordinary obstinacy. The factors which decided the election of 1784 have often been debated. Some historians have attributed the result chiefly to popular weariness with the methods of the Opposition, and particularly the bizarre temporary alliance made between Fox and North; others have decided that the result was procured by the skilful financial management of John Robinson, who for many years was Secretary to the Treasury; and the influence of the reaction to the Gordon riots was probably considerable. But there could be no doubt about the nature of the result. When the new Parliament met in May, Pitt had a substantial majority in the first division. He was to remain Prime Minister for the next seventeen years.

The beginning of Pitt's long premiership ended the period in which the King had been served by inferior Ministers, who either did not believe in his policy or else did not enjoy his confidence, and in which virtually all the debating honours had gone to the Opposition. The election of 1784 might well have seemed at the time a crushing victory for the King over the Whigs. In fact it was the beginning of a new period in parliamentary history, a period in which for the first time during the reign a Prime Minister remained in office long enough to establish a policy which was his own.

During this period the voice of the Opposition tended to be more and more the voice of Fox, reinforced by the voice of Richard Brinsley Sheridan, who was by then choosing politics rather than the drama as a means of showing how he could achieve almost every success in life except solvency.

The parliamentary question, now established as a proper form of procedure, was among the weapons used by this Opposition, but during the twenty years following the Speaker's rulings of 1783 questions were still put sparingly. They were seldom asked on the routine affairs of Government, being resorted to rather for expressing anxiety or disagreement over the major political issues of the time.

One such issue, to which Parliament devoted many hours, was the conduct of the Heir to the Throne, the future King George IV, who, as he grew up, accepted the traditional part played by Hanoverian Princes of Wales, that of a patron of the King's political opponents. In April 1787 Alderman Newnham put a question to Pitt, which, he said, did not 'arise from personal curiosity.' This was whether it was 'the design of Ministers to rescue the Prince of Wales from his present very embarrassed situation.' He went on to say that the Prince's conduct during his difficulties had 'reflected greater honour and glory on his character than the most splendid diadem in Europe has upon the wearer of it,' and declared that if the Prince of Wales continued to be financially embarrassed, 'it would be an indelible disgrace upon the country.'[6]

This was an interpretation of events which made little appeal to Pitt, who, after all, knew the Prince of Wales. He answered simply that it was not his duty to bring forward such a subject except at the command of His Majesty, and he had not 'been honoured with such a command.' Newnham then gave notice of his intention to raise the matter at a later date—the procedure now commonly adopted when an answer to a parliamentary question is considered unsatisfactory—and this opened the way for Parliament to investigate the private life of the Prince of Wales in some detail.

When Newnham instituted a debate a week later, John Rolle, a firm supporter of Pitt and the man who had questioned Burke about irregularities in the Pay Office, made an insinuation which the House had little difficulty in understanding. He spoke of a matter 'affecting Church and State,' which, he said, particularly concerned 'that description of persons, the country gentlemen.' The atmosphere became tense at once. Rolle was clearly referring to the report that the Prince of Wales had married Mrs. Fitzherbert, a woman who had been twice widowed, was a commoner and, most important of all, was a Roman Catholic. Sheridan came to the Prince's defence, and three days later Fox went even further than Sheridan had done. Announcing that he was speaking 'from the immediate authority of the Prince of Wales,' he said there was 'no part of His Royal Highness's conduct that he is either afraid or unwilling to have investigated in the most minute manner.' Fox also described Rolle's insinuation about a matter affecting Church and State as a 'low, malicious falsehood.'[7]

With this the House seemed to be satisfied—surprisingly, perhaps, since the Prince of Wales had been married to Mrs. Fitzherbert for rather more than a year. Mrs. Fitzherbert was rather less pleased with the denial of the propriety of her connection, and was reputed to have said that Fox had rolled her 'in the kennel like a street-walker.'

The other immediate outcome of the affair gave considerable satisfaction to the Whig supporters of the Prince of Wales. Almost exactly a month after Newnham had asked his question, Pitt presented a message from the King. This contained not only a request to the Commons to vote enough money to pay off the Prince's debts, but also a statement that a further £10,000 a year would be paid to the Prince out of the Civil List, and a promise that an estimate of the cost of completing Carlton House, an undertaking which the Prince was finding an embarrassment, would be laid before the House. Newnham thereupon rose to say: 'I do not pretend to arrogate to myself that anything which I have done has promoted this happy event; but it is my boast that nothing I have done has prevented it.'[8]

Alderman Newnham had good reason to be pleased with the outcome of the question he had asked, but the Commons had not finished investigating the private life of the Prince of Wales. On two separate occasions in 1789, when proposals to establish a Regency because of King George III's access of lunacy were discussed, Rolle challenged Fox's denial of the marriage with Mrs. Fitzherbert. And fourteen years later Colonel Stanley was to ask what had by then become a familiar question. This was whether it was intended to 'raise money for the purpose of relieving the embarrassments of the Prince.' Henry Addington, the former Speaker, who was then Prime Minister and Chancellor of the Exchequer, answered the question, and moved that a sum not exceeding £60,000 a year should be paid to the Prince of Wales out of the Consolidated Fund. He advanced as one of his arguments 'the great change which has taken place in the value of money during the last eight years.' The motion was carried, and once again Parliament came to the Prince's rescue.[9]

The Government's conduct of foreign affairs, and particularly the alliance with Prussia, also gave rise to a number of searching questions. In May 1789 Lord Stormont, who had himself suffered when in office from the embarrassment which direct questioning could cause, asked a question in the House of Lords about a treaty with Prussia, a copy of which had just been laid on the table. He wanted to know whether this treaty, which was ostensibly of a defensive nature, contained all the commitments entered into by the Government. The Duke of Leeds, one of the many peers whom Pitt had chosen as Ministers, described this as a most improper question from one who had 'set himself up as the oracle of everything that concerns diplomatic duty and etiquette,' and refused to answer.

Stormont complained that the Duke's conduct was 'unparliamentary,' and said Ministers were bound to lay on the table a complete copy of a treaty or none at all. The Duke of Leeds was rescued by the Lord Chancellor, Lord Thurlow, at that time still a supporter of Pitt's, but later to change his allegiance. Thurlow evidently attached more importance to the secrecy of diplomacy than to the rights of peers to ask questions, for he described Stormont's as 'the most obviously irregular question that has ever been put to a Secretary of State in Parliament.' He added: 'If the noble Duke had answered it, he would have been guilty of a high misdemeanour.' From one whose office gave him the right to speak with authority on the procedure of the House of Lords, this was a remarkable ruling.[10]

The problem of how far Britain was in fact committed to further the interests of Prussia continued over a number of years to provide the Opposition with material for discrediting the Government. Fox had raised the subject in debate in 1785 and been reproached by Pitt for going to 'most improper lengths,'[11] and six years later the issue became a critical one.

At that time Russia was at war with Turkey—a war which was largely concerned with the Black Sea fortress of Ochakov—and Turkey had an alliance with Prussia. The Opposition feared that Britain would be drawn into war with Russia, and their fears were heightened when in March 1791 a message from the King was read, announcing the need to strengthen British naval forces. This was openly admitted to be a direct consequence of the Russo-Turkish war.

Although an assurance was given that the strengthening of the Fleet was 'not the result of any obligation entered into by any specific treaty,' the Opposition launched one of the most formidable attacks ever made on Pitt's conduct of affairs. Stormont insisted that the alliance with Prussia was an offensive one, and declared: 'We are about to hold a conduct with respect to Russia, which Louis XIV, in the plenitude of his prosperity, when surrounded by sycophants and revelling in all the lust of lawless power, would have been ashamed to adopt.'[12]

In a debate in the Commons on the same day W. H. Lambton opposed participation in a war with Russia on rather different grounds. Such a war, he said, would not 'hold out the usual incentives which call forth the exertions of the British tars. There are no galleons in the Baltic, no one has ever heard of Russian dollars or of the ingots of the Cossacks or Calmucks. We have little to expect except bear-skins.' The best that Pitt could do in reply was to give an assurance that 'Ministers are bound by no engagements to Prussia but such as have received the sanction of Parliament, and by their unbiased sense of the British interests.'[13]

The Opposition continued the onslaught for several months. Charles Grey, later to become the champion of parliamentary reform, asked in the Commons whether it was prudent to interrupt a trade with Russia whose value was £2,000,000 in exports and £1,000,000 in imports. He then moved a number of resolutions on the subject. They were defeated, but the closeness of the divisions led Fox to declare that Pitt had now to account to an 'awakened country for the deceptive language which from year to year he has put into His Majesty's Speeches from the Throne.'[14]

When Parliament reassembled the next year, the Speech from the Throne contained a reference to intervention 'to promote a pacification between the Empress of Russia and the Porte.' Fox could then claim, fairly convincingly, that 'in warning the people of their danger and obliging the Minister to abandon the most absurd and impolitic attempt that ever was conceived, we did our duty then, and have now the consciousness of having done signal service to the nation.'[15] But a bigger political triumph was still to come.

On 20th February 1792 the Duke of Leeds, who had been Secretary of State for some eight years, announced to the House of Lords that he had resigned. In explanation he said: 'I was wrong, in common with my colleagues, in resisting all explanation and for not meeting the question fairly. . . . On a subject so important as a message announcing an armed interference with a foreign power, the nation has an undoubted right to explicit explanation.'[16] The resignation of the Minister, who had been responsible for the conduct of foreign affairs, for the express reason that the Government had failed to provide satisfactory answers in Parliament was, perhaps, the most triumphant vindication afforded until then of the Opposition's right to ask questions.

No other aspect of foreign policy provided opportunities for such searching questions during Pitt's Ministry as the alliance with Prussia. But a foretaste of future events was given by a question put by a Member named Pulteney on 6th July 1789. After mentioning a 'report in circulation' of a great scarcity of corn in France, and of an application made for supplies from Britain, he asked what steps the Government were taking in the matter. Pitt admitted that such an application had been made, and went on to give an answer of a kind which was to become stereotyped in a later age. The application, he said, was being considered by a committee of the Privy Council, and the Government had not yet reached a decision. William Wilberforce, at the time still a comparatively junior Member, thereupon advocated the sending of supplies, mentioning as a reason for doing so 'the state of perturbation in which that kingdom is well known to be at present.'[17]

The consequences of the state of perturbation in France in 1789 were to provide the subjects of a number of the most important questions put to the Government while Pitt was Premier. As the probabilities of war increased, the danger of invasion by the French revolutionary armies and the growing political conspiracies at home were regarded, not unreasonably, in Government circles as two aspects of the same problem. It was on the subject of the security measures adopted to meet these two threats that a somewhat unusual question was asked in December 1792.

On 13th December the Speaker was about to read the King's Speech, when he was prevented from beginning by Joseph Jekyll, a Whig Member who had a reputation as a wit. Jekyll put a question to 'those who are best qualified to clear up what is obscure and doubtful.' His question was by what authority Parliament was then sitting. Parliament, he claimed, could not be called together at an earlier date than that to which it had been prorogued, and no prorogation could be shorter than forty days. He quoted the recognized parliamentary authority of the time, Hatsell, as evidence that the only exception made to this rule had been in the reign of King Charles II, when the Dutch had sailed up the Medway.

Jekyll was answered by Henry Dundas, Secretary of State for the Home Department, the Government being temporarily at a disadvantage because Pitt had not yet been re-elected after accepting the office of Lord Warden of the Cinque Ports. Dundas pointed out that the King had exercised his powers to call out the militia during the prorogation, and that on doing so, he was bound to summon Parliament within fourteen days.

After this the King's Speech was read, and its references to 'seditious practices and insurrections' were evidently borne out by the dramatic entrance of the Lord Mayor of London, Sir James Saunderson. Saunderson had arrived in the House late because of what he called 'an interruption in the streets,' and as soon as he was able to do so, he moved an address declaring that the House had learnt with concern that 'a spirit of tumult and disorder . . . has shown itself in acts of riot and insurrection.' Lord Fielding gave notice that he would move for leave to bring in a Bill for suspending the right of Habeas Corpus for foreigners; Fox described the occasion as 'the most momentous crisis' in the history of the country; and the great battle over the security of the constitution began.

Fox excelled even his own standard of oratory in a speech which included the famous sentences: 'Our constitution was not made, thank God, in a day. It is the result of gradual and progressive wisdom. . . . You neglect in your conduct the foundation of all legitimate government, the rights of the people.'[18] But the Bill restricting the liberties of aliens soon became law; the Government set up a committee to consider seditious practices, and early in 1793 the issue was clarified by a declaration of war against revolutionary France.

When Pitt presented the second report of the Committee on Seditious Practices, Sheridan rose to ask a question. Among the political organizations whose activities had been investigated by the Committee was a society known as the Friends of the People. This body advocated parliamentary reform, and it had a petition presented to Parliament, in which the claim was made that 71 peers and 91 commoners between them procured the return of a working majority of 306 M.P.s.

Unlike other political organizations formed at the time—such as the London Corresponding Society—the Friends of the People were socially thoroughly respectable, and their secretary, Daniel Stuart, later became the proprietor of the Tory *Morning Post*. The question asked by Sheridan was why Daniel Stuart had not been examined by the Committee. Pitt's answer was somewhat evasive, and was construed by Sheridan to indicate that the Committee had deliberately tried to misrepresent the aims of the Friends of the People. Something of a sensation was caused when Philip Francis, commonly believed to have been the famous pamphleteer *Junius*, had the courage to admit that he was himself a member of the society. Sheridan's question and the discussion which followed at least had the effect of showing that the Friends of the People were rather less traitorous than had been commonly supposed.[19]

A much more alarming occurrence than the formation of a few political societies took place in 1797. This was a serious mutiny in the Navy, and again it was through the procedure of questioning that Parliament came to consider the subject. On 1st May 1797 Fox rose and asked for official information on what had happened at Portsmouth. Pitt refused to say anything except that Parliament would be called upon to vote a sum of money in connection with the subject of Fox's question 'in a day or two.'[20]

On 3rd May the fifth Duke of Bedford, a Whig peer, asked a similar question in the House of Lords. Earl Spencer, First Lord of the Admiralty, said that he had not been commanded by His Majesty to make any communication, nor did he foresee that any communication would be made. But five days later the Government had no choice but to ventilate the subject in Parliament.

Some three weeks before, on 18th April, delegates of the sailors at Portsmouth had presented a petition to the Lords Commissioners of the Admiralty, demanding an increase in their wages, which, they said, had been fixed at a time 'when the necessaries of life, and slops of every denomination, were at least 30 per cent cheaper than at the present time.' They also demanded other concessions, including an adequate supply of vegetables and a provision that 'if any man is wounded in action, his pay be continued until he is cured, and discharged.' Four days were allowed to pass, and then the seamen's delegates announced that unless their demands were satisfied, the fleet would not lift anchor. This was mutiny, and the consequence was fighting and bloodshed. But eventually the Government agreed to meet the seamen's demands, and it was to raise the money for the increased wage-bill that they had to apply to Parliament.

When the application was made, Pitt asked for the 'silent

indulgence of the House,' but Fox would not agree. The cause of all the trouble, he insisted, was the Government's 'scandalous delay,' and he declared it to be the duty of the House 'to call for a full explanation of the discontent.'[21]

The next day Samuel Whitbread asked another question. This was why Pitt had not made an application to Parliament earlier. Pitt's answer was that the memorial of the Lords of the Admiralty of 26th April—that was to say eight days after the presentation of the seamen's demands—had been referred to a committee of the Privy Council, which in turn had had to make a report. 'All these forms,' he said, 'which the regular conduct of the business required, necessarily consumed some time.' Once again, as in 1789, Pitt had been forced to admit the cumbersome nature of the bureaucratic machine to justify the Government's failure to act quickly.[22]

The Government made an even worse showing in the House of Lords on the same day. Again it was the Duke of Bedford who asked a question. He wanted to know whether the Government intended 'to carry into execution all the promises made by the Lords Commissioners of the Admiralty to the seamen.' The answer came from Lord Grenville, one of the Secretaries of State, who said he considered it 'necessary to deny in the most express terms that I am in my official capacity bound to answer any question that may be put to me, however unseasonably, by individuals. . . . It would be peculiarly hard if Ministers were to be tried on the grounds of answers extorted from them by questions insidiously and irregularly put, and then carefully conveyed to the public. From answers extorted in this way the grossest misrepresentations go abroad through those disorderly and unconstitutional channels, though acquiesced in, the public papers.'[23] This answer, apart from the doubts it must have aroused about the Government's good faith, was as clear an admission as could have been afforded of the telling use made by the Opposition of their questions.

The Government survived the attack. The next day in the Commons Whitbread moved a vote of censure on Pitt personally, but the motion was defeated. However, Pitt's ministry was considerably discredited, and its prestige was restored only when the seamen at Portsmouth became so violent that measures taken to suppress them were approved by the Commons with only one dissident voice.

The use made by the Opposition of the parliamentary question during Pitt's long premiership confirmed it for all time as an indispensable weapon of attack on major political issues. But it was seldom used during this period for investigating the routine affairs of administration. The explanation may lie partly in the natures of the Opposition leaders. Fox, for instance, could write to a friend: 'Though I like the House of Commons itself, I hate the preparatory business of looking at accounts, drawing motions, etc.' Sheridan too achieved his greatest parliamentary distinction with a speech lasting five-and-a-half hours on the subject of the Begums of Oude.

To such men, who were incapable of doing anything on a small scale, who were made for Opposition rather than Government, pulsating oratory had more appeal than attention to administrative detail. At times their methods were deplored even by their fellow Whigs. In 1796 Grey spoke of 'the unexampled power which the present Ministers possess, and the little disposition the House discovers to enquire into any part of their conduct.'[24] Two years earlier Francis had complained of the prevailing practice, whereby a few distinguished Members occupied 'the whole time of the House with speeches of many hours,' with the result that the constitutions of the others 'sink under the intolerable burthen imposed upon their faculties.'[25]

On matters of administration the older method of obtaining information on a specific subject, or of airing a particular grievance, still continued in use. This was to move for papers rather than to ask a direct question. In 1796, for instance, General Macleod, after mentioning newspapers' reports and quoting from a private letter, moved for a humble address for copies of 'such intelligence as has been received by any of His Majesty's Ministers' on the use of bloodhounds in the prosecution of the war against the Maroons in Jamaica.[26]

One question of importance on the rights of an individual was, however, asked during Pitt's long premiership. This concerned the treatment of a Member of the Irish Parliament, Arthur O'Connor, who, after being acquitted following a trial at Maidstone, had actually been arrested in court by Bow Street officers on a warrant issued by the Secretary of State.

The first question on the subject was put by Lord Holland, the nephew of Charles James Fox, in the House of Lords in 1798, and a further question was asked in the Commons some three weeks later. The questioners gained little satisfaction beyond eliciting the information that the new charge against O'Connor was one of treason. But the Lord Chancellor, Lord Loughborough, was drawn into a display of ill humour, when he said that Holland's action in asking a question was 'contrary to the established rules of the House,' and that he was a young Member, who would 'possibly receive and follow better information.'[27]

Two questions on matters of administration were also asked on 28th November 1803—that was after Pitt had resigned from office and been succeeded by Addington. One was put by Alderman Combe, who asked whether the Government intended to bring in a Bill to simplify the Act relating to income tax, a subject on which feeling ran high. Combe's contention was that 'much difficulty is at present felt in making out the returns.' The other question related to the expenses of barracks.[28]

These questions were of importance in the development of the procedure of questions, for they provided the first recorded instance of two questions on unrelated subjects being asked one after the other in the House of Commons on the same day. This may well be regarded as the beginning, by accident rather than by regulation, of setting aside a special period for the asking of questions, the period which later came to be known as Question Time.

IV

War and the Change of Emphasis (1803–1815)

ALDERMAN COMBE'S question about income tax in 1803 was the first of a number asked during the next ten years on the same subject—a tendency which was indicative of a new development in the use of questions, which occurred during the Napoleonic wars. This was the practice of submitting Governments to much more searching interrogation on administrative, as opposed to primarily political, matters.

In 1804 Earl Temple suggested in the House of Commons that excessive deductions for income tax were being made from the pay of officers of the militia, and in doing so, he explained how he had investigated the matter. He had first written to the Secretary at War, Charles Bragge, and receiving no satisfaction, he had asked a question in the House. Bragge's answer on that occasion, namely that if the revenue commissioners 'should be found to have exceeded their trust, the law is open to correct them,' was clearly no more satisfactory than his letter had been. A month later Temple moved for an account of all sums paid by officers in income tax. Addington opposed the motion, pointing out that Temple's real object was not to obtain information, but to have subalterns exempted from income tax.[1]

Temple admitted this was true, and the motion was defeated. But his explanation of his conduct in this affair showed that he followed in detail what is now considered the proper course for M.P.s in such circumstances: the letter to the appropriate Minister, followed by a question, followed, if necessary, by a motion.

In 1810 the methods by which taxes were collected were again brought forward in the Commons in the form of a question. Lord Mahon asked how it was that whereas Pitt, when first imposing the income tax, has estimated the taxable revenue of Scotland to be one-eighth of that of England, yet in the preceding year the total of the taxes imposed in England amounted to £59,000,000, and in Scotland to only £4,500,000. This was the kind of question which, under the system prevailing at the time, whereby Ministers usually had to answer impromptu and from their own personal knowledge, was clearly baffling.

Spencer Perceval, the man who, as Prime Minister, was to be murdered two years later by a lunatic in the lobby of the House of Commons, made an enterprising attempt. He said he thought the disparity arose not 'from any neglect in the collection of taxes in Scotland,' but 'from the increased prosperity of England, from which the taxes produced much more than was expected.'[2] Nearly three weeks passed before Mahon was given a detailed answer in the House. Then it was explained to him that he had been making comparisons between two different years, when the rates of income tax had not been the same, and that certain taxes assessed in Scotland were, in fact, collected in England.[3]

A high proportion of the questions on administrative matters during the decade which ended in 1815 were concerned, naturally enough, with the conduct of the wars themselves.

The appointments of the supreme commanders for some of the major campaigns were, for instance, among the subjects raised in questions. In 1808 the Earl of Suffolk stated in the House of Lords that it was generally believed that 'a large armament' was to be sent to Spain, and asked who was to command the expedition.

The next year the Earl of Buckinghamshire asked a question about the choice of Sir Arthur Wellesley, the future Duke of Wellington, for the supreme command in Portugal, and suggested it might well reflect discredit on Sir John Cradock, who had been in command until then. The Earl of Liverpool, the son of King George III's confidant, Charles Jenkinson, and himself a future Prime Minister, objected to this question as an attack upon the prerogative of the Crown. He also protested against 'such questions being addressed to Ministers, lest it should be drawn into a precedent, and that upon occasions when it might not be in the power of Ministers to speak of the commander then alluded to' in quite such favourable terms as he was himself prepared to speak of Cradock.[4]

Such retreats behind the prerogative of the Crown, while considered permissible on the subject of personal appointments, were not admitted as a defence against questions on the general administration of the Army and the Navy, and a number of searching questions on the conditions of soldiers and sailors were asked during the war period.

In March 1812, when the need for fighting manpower was being felt, Earl Grosvenor asked in the House of Lords whether it was true that criminals sentenced to imprisonment on board the hulks were being drafted into the Army instead. He also wanted to know whether orders had been issued to the recruiting sergeants of certain regiments not to enlist Irishmen, while foreigners were admitted without scruple. Liverpool admitted that a limited number of convicts, 'who were known to be penitent,' had been allowed to join the Army. But he vigorously denied the charge about Irishmen, saying that 'the people of that country form the great strength and stamina of the British Army.'[5]

Liverpool answered these questions about the quality of new recruits fairly successfully, but in June 1814 a less skilful defence was put up by Charles Manners Sutton, later to be Speaker of the House of Commons, and at that time Secretary at War. He was asked by Henry Bennet, Member for Shrewsbury, whether he had any information about a soldier named Greenfield. Greenfield was the servant of a regimental surgeon, and he had been sentenced by a court-martial to receive three hundred lashes. After more than a hundred lashes had been delivered, Greenfield, it appeared, had become insensible. Manners Sutton disclaimed any knowledge of the affair, and added that this was not surprising, as the man had evidently been tried by a regimental court-martial, the returns of which would not normally be sent to his office.[6]

Four days later Manners Sutton reversed the normal process by asking Bennet a question. This was whether he had got his information about the flogging of Greenfield from a Sunday newspaper. Bennet said that he had, and Manners Sutton, knowing then that they were speaking of the same case, offered his explanation. Greenfield, he said, had fainted because he had stuffed some clothing into his mouth in the belief that this might make the pain more bearable, and as a result he had been nearly suffocated. When the clothes were taken out of his mouth, he had been able to walk to hospital, 'where he remained, subject only to such inconvenience as might be expected to arise from the lashes he had received.'⁷ Bennet did not find this a very satisfactory answer, and for many years the House was to hear a great deal from him and others of its more radical Members about flogging in the Army.

The treatment of an individual sailor also provided the subject of a question which brought to light an ugly and strange story. The questioner in this case was Sir Francis Burdett, the outspoken champion of parliamentary reform, who was himself imprisoned for his political opinions.

In February 1810 Burdett asked what was intended to be done about a sea-captain named Warren Lake, who had punished one of his sailors by putting him ashore on a barren rock in the West Indies without provisions of any kind. Knowledge of this affair had reached the Government by accident through a report in an American newspaper, and Captain Lake had been dismissed the service.

Burdett wanted to know whether any further action was contemplated. The reply he got was that the court-martial which had imposed the sentence of dismissal 'had not it in its power to do more.' Burdett became rather angry and had to be called to order by the Speaker, in spite of his protest that 'a matter of convenience ought to give way to a matter of life and death.'⁸

But some six weeks later he had a chance to raise the matter again. He then moved for the appointment of a committee to consider Lake's conduct, saying his first idea had been to move for an address praying for the prosecution of Lake, but that the absence of the seaman's body offered an obvious difficulty.

The seaman who had been punished, Robert Jeffery, was suspected of having stolen some spruce beer. For this Lake had ordered him to be left without food, money, and the greater part of his clothing on the barren island of Sombrero, which was thirty miles from the nearest inhabited land. Lake, when ordering this punishment, was believed to have been either drunk or insane.

The incident was not kept altogether quiet, and Sir Alexander Cochrane, the Admiral commanding the station, had admonished Lake, and ordered a search to be made on Sombrero. But this was two months after the incident had taken place, and the search was carried out by the very men who had set Jeffery ashore. In carrying out their search, two members of the crew, who had taken with them, in Burdett's words, 'the materials for enjoying the diversion of shooting the birds upon the island," had found by accident parts of Jeffery's trousers. There was a strong presumption that Jeffery was dead, although the American paper which had reported the affair, but to which Burdett attached little credence, suggested he had escaped.

Spencer Perceval, the Prime Minister, did not attempt to defend Lake, but said he did not know what a committee of the kind proposed by Burdett could achieve. Without a body, no charge of murder could be brought, and for the offence known to have been committed Lake had already been tried. If Jeffery were still alive, Perceval pointed out, he could bring a civil action for damages.

Samuel Whitbread, who for many years was to be one of the most formidable parliamentary questioners of those in authority, then called attention to the action of Admiral Cochrane, who, between first hearing of the affair and the holding of the court-martial, had actually promoted Lake to a higher command. In the end the House agreed to order the laying of all communications between Cochrane and the Admiralty on the subject and a further minute and accurate search of Sombrero.[9] It must have been a strange search, and there is no record that it produced any satis-factory results.

The fate of the widows of naval officers killed at Trafalgar and the treatment of a British prisoner of war in French hands were among other subjects on which the wartime Governments were questioned. John Bastard, Member for Devonshire, elicited the information, shortly after the battle of Trafalgar, that it was 'not customary on such occasions to make any particular provision for the widows of naval captains,' although an application could be made to the King's Bounty.[10]

In 1804 William Windham, who had himself held office under Pitt and who was an uncompromising enemy of Bonaparte and Bonapartism, asked a question about a certain Captain Wright, who was said to have been harshly treated by his French captors. Wind-ham's suggestion was that Wright was being punished either because he had landed on the French coast with the object of inciting insurrection, or because he was a personal friend of Sir Sidney Smith, the hero of the defence of Acre, who had succeeded in escaping from captivity.[11] The next year the House learnt that the British Government was in communication with the French

Government on the subject of Wright's treatment. It also learnt that in spite of the allegations of cruelty, the French were sufficiently indulgent, or sufficiently careless, to allow details of how Wright was faring to be sent in a letter from one of his fellow-prisoners to Sir Sidney Smith.[12]

On wider issues of policy, as well as on matters of detail, the conduct of the war, and of the closely related subject of foreign affairs, by the administrations of Addington, Pitt, Grenville, Perceval, and Liverpool was frequently called into question.

In March 1805 Philip Francis asked a question about the origin and motives of the war against Holkar in India, and three weeks later, by raising the subject on a motion, he put the Government in the position of having to deny, by a majority vote, the proposition that 'to pursue schemes of conquest and extension of dominion in India are measures repugnant to the wish, the honour, and the policy of this nation.'[13]

In 1810 a question asked in the House of Lords elicited the information that from April to August 1809 the British Minister in Madrid received only one letter of instruction from the Foreign Secretary although at the time, as the questioner, the Marquis of Lansdowne, quite reasonably asserted, 'the most important transactions were going forward in the peninsula.'[14]

From 1807 to 1812 several questions on British relations with America were asked, culminating in the announcement of the American declaration of war against Britain; and on one occasion Canning, as Foreign Secretary, was brought to say of David Erskine, who had been conducting negotiations as British Minister Plenipotentiary in Washington, that 'the proceedings of that gentleman were productive of very great embarrassment to His Majesty's Ministers.'[15]

A number of attacks were made on the Government in 1814 on the grounds that the object of blockading Norway was to force the Norwegians into a union with the Swedish Crown, this matter having been raised in Parliament for the first time in the form of a question asked by Samuel Whitbread 'for the sake of humanity.'[16] And one of the most dramatic moments which the House of Commons was to experience during the war occurred on 10th March 1815, when Whitbread, after asking a question about the Treaty of Chaumont, added: 'Being on my legs, I beg to be informed whether the Government has received any intelligence respecting the landing of Buonaparté in France.'[17] Castlereagh, the Foreign Secretary, admitted the Government had received reports of the landing, and the signal for a prolonged series of attacks on the Government's handling of the Elba episode was given. A month later the Duke of Wellington's brother was to declare: 'I should have granted a handsome, nay a noble provision to Buonaparté, but I should have taken care to make due provision against his return to power.'[18]

Between 1803 and 1815 there was, in fact, not only a new emphasis on administrative rather than political matters in the use of the parliamentary question, but also a great increase in the range of subjects on which questions were asked. This new range extended from the problem of how the country was to be governed during the periods of King George III's lunacy to a proposed building in the grounds of Chelsea Hospital; from a major constitutional issue involving the relationship of the executive Government with the Lord Chief Justice to the debauching of a female prisoner in Cold Bath Fields.

The problem of how the country was to be governed was raised in December 1810, when Earl Spencer asked in the House of Lords 'what course of proceeding it is intended to propose on the present melancholy emergency.' It was already clear by then that King George III was unlikely to be able to exercise the royal powers again, and from the answer to the question the Lords learnt that it was proposed to put forward a number of resolutions for the establishment of a Regency. Certain objections to this procedure were made on constitutional grounds, Earl Fitzwilliam even objecting to the formal use of the words, 'present session,' since in the absence of any summons by the King, he pointed out, 'the present assembling of the estates can in no sense be denominated a session of Parliament.'[19] In the end the resolutions were carried, and in February 1811 the Regency Bill received the assent of a commission consisting of five peers, with a somewhat curious use of the words, 'Le roi le veut.'

Another subject of major constitutional importance was raised by means of a question in February 1806, when Spencer Stanhope asked 'whether Lord Ellenborough, who is one of the Privy Council, is also allowed to sit in that department of the executive Government which is in common called the Cabinet Council.' The significance of this question was that Lord Ellenborough was the Lord Chief Justice, and the Earl of Bristol, when asking a similar question in the House of Lords a week later, described it as 'a topic of great constitutional importance.' Lord Grenville, the Prime Minister, answered Bristol's question and denied that Ellenborough's position was either unconstitutional or unprecedented. He added: 'What is generally or usually known as 'the Cabinet' is, under that appellation or description, unknown to the constitution. Indeed it should rather be considered as a committee of the Privy Council that is more frequently called upon by His Majesty for advice.'[20]

In a literal sense this was sound doctrine, but Bristol was concerned with the fundamental problem of the independence of judges from the executive Government, and he gave notice that he would raise the matter again. When he did so in March, he moved that 'it is highly inexpedient and tends to weaken the administration of justice to summon to any committee or assembly of the Privy Council any of the judges of His Majesty's courts of common law.' In support of his motion he declared: 'Far am I from being one of those who think the atmosphere of Downing Street and St. James's so impure that nothing can escape it unpolluted. But of this I am sure, that neither the Palace nor the Treasury are fit to be the daily resort of British judges.'[21]

The debate was a long one, and in the course of it the Lord Chancellor Erskine stepped from the Woolsack, and said the King had a right to choose those whom he called to his councils. Bristol's motion was defeated, and on the same day a similar result took place in the Commons on three resolutions moved by Spencer Stanhope. On this occasion the viewpoint of the Government was expressed by Fox, who had shortly before achieved the miracle of a return to office in spite of his outspoken opposition to so many aspects of the war with France. 'From what parts of our statutes or of the recorded proceedings of this House,' Fox asked of Stanhope, 'has he learnt that the Cabinet, or any individual belonging to it, has been, as such, held to be legally responsible? . . . For any act done in my office I am directly responsible to Parliament and the country.' Stanhope's motion was defeated by 222 votes to 64, and Parliament thereby not only refused to acknowledge the legal existence of the principal organ of the Government, the Cabinet, but in effect went on record as denying that there was such a thing as collective Cabinet responsibility.[22]

By contrast with issues such as these, which would have excited Parliament at any period in its history, a question asked, following the presentation of a petition by Sheridan, led to the announcement that a commission would investigate conditions in Cold Bath Fields prison, where happenings were such that a female prisoner had had, by the son of the chief gaoler, a child which was 'burdensome to the parish of Kensington';[23] and in 1809 a question asked by Burdett led to an agreement between the Government and an individual landowner for altering the site of a house which was to have been built in the grounds of Chelsea Hospital.[24]

One event which led to a sudden extension in the range of questions asked in the first years of the nineteenth century was the union with Ireland. For the first thirty or more years, following the Act of Union and the destruction of Grattan's Parliament, the Irish Members at Westminster were much less formidable critics of established government than their successors were to be, in spite of Grattan's threat to 'send into the ranks of your Parliament, and into the very heart of your constitution, a hundred of the greatest scoundrels in the kingdom.' For one thing, the Catholic Irish remained unrepresented by anyone except Protestant Members. But Irish affairs, and questions on Irish affairs, came to occupy more and more time in Westminster.

In 1809, for instance, Sir John Newport, M.P. for Waterford, asked whether any steps had been taken 'for the criminal prosecution of the late collector for Cork in consequence of his embezzlement of the public money.' To this the future Duke of Wellington, in his capacity of Chief Secretary for Ireland, answered with characteristic brevity: 'I do not understand that any steps have been taken for his prosecution. He is now, however, in gaol.'[25]

Five years later the same questioner wanted to know why no account of the population of Ireland had been laid, and was told by Sir Robert Peel, who had then succeeded to the Irish Secretaryship, that the census returns 'were in such an imperfect state that they were utterly unfit to be laid on the table of the House.'[26]

With the steady increase in the number of questions asked during the war period, a feeling developed among certain Members that

5

better provision ought to be made for supplying answers. In 1804 Admiral Berkeley, Member for Gloucester, announced that he had attended 'almost daily for some time in the hopes of seeing some of the Lords of the Admiralty in their places in the House to obtain an answer to a question.'[27]

Eight years later Whitbread asked Perceval whether Richard Ryder, the Home Secretary, had informed the Prince Regent that there were petitions ready to be presented to him. Perceval, after saying that petitions were normally presented on levée days and no levée had yet been appointed, added that it was a singular action on Whitbread's part to ask him 'what somebody else has done, with whose department I am not connected.' To this Whitbread replied: 'It is the duty of the Secretary of State, as a Member of Parliament, to attend in his place; and in his absence it is the right of any other Member of Parliament to ask for information from those who, it is probable, can afford it on any subject upon which the public interest demands explanation.'[28] The upshot was that Perceval promised that Ryder would be present the next day, but the uncertainty of finding the appropriate Minister in the House when an urgent question was to be asked remained a source of dissatisfaction.

In consequence the practice developed, as a convenience but not as an obligation, of giving advance notice of certain questions. In 1812 Lord Holland, after asking an embarrassing question in the House of Lords about the activities in the United States of a British secret agent named Captain Henry, said that he had delayed his question for twenty-four hours to give Liverpool 'time to refresh his memory on the subject.'[29] A month later in the House of Commons Stuart Wortley spoke of having given advance notice of a question as he 'would have done to any other Member of Parliament.'[30]

The lack of any arrangement, whereby Ministers could be relied upon to be present, was not the only obstacle to the provision of satisfactory replies. In answering questions on foreign affairs, Ministers were necessarily handicapped by the poverty of communications, which wartime conditions accentuated, and for answers on all subjects outside their immediate knowledge they had to depend on an unsystematically organized administrative machine.

Nearly three months after his motion on the war with Holkar had been defeated, Francis asked whether any despatches on the subject had yet been received, and was told by Castlereagh that 'the packet containing these despatches was taken by the French on its passage to Europe.'[31] Two years later Humphry Howorth, Member for Evesham, who had himself served as an Army surgeon in India, asked for information about the mutiny at Vellore, and in particular whether any steps had been taken 'either to remove those persons who were so obnoxious to the natives, or to attempt to conciliate those who were so much irritated.' Robert Dundas, who not long before had assumed the office of President of the Board of Control for the Affairs of India, answered, with some frankness, that on the immediate causes of the mutiny the members of the Board then in office had not had time to make up their minds. It was then agreed that action should be deferred until the return of Sir John Cradock from Madras.[32]

A number of reforms in the civil administration had been carried out following the alarming revelations made by Burke and others some twenty years earlier. In 1802 a clearer form of estimates and accounts was instituted, and there was an effective division between the King's personal and administrative expenditure. The number of sinecures had also been substantially reduced. Yet in 1806 Henry Petty-Fitzmaurice, generally known as Lord Henry Petty, could state, when he was Chancellor of the Exchequer, that 'the arrears make the enormous sum of £445,000,000 of public money unaccounted for, that is to say a larger sum unaccounted for than comprises the whole of the national debt'; and when the affairs of a First Clerk of the Treasury named Chinnery, who had converted £70,000 to his own use, were investigated, Perceval admitted that Chinnery's manipulation of the accounts had gone on so long that 'it was a matter of little surprise that the auditors were deceived.'[33]

On matters of major importance the Government often found itself in the position of simply having no information. Considerable interest, for instance, was aroused in the affair of a Portuguese spy, who was described by the name of Colville and who had been arrested. Whitbread called attention to his case in Parliament on more than one occasion in 1811; yet three years later, when Whitbread asked whether Colville was still alive, and if so, whether he had been released, Goulburn, answering for the Government, said he could not take it upon himself to state whether he was alive or not. Peel came to Goulburn's help by saying he believed Colville was alive, but he could not say whether he would be liberated.[34]

In these circumstances, and with such inadequate sources of information on so many subjects, it is perhaps remarkable that on 1st December 1814 the Government could supply satisfactory answers to five questions asked in rapid succession on such varied subjects as the disembodying of the militia, a loan to Spain, the household establishment of the Princess Charlotte, the sale of frigates by the Admiralty, and the problem of whether refugees from Spain would be handed over to the Spanish Government.[35]

The practice of giving notice of questions, which greatly facilitated the business of answering, developed informally for some time, without rulings from the Chair or Standing Orders on the subject. But during the period of the Napoleonic wars a number of pronouncements, of a more or less official nature, served to fashion the forms which questions were or were not allowed to take.

The right to ask questions was still resisted on certain occasions. In 1805 Lord Eldon followed the example of more than one Lord Chancellor before him in opposing what he regarded as an irregular innovation in procedure. The Duke of Clarence, the future King William IV, who normally at that time distinguished himself in the House of Lords by resisting attempts to abolish the slave trade, had asked two questions on different subjects in rapid succession. After the answers had been given, Eldon delivered what he called 'a serious protest against questions and conversations which are inconsistent with the order and regularity of your Lordships' proceedings.'[36]

The Duke of Clarence did not accept the rebuke willingly, and Eldon's assertion accorded neither with the practice of the House of Lords nor with the fully recognized procedure of the House of Commons. In 1807, when a Member named Dickenson apologized in the Commons for asking a question about the Government's intention to allow Catholics to serve in the Army and Navy while taking an oath consistent with their religion, he was told: 'No apology is necessary from the hon. gentleman for the exercise of one of the first privileges of a Member of Parliament, that of calling upon His Majesty's Ministers for explanation upon any great and important subject.'[37]

More than one Speaker's ruling on the propriety of a particular question was given during the war period. When Fox, after his return to office, was asked in 1806 to elaborate an opinion he had expressed a fortnight earlier on the Act of Union with Ireland—an event which he had described as 'one of the most disgraceful that ever happened to that country'[38]—the Speaker, Charles Abbot, intervened to say: 'For any Member to put a question to another with reference to any expressions that may have been used by him in a former debate is wholly irregular and inconsistent with the received practice of the House.' The Speaker left it to Fox to decide whether he would reply, and Fox duly accepted the challenge.[39]

Five years later a Member named Prendergast read a newspaper account of the proceedings at a public dinner of the Missionary Society. At this affair a number of M.P.'s, including Wilberforce, were reported to have agreed to a resolution that £250 should be given to persons 'reading the Scriptures in the market-places of the populous cities of Asia.' Prendergast asked whether the report was true. At this point the Speaker ruled: 'It is certainly quite new in the proceedings of Parliament for Members to be questioned in this House about what passed at tavern dinners.'[40]

The extent to which a discussion could be allowed to arise out of the answer to a question was also the subject of two important rulings made on occasions when the House of Commons was in a state of some excitement. In April 1810 disturbances of an alarming nature to a country at war had taken place in Piccadilly. A detachment of the Life Guards, while marching down the street, had been pelted with stones and mud, and then fired on; a Member of Parliament, who had been on duty with his troops at the time, described how a soldier near him had been shot with a ball through the jaw; one of the crowd around the soldier had been killed, and at the coroner's inquest a verdict had been returned of 'wilful murder' against 'a life-guardsman unknown.'

More than one question was asked about this affair, and when Whitbread was called to order by another Member for prolonging the discussion, Speaker Abbot stated: 'It has been deemed generally convenient to the House to extend a conversation of this nature beyond the mere answer to the question.'[41] Whitbread thereupon took advantage of his right to propose a motion on the subject without notice, a right which was still occasionally claimed, although four years earlier Speaker Abbot had stated that it was 'the recent practice ... on every proposition for bringing forward any measure on which the House is to act, to give notice of its being intended to be brought forward.'[42]

The other ruling on supplementary questions and discussions was given in March 1808. On this occasion the original question, asked by Lord Henry Petty, was an enquiry about the Government's intentions regarding the blockade of enemy ports, with particular reference to the action to be taken in Ireland. After the answer had been given, George Tierney, a combative politician, who had once fought a duel with Pitt, complained of delays in acting. He in turn was answered by Perceval, and when several Members, including Tierney, rose, Speaker Abbot called the House to order, pointing out that there was no motion before it. John Foster, Chancellor of the Exchequer for Ireland, declaring the 'conversation' at an end, then moved the order of the day for going into committee.[43]

At this point Tierney announced that he would later call the attention of the House to the manner in which he had been 'prevented from replying to a personal observation.' This was clearly a reflection on the Speaker, and in view of the somewhat haphazard manner in which questions and answers were still given, it could be expected to be both personally and procedurally a serious matter.

Later that evening, just before the House was due to rise, George Canning, who was then Foreign Secretary, asked Tierney whether he proposed to give notice of any motion on the subject of the Speaker's conduct. Tierney appeared rather flustered by these tactics, and shifted his ground in the course of his answer. On the one hand he complained of the inconvenience he had suffered at being interrupted, and on the other he declared his 'intention in future to prevent that species of debate which is called conversation, unless there is some specific motion before the House or some understanding established as to the latitude which should be allowed in it.' His argument was not an easy one to sustain, for he was both objecting to the practice of supplementary questions, and complaining of being interrupted when himself indulging in that practice. But he was at least pointing to the need for a clearer understanding of what was and what was not permissible in questions.

Speaker Abbot accepted Tierney's complaint as a personal stricture on himself, and took some trouble to justify what he had done. 'It has ever been the usage of the House,' he said, 'and it has been found a most convenient usage, to permit questions to be asked tending to facilitate the arrangement of business.' This usage, of whose history he could not have been very well informed, had, he pointed out, been duly followed earlier that day, but when several Members had risen, he had felt obliged to end the discussion. He then added that when Foster 'distinctly spoke of the conversation, no choice was left me on the subject.'

Abbot went on to state that he had been chosen Speaker four times, and had occupied the Chair for seven years, and that this was the first imputation of its kind made against him. He must, he said, leave it to the House to decide. Canning thereupon moved 'that this House does highly approve of the upright, able and impartial conduct of the Right Hon. C. Abbot in the Chair of this House.' Abbot had to put the question himself, and he did so in a low voice and in a visible state of emotion. There was a loud shout of 'Aye!' from all parts of the House, and Tierney alone opposed the motion.[44]

Tierney's ill-tempered outburst led to the overwhelming vindication of the conduct of Charles Abbot, who had guided the practice of questions during some of the most important years in the development of the procedure. The division on Canning's motion also served as a vote of approval, by implication, of the practice of allowing supplementary questions to be asked, in so far as the Speaker chose to permit them. From then on the ways in which successive Speakers carried out this duty was to shape, with growing precision, the procedure of Question Time in the nineteenth and twentieth-century Parliaments.

V

The Growing Force of Public Opinion
(1815–1832)

IN the twenty years following the Speaker's ruling of 1783, questions asked in Parliament had been developed as a weapon of opposition by eloquent orators on major political issues. During the Napoleonic wars they had come to be used more and more as a means of probing various aspects of administration. Between 1815 and the Reform Act of 1832 the parliamentary question gained a new significance as a method by which public opinion, as formulated over wider and wider areas, could be expressed.

Before 1815 the subjects on which questions were asked, although extensive in range, were mostly such as might have been expected to come to the knowledge of Members of either House in the course of their normal social lives. Those topics of war and foreign affairs which gave rise to questions were, no doubt, discussed and—with the increasing influence of newspapers—read about in London clubs; and the alarms and scandals to which attention was called were of a predominantly metropolitan character: a riot in Piccadilly, costly works in St. James's Park, the birth of a bastard in Kensington, an architectural threat to Chelsea.

After 1815 a change came over the character of questions, which was a reflection of the change in parliamentary discussions as a whole. Lord Egremont, who had been a friend of Fox, gave expression to one aspect of this change in 1827, when he declared: 'The business and eloquence of Parliament have undergone a total change within the short period of my remembrance. . . . The flights of Demosthenes are as little suited to sinking funds and paper money, and corn and fir, timber and cotton, as a trumpet would be to a Quakers' meeting.'

72

Another aspect of the change which was to occur was indicated in a question asked by Lord Holland in the House of Lords as early as February 1812. Holland asked whether it was intended to give any explanation to Parliament about the disturbances in and around Nottingham, which had continued for a year. This was the beginning of a long series of questions which were to be asked about a world of which few Members of Parliament had first-hand knowledge, but of which they were to become increasingly aware, the world of the poor in the large provincial towns.

Ten days after Lord Holland had asked his question in the Lords, Richard Ryder, the Home Secretary, moved in the Commons for leave to bring in a Bill 'for the more exemplary punishment of persons destroying or injuring any stocking or lace frames or other machines or engines used in the framework knitted manufactory.' In explanation of the Government's proposals he said: 'It is notorious that houses have been broken open, and machinery of different kinds destroyed, and that a system of riots has existed for the last three months, a system bordering on insurrection.'[1]

The riots were not confined to Nottingham, but were expected to spread to Leicestershire and Derbyshire, and the existing laws were considered too lenient for those who set out deliberately to destroy machinery. Before the introduction of his Bill, the breaking of frames, Ryder explained, had been 'a minor felony, punishable with transportation for fourteen years.' He went on to say: 'That enactment has proved completely insufficient to deter from the commission of the offence which it was meant to guard against, and it is my intention to propose that the offence should now be made capital.' Within three weeks, despite Whitbread's vigorous protest that the death penalty was already imposed too lightly, the Bill passed through all its stages.

The revelations of what was going on in Nottingham, which followed from Lord Holland's question, filled in only one part of the picture of the life of the poor in Britain which was to be depicted by Members of Parliament during the next twenty years. Many other questions, prompted by an increasingly restive public opinion, were asked on the subject, most of them, though taking the form of questions, being in effect demands for action.

Between 1815 and 1832 the parliamentary question came to be more and more a method of insisting on what was known as

'reform.' 'Reform' was a catchword; what was meant was the
creation of new safeguards, a new kind of Government and new
institutions, all of which would respond to the fact that Britain had
undergone an industrial revolution.

One of the most insistent demands was for reforms in the system,
or lack of system, whereby relief was given to the poor. Questions
on this subject were asked repeatedly between the end of the
Napoleonic wars and the eventual passage of the comprehensive
Poor Law Amendment Act of 1834. Governmental pronouncements on the condition of the people, except when major disturbances occurred, tended to be bland and reassuring. In 1819 'our
internal prosperity' was mentioned in the Speech from the Throne;
in 1824 it was stated that agriculture 'by the steady operation of
natural causes is gradually reassuming the station to which its
importance entitles it'; and the next year it was actually asserted in
the King's Speech that 'there never was a period in the history of
this country when all the great interests of the nation were at the
same time in so thriving a condition, or when a feeling of content
and satisfaction was more widely diffused through all classes of the
British people.'[2] The more radical Members were not convinced by
these analyses, as the questions they asked continually showed.

In 1816 John Christian Curwen, M.P. for Carlisle, who advocated
revision of the Poor Laws with some persistence, asked Castlereagh
whether the Government would propose any new measures in this
field. Castlereagh disclaimed any such intention on the part of the
Government, but he expressed the hope that this would not deter
Curwen, whom he described as 'very well informed on the subject,'
from bringing forward a motion himself.[3] This attitude of benevolent neutrality, whereby the responsibility for initiating action
remained with private Members, continued to be adopted by the
Governments headed by the Earl of Liverpool and the Duke of
Wellington on almost every occasion when the subject of the Poor
Laws was raised.

Curwen, after stating that 'from 1760 we may date a great revolution in the state of the country,' and revealing that 3,000,000 people,
or nearly one-third of the population, were in 'the degraded state of
pauperism,' moved successfully for the appointment of a select
committee to consider the Poor Laws.[4] But the most comforting
assurance he could extract from Castlereagh was that 'His Majesty's

Ministers will most cheerfully dedicate so much of their time as they can possibly withdraw from other duties to assist in the investigation of this most important subject.'[5] These other duties at the time consisted, to a great extent, of preventing seditious meetings, suspending the Habeas Corpus Act, and increasing the penalties for poaching.

The Committee and its successors, to whose appointment the persistent questioning by Curwen gave rise, were by no means ineffective. In February 1818 Castlereagh agreed that 'great good has resulted from the report of the former Committee—even if no legislative measure should follow—from the facts which it disclosed';[6] and legislation did indeed follow in time. A measure enabling relief to be administered under a less rigorous system of residential qualification, and another empowering bodies of responsible people in every parish to appoint paid overseers of poor relief, both came into force in 1819. Both could be claimed as direct results of the work of one of the Committees. An Act of 1817, designed to encourage savings banks, had a similar inspiration.

Curwen's successors as leading advocates of reforms in the Poor Laws, William Sturges-Bourne, who in 1827 became Home Secretary for a short time, and Henry Brougham, later to become Lord Chancellor and the champion of Queen Caroline, found that without the active assistance of the Government they could achieve only limited successes. In 1819 Sturges-Bourne, when moving the second reading of the Poor Rates Misapplication Bill, complained that 'whilst the nation considers this as the most momentous question, and the one that presses hardest on them, such is the apathy and indifference of Ministers that not one of them has thought it incumbent upon them to attend.'[7]

But the effect of continual questions and motions on successive Governments was cumulative. When Peel was asked in 1830 whether the Government proposed any measures 'with a view of relieving the extreme pressure of the lower and also of the middling classes,' he protested somewhat irritably against 'this course of asking day after day questions with regard to the measures contemplated by the Government.' He added that many measures could be cited as serving the purpose mentioned, and included among these the removal of the duty on beer and the employment of the Irish at home to prevent them from migrating to England.[8]

It was too a question asked in the House of Lords in February
1832 which led to the announcement that a commission would be
set up to enquire into the practical application of the Poor Laws. By
the time this question was asked, the complexion of the Government
had changed, Brougham was in office, and it was he who gave the
answer.[9] The recommendations of the 1832 Commission provided
the basis for the Act of 1834 and the first complete overhaul, on a
stern and utilitarian basis, of the Poor Laws dating from the reign of
Queen Elizabeth.

The conditions of the poor in England gave rise to many questions which revealed a striking contrast between the standpoint of
Liverpool and his colleagues and that of their most persistent
interrogators. But the contrast was even stronger on the subject of
the poor in Ireland. In 1822, for instance, members of the Government in both Houses faced a barrage of criticism for their failure
to relieve the Irish famine, after a question had been asked by the
Earl of Darnley in the House of Lords in April.

Darnley's question was whether the attention of the Government
had been called to the distress prevailing in Ireland, and whether any
measures of relief had been adopted. Liverpool admitted some
knowledge of the conditions, and added that 'measures, comparable
to precedents established on former occasions and found sufficient,
have been resorted to.' In explanation of this somewhat chilling
answer he added: 'Nothing, except in extreme cases, could be more
improper than the interference of Government with the subsistence
of the country.'

This was an expression of a political philosophy, in extension of
which Liverpool told the House of Lords a story of a foreigner, who
had expressed surprise that 'so great a city as London should be
so well supplied without any regulations.' The answer given to the
enquiring foreigner had been that 'the reason of its being so well
supplied was precisely because there were no regulations for that
purpose.'[10]

Liverpool's personal interpretation of the doctrine of *laissez-faire*
was not considered by certain Irish Members, and by some of his
Whig and Radical opponents, wholly applicable to Ireland in 1822.
One Irish M.P. pointed out that thousands of people in Ireland
lived on one dish of oatmeal and water a day, and that whereas

normally the whole of Southern Ireland lived on potatoes for the greater part of the year, the famine had prevented them even from doing that. Henry Goulburn, the Chief Secretary for Ireland, answered this attack by saying that 'agitation of the subject would augment rather than alleviate the evils.'[11]

Later Thomas Spring-Rice, the Whig Member for Limerick, revealed that one-third of the population of that county subsisted on charity.[12] But the most that could be drawn from Liverpool was an announcement that the Government had sent an unspecified sum of money to buy both provisions for the destitute and seed to prevent a recurrence of famine, and a subsequent statement that the Government had 'cautiously' sent a supply of food, but considered 'other sources as a much more eligible mode of relief.'[13]

For a variety of reasons the state of Ireland between 1815 and 1832 provided grounds for parliamentary questions to be asked as a means of demanding reforms, and for the greater part of the period the main emphasis was put on reforms which would increase the liberties of the individual rather than those which would alleviate the distress of the poor. Between 1810 and 1833 Parliament appointed 114 commissions and 60 select committees to investigate Irish affairs. But as was generally recognized, even by the bitterest antagonists, the principal issue was a religious one.

The main subject of dispute was the discrimination sanctioned by laws, which had originally been designed for purely English purposes, against persons of the Catholic faith, and therefore against the overwhelming majority of Irishmen. Sir Robert Peel, when stating to the House of Commons in 1827 the reason why he had resigned from the office of Home Secretary, expressed with some clarity the policy followed by himself and most of his colleagues. 'For a space of eighteen years,' he said, 'I have pursued one undeviating course of conduct, offering during the whole of that time an uncompromising but a temperate, a fair and, as I believe, a constitutional resistance to the making of any further concessions to the Roman Catholics.' The opposite view was put with equal clarity by the Earl of Donoughmore, when he said: 'Englishmen talk of liberty and freedom and so forth more than any other country of Europe, while they deprive six millions of Catholics of their freedom of conscience.'[14]

The battle over the subject of discrimination against Catholic was one in which there could hardly be any compromise, and the questions asked on the subject, especially during the last two years before Wellington and Peel made their ultimate and reluctant concession, varied little in either form or content. In 1827 Joseph Hume, Member for Aberdeen, whose numerous questions were usually concerned with what he considered to be administrative extravagance, asked Peel in the course of a debate whether he would give his support to a Bill for annulling the main Acts which penalized people for their religious beliefs. Peel refused to be drawn, and said: 'I think it rather hard that I should be punished with a question because I happened to be paying attention to the debate.'[15]

In January of the next year Lord Clifden, using the normal form of the parliamentary question, asked the Duke of Wellington whether it was 'intended during the present session to introduce a Bill for the repeal of the existing penal laws affecting the Roman Catholics.' Wellington replied: 'Government has no intention of bringing forward any such measure.'[16] But less than a fortnight later Wellington, answering a similar question from the Earl of Darnley, admitted that 'there will be measures brought forward in the course of the session in the other House.'[17]

The principal measure brought forward in the House of Commons was a motion by Lord John Russell for setting up a committee to consider the repeal of the Test and Corporation Acts of King Charles II's reign, which were the main sources of authority for religious discrimination. The motion was carried, but it was not until the next year that the Duke of Wellington felt ready to accept a formula which would enable the growing public demand to be met.

In the Speech from the Throne at the opening of the session of 1829 it was stated that 'His Majesty recommends that . . . you should take into your deliberate consideration the whole condition of Ireland, and that you should review the laws which impose civil disabilities on His Majesty's Roman Catholic subjects.'[18] When the Duke of Newcastle asked Wellington whether he intended to move for a committee to consider the subject, the answer given this time was that 'a measure for the adjustment of what are called the Roman Catholic claims' would be 'brought forward in a substantive shape by His Majesty's Ministers without going through a committee.'[19]

A month later Peel was explaining to the House of Commons that the government of the country was being paralysed by the failure to settle the Catholic issue, and speculating on 'what becomes of Ireland, and what may become of her, if these party conflicts without a result continue beyond the present session of general tranquillity.' His concluding argument was that by acting as the Government then proposed, 'we shall have dissolved the great moral alliance that has given strength to the cause of the Roman Catholics; we shall range on our side the illustrious authorities which have heretofore been enlisted on theirs; the rallying cry of "civil liberty" will be all our own.'[20]

The man whom Disraeli was one day to describe as 'the greatest Member of Parliament that ever lived' had shown a talent for adjusting his opinions, of which Parliament would learn more later; the Bill, which the Duke of Newcastle in a last-ditch stand described as one 'for oppressing and injuring the King and for introducing Popery and arbitrary power,'[21] was passed; and a new phase in parliamentary history opened on 6th May 1829, when the Earl of Surrey took his seat as Member for Horsham and the first Catholic to sit in the House of Commons since the disqualification.

The cause of the rights of the individual, which had inspired so many questions about the disabilities of Catholics, prompted a number of other questions demanding action. In particular, demands were made for just treatment of those who were in prison, either for political or for other offences.

In 1817 Henry Bennet asked a question about a man named Thomas Evans, who, he claimed, had been summoned to appear six times before the Privy Council, merely to be asked whether he knew the notorious insurrectionary, Arthur Thistlewood. Other complaints made about Evans's treatment were that he had been put in irons, that he had not breathed fresh air for months, and that he had been deprived of his only source of amusement, his flute.[22] The case of Evans was raised several times, and eventually Castlereagh was drawn into saying: 'Circumstances have arisen in this case which could lead to a correction of the evil, and the presumption is that wherever an abuse does exist, it will not be long before it comes to the knowledge of the Government, who, I can assure the House, will pay the utmost attention to it.'[23]

Earlier Bennet had called attention to the fate of fifty-eight prisoners under sentence of death in Newgate gaol, by asking why it took so long to decide their fates. Castlereagh attributed the delays to the indisposition of the Regent and 'the difficulty and inconvenience of assembling the law officers at Brighton who ought to be present in Council on these occasions.'[24]

Bennet was not satisfied, and nearly a year later he moved successfully for a return of the numbers under sentence of death in the same prison.[25] When the return was made, he described a visit which he had himself paid to Newgate, where he had found many of the prisoners 'senseless and half-intoxicated' and looking forward to the carrying out of the death sentence as a relief from suspense. Bennet's agitation was so far effective that Castlereagh gave a promise that decisions on the death sentence would be speeded up, and it was announced that a meeting of the Privy Council in that connection would be held the next day.[26]

Better treatment for soldiers, the protection of working men from what was considered to be the tyranny of political unions, and justice towards a member of the Royal Family, who was widely believed to be suffering from persecution, were among other demands stated in the form of parliamentary questions, and put forward in response to different expressions of public opinion.

The more radical Members continued year after year to agitate the subject of corporal punishment in the Army, frequently by means of questions, and there could be no doubt that their exertions were beginning to produce results. During a spirited debate in the Commons in 1824 a certain Colonel Dawkins stated that the number of floggings inflicted in the Army had lately become fewer, owing to 'the liberal regulations of the Duke of York.' To this Hume replied : 'The diminution in the number of floggings is not so much owing to the regulations of the Duke of York as to the exertions of my hon. friend, the Member for Westminster.'[27]

The Member for Westminster referred to was Sir Francis Burdett, and the truth of Hume's statement was illustrated three years later during a debate on the Mutiny Bill. A Member named Sir Henry Vivian then said that when he had himself held an Army command, he had found it commonly believed that through the efforts of Burdett corporal punishment had been abolished; in consequence he had had to have one man flogged in order to restore order. When, therefore, Burdett in 1830 asked Sir Henry Hardinge, the Secretary at War, whether he would object to having a return made of the number of corporal punishments inflicted in each regiment of the line respectively during the past year, Hardinge replied that he would object most strongly. He did undertake to supply Burdett with the information privately, but insisted that the making of any public return would be 'a proceeding of a most invidious character.'[28]

Questions about the power of unions were asked in 1832, after Earl Grey's Government had come into office. The incident which gave rise to one question was a murder committed at South Shields, for which two miners, who were union members, were believed to be responsible. After it had been stated in an answer given in the Commons that the affair was being investigated by the Home Office, Peel, who was then in opposition, declared: 'What I have always felt about the subject of these unions is that the industrious classes are more interested in their suppression than the higher classes, because we can always escape, to a certain extent, from their effect. But those in humbler life, whose only dependence is their labour, are subjected to the full brunt of their tyranny, and are not allowed to take their labour to the best market. I am therefore certainly of the opinion that some legislative enactment should be introduced for the purpose of remedying this evil.'[24]

With a similar intention the Marquis of Londonderry asked Grey the next day in the House of Lords whether he would be prepared to 'adopt some more efficacious means of putting an end to political unions.' Grey replied that he had no intention of introducing any new legislation on the subject of unions, and that he looked to 'the good sense of the people to put an end to them.'[30]

Public opinion was at no time during the period so vociferous on the subject of unions as it was on the subject of Queen Caroline, the wife of King George IV. In February 1820, shortly after the death of King George III, but before the dissolution of Parliament which followed in consequence, Joseph Hume asked what provision was to be made in the future for the new Queen. An Act, whereby she had been provided with £30,000 a year, expired on the death of King George III, and this prompted Hume to ask: 'Is it now intended to leave her unprovided for? In what situation is it meant that the Queen of England shall stand? Is she to be left a beggar on the Continent?'

Hume was asking a dangerous question. It was notorious that the relations between the new King and Queen were nearly as bad as they could be, and although those who were well informed knew that the Queen's conduct during her European travels had been openly scandalous, her name was already becoming a rallying-point for radical opposition. Castlereagh expressed regret that any attempt should be made 'to press into discussion the very delicate question alluded to.'

This immediately roused Tierney. He stated openly that he would not vote for any sum to be allowed to Queen Caroline 'until some explanation shall be given or promised as to the rumours which have gone abroad with respect to her conduct upon the Continent.'[31] The storm which was to occupy most of Parliament's attention and become the subject of frenzied public interest throughout the year 1820 was thereby set in motion.

In July a report of a secret committee, which had been set up by the House of Lords, was published. Reference was made to allegations, well supported by evidence, charging the Queen with 'an adulterous connection with a foreigner, originally in her service in a menial capacity.'[32] The Queen decided to fight the issue, Brougham conducted her case energetically, and Parliament—and, of course, the public—learnt the most intimate details of the Queen's affair with a footman named Bergami.

Neither Queen Caroline nor the Government gained much advantage from the business. The Queen had her private life made into a public scandal, and the Government, for its part, was considerably shaken by the extraordinary popular enthusiasm for the Queen's cause. During the debate in the House of Lords on the third reading of the Bill to deprive the Queen of her title, Earl Grey summed up what the Government had done in damning words: 'They have thus for many months agitated the nation, they have produced a general stagnation of private and public business, and they have given a most favourable opportunity, were it desired, to the enemies of peace and tranquillity. They have betrayed their King, insulted their Queen, and have given a shock to the morals of society by the promulgation of the detestable and disgusting evidence, in the hearing of which the House has been so long occupied.'[33]

Queen Caroline's name proved in time to be a poor rallying-point for those who considered themselves oppressed by the Government in other ways. Once the scandal had died down, the popular demands for reform became more practical and less emotional in nature, and of all the demands none was voiced more persistently than that for the reform of Parliament itself.

The problem of whether the manner in which Parliament was elected should be altered was an ancient one. Even Locke, the prophet of so much of the political theory which was to be put into practice in the eighteenth century, had admitted the illogicality of the existing system; both the Earl of Chatham and his son had advocated measures of electoral reform, which, had they been carried, would have been considered sweeping; and in the quarter of a century following the outbreak of the French Revolution more and more societies had been founded in England to promote reform. But agitation on the subject did not afford a widespread and genuinely revolutionary threat until the eighteen-twenties.

Then the belief developed that there was no hope of an improvement in the conditions of the new industrial towns until there was a complete overhaul of the electoral system. Many of these towns returned no Members at all, for in England, Scotland, and Wales the constituencies were virtually the same as they had been at the time of the union with Scotland. Changes were called for not only in the distribution of seats; there were also demands for a new system of what was sometimes scornfully referred to as 'democracy.' In 1830 the political union founded by Thomas Attwood in Birmingham passed a resolution in favour of 'such a reform in the Commons' House of Parliament as may ensure a real and effectual representation of the lower and middle classes of the people in that House.'

Proceedings in Parliament reflected the growth of public opinion on the problem of reform, but the normal method by which it was brought forward was the presentation of petitions, often signed by huge numbers of people, rather than the parliamentary question. The volume of these petitions soon became indigestible, and after Speaker Manners Sutton had agreed to take the Chair at noon on Saturday, 26th February 1830, for the express purpose of receiving petitions on reform, Parliament earnestly set itself to devise methods for keeping the discussion of petitions within reasonable bounds.

Although the petition continued to be the chief method of parliamentary agitation, questions on reform became more frequent from 1829 onwards, when the Whig Opposition began to feel more confident of its strength as the reforming party. But the answers extracted from Peel gave little away. In March 1830, for instance, replying to a question from the Marquis of Blandford, he said that it was impossible to make a return of the number of qualified voters, and that it would be 'a most dangerous practice to allow the returning officer to decide upon the number of persons entitled to vote in any particular borough or city.'[34] The argument of administrative difficulty could be used as readily as that of constitutional danger to block the provision of information tending to favour reform.

When Earl Grey's Government came into office, pledged to a policy of reform, its Ministers began with a number of unequivocal statements. In November 1830 Grey told the House of Lords: 'It is necessary that the Government . . . should take into immediate consideration the state of the representation, with a view to the correction of those defects which have been occasioned in it by the operation of time, and with a view to the re-establishment of that confidence upon the part of the people which, I am afraid, Parliament does not at present enjoy to the full extent that is essential for the welfare and safety of the country and the preservation of the Government.'[35] This policy was quickly translated into action, and in March 1831 a triumph for the reforming party occurred. The Reform Bill passed its second reading with a majority of one, and a scene took place described in the famous words of Macaulay: 'And the jaw of Peel fell, and the face of Twiss was as the face of a damned soul. . . .'

But the battle was still undecided, and with the House of Lords likely to prove intractable, there were rumours of a possible dissolution. By this time Grey had become cautious about announcing the tactics he intended to adopt. In April a question addressed to Ministers in general was asked in the House of Lords by Lord Wharncliffe, a Tory politician, who had sat in the House of Commons for more than twenty years. Wharncliffe wanted to know 'whether there is any truth in the statement that they have advised His Majesty to dissolve Parliament, and that it has been resolved to adopt that course.' Grey answered: 'I believe the noble Lord's question will be admitted to be one of a very unusual nature, and I can hardly bring myself to believe that when he put it the noble Lord expected an answer. But whatever the noble Lord's expectation may have been, I have only to say I must decline answering his question.'[36]

A more explicit answer was given the next day, when Lord Lyndhurst insisted, with evident meaning, on the Crown's right to dissolve Parliament. Almost at once an uproar, which was probably unique in the history of the House of Lords, broke out, and a scene developed which was described by Brougham as a 'bear-garden exhibition.' The highlight of the occasion was provided by the Marquis of Londonderry, who, according to the description left by Greville in his diary, 'rose, roared, gesticulated, held up his whip, and four or five Lords held him down by the tail of his coat to prevent his flying on somebody.' The closing scene of the drama was the sudden appearance of King William IV, who announced: 'I have come to meet you for the purpose of proroguing this Parliament with a view to its immediate dissolution.'[37]

The King's professed object in agreeing to the dissolution was, in his own words, that of 'ascertaining the sense of my people.' A tumultuous election followed. There were riots in many parts of the country; the Duke of Northumberland was reported to have promised £100,000 in support of one candidate; working men subscribed from their wages to help those who stood for reform; and in spite of the allegedly corrupt nature of the system, the reform party gained a clear victory. Earl Grey formed another Government, and Lord John Russell was given the task of steering a Reform Bill through the House of Commons.

Russell carried out his task successfully, but in May 1832 the Government was defeated in the House of Lords. Grey offered to resign; the King, in spite of having ascertained the sense of his people, accepted his resignation; petitions poured into Parliament calling upon the Commons to withhold supplies; many middle-class citizens refused to pay taxes; and there was a threat of a run on the banks. Revolution threatened, but for some ten days no effective decision was taken. Then Lord Althorp, who had been Chancellor of the Exchequer in Grey's Government, gave an answer to a question asked by Hume in the Commons. In this he said: 'His Majesty's Ministers conceive they have secured for the passage of the Reform Bill such an arrangement as they deem sufficient, and therefore that we continue to hold the offices we are now in possession of.'[38]

The arrangement Althorp referred to was the King's undertaking to create, if necessary, a sufficient number of peers to ensure the passage of the Bill, although three days later, in answer to a question from the Duke of Newcastle, Grey denied the authenticity of a letter which had appeared in the *Morning Chronicle*, and which purported to be the King's express undertaking to this effect.[39] The threat to swamp the House of Lords with new peers did not have to be carried out. Under the guidance of the Duke of Wellington, the Lords arranged to have the Bill passed, and it became law on 7th June 1832. It was an Act designed, as its preamble stated, for 'correcting divers abuses' and to deprive 'many inconsiderable places of the right of returning members,' as well as 'to grant such privilege to large, populous and wealthy towns,' 'to increase the number of knights of the shire,' 'to extend the elective franchise to many of His Majesty's subjects,' and 'to diminish the expense of elections.'

The great parliamentary issues on which questions were asked between 1815 and 1832 were mostly home affairs. Events which took place overseas, even while peace negotiations were being conducted in Vienna, gave rise to relatively few important parliamentary occasions. In 1818, for instance, Humphry Howorth, who maintained a constant interest in the subject of India, asked Canning whether he had any confirmation of reports that Company troops had been attacked by Mahratta forces, and that Poona had subsequently been captured by the Company. Canning disclaimed any wish to withhold information, but added: 'Little interest is excited here by occurrences in that quarter of the globe. Singular as it may seem, it has never been the practice to communicate to Parliament intelligence from India, except in cases of a very extraordinary nature.'[40] This statement about lack of interest could hardly have been made some thirty years earlier, when nothing had inflamed parliamentary passions more violently than the affair of Warren Hastings.

In spite of Parliament's preoccupation with the internal condition of the country, the character of questions asked on foreign affairs during this period had something in common with that of many of

the questions on domestic subjects. The tendency for the question
to become in effect a demand for a foreign policy which would
accord with popular opinion became steadily more evident. In 1830
Greville shrewdly noted in his diary: 'It is astonishing the interest
the people generally take in the slavery question, which is the work
of the Methodists, and shows the enormous influence they have in
the country.' As Greville suggested, the kind of foreign policy for
which there was the most vociferous popular demand was a radical
one, which would be strongly influenced by moral considerations.

Religious practices in India, the fate of the Christian peoples of
the Eastern Mediterranean in their struggles with the Turks, the
pretensions of Imperial Russia, and discrimination against persons
of colour in the State of Georgia all gave rise to questions asked
between 1815 and 1832.

Thus it was through an answer to a question put by Hume that
the Commons learnt that in five years some 10,000 widows had
been immolated on funeral piles in Bengal alone; and in 1819 a
question asked by Frederick Douglas, Member for Banbury and
himself something of a Hellenist, led to a prolonged attack on the
Government over the fate of the people of Parga on the coast of
Albania. Douglas's question was whether the Government had
'adopted any proceeding to prevent the surrender of Parga to the
Ottoman Porte.'

Parga had been at various times under Venetian, French, Russian,
and Turkish control, and in 1814 it had been occupied by a British
force under General Campbell, when a specific engagement had
been made to the people that they could look forward to the same
fate as that of the Ionian Islands.

This undertaking later caused some embarrassment, as Castlereagh showed when he answered Douglas's question. 'The hon.
gentleman must,' he said, 'see that it would be attended with great
inconvenience if Ministers were called on to answer in the progress
of their duty whether they had or had not sent out certain instructions. An answer to such a question necessarily involves some
notice of the instructions themselves, and is in fact such an interference with the official duties of Ministers as, I conceive, with all
due deference to the hon. gentleman, could not be considered fair
and proper.' Douglas said he had no wish to elicit the secrets of
Government or do anything improper, and Castlereagh then

assured him that 'His Majesty's Government will pursue that course which appears to them correct.'[41]

The course which appeared to the Government correct was disclosed nearly a fortnight later, when Castlereagh, in presenting papers on Parga, said he wished to 'undeceive the House on the part which our Government has acted.' He went on: 'We have never delivered Parga up to the Turks; all we have agreed to in the treaty is to withdraw our troops from the town and leave the inhabitants to themselves.'

In a literal sense it was true that the inhabitants of Parga were not left entirely to the mercy of the Turks. They were given the opportunity of migrating to the Ionian Islands, then under British rule, an opportunity which many of them took; for the loss of their property and territory they received from the Turks an indemnity of less than £150,000. Castlereagh compared their fate, and the sympathy which would be shown them, with that of the American loyalists who had fought on the British side against the colonial forces. To this Lord John Russell replied that what the British Government had in effect said was: 'We have discovered your position to be indefensible, and therefore we surrender you to the Turks.'[42]

The divergence between popular opinion and British diplomatic policy was even more strikingly revealed during the Greek War of Independence. In April 1826 Earl Grosvenor asked in the House of Lords whether the Government had any information about the fall of Missolonghi, and whether there was any hope that the Greek cause would be taken up. Liverpool answered that he believed the report of the fall of Missolonghi to be true, and then added: 'The contest being one with respect to which this country is perfectly neutral, I do not consider it a subject for discussion in this House.'[43]

This rather deflating answer from a fellow-countryman of Lord Byron's did not go unchallenged. A month later a petition was presented in the House of Commons from the people of such a small place as White Roothing in Essex, demanding 'firm expostulation and prudent negotiation' on the subject of Greece; Sir Robert Wilson, who had himself been a distinguished soldier, said the time had come for something to be done 'to save a Christian people from extermination'; and William Smith, one of Wilberforce's chief associates in the campaign to abolish slavery, spoke of the popular feeling which was by no means indifferent to the fate of the Greeks.[44]

Indignation about Russian territorial demands was voiced on more than one occasion in questions asked by Sir James Mackintosh, a distinguished lawyer, who was to become President of the Board of Control, about a Russian Imperial ukase, which claimed as parts of the Russian dominions coastal stretches in North-east Asia and North-west America measuring some 5,000 miles.[45] And the denial of human rights in the State of Georgia was brought to the attention of Parliament by Daniel O'Connell, the first leader of the Catholic Irish in the House of Commons. O'Connell, who raised this subject on more than one occasion, asked in February 1830 'whether His Majesty's Government have been apprised of a law passed by the State of Georgia, imposing quarantine upon foreign vessels having on board free men of colour. By this regulation it would seem as if British subjects, not being white, were considered by the State of Georgia as a sort of pestilential objects.' Peel agreed that the law existed, and said the matter was being investigated.[46]

The next day Peel decided to make use of the nature of Georgia's legislation in a somewhat curious manner. A debate was taking place on the subject of parliamentary reform, and in the course of it he drew attention to a number of statutes which were in force in Georgia. The effect of one of these was that circulating, or causing to circulate, any paper inciting slaves to insurrection was punishable with death; and of another that any negro or white person who taught a negro to read or write would be guilty of a misdemeanour, punishable by a fine and whipping or a fine and imprisonment, at the discretion of the court. Such laws, Peel claimed, could never have been passed by any House of Commons elected under the existing system, yet they had been passed by a State which enjoyed universal suffrage.[47] This was among the stranger arguments advanced against parliamentary reform in Britain.

While questions on both home and foreign affairs tended to become more representative of that section of public opinion which demanded reform, the practice also grew up between 1815 and 1832 of asking questions in order to elicit answers which could be expected to influence a wide public. The audience for question and answer was no longer regarded as consisting almost exclusively of the ruling classes, and the value of the parliamentary question as a form of publicity was increasingly appreciated.

One reason for this was that the reporting of proceedings had become both more extensive and more accurate. The sevenpenny newspapers sometimes devoted three-and-a-half of their four pages to proceedings in the two Houses, and as a permanent record the *Parliamentary Debates*, which were begun by William Cobbett in 1803 and were later taken over as an enterprise by the printer, Thomas Curson Hansard, came to be recognized as an authoritative source. A shorthand writer had been appointed for both the Lords and Commons in 1813 'to attend when required,' and gradually more attention was paid to the difficulties of those who had to report the debates for the newspapers. In 1830 Colonel Sibthorp, the Member for Lincoln, who was later to acquire a reputation as a die-hard, made proposals for improving the reporters' facilities, and declared: 'The accurate reporting of debates is of great consequence to the country.'[48]

On more than one occasion during this period Members, when asking questions, made it clear that they were doing so chiefly because of the effect the answers might have on public opinion. In 1819 Vesey Fitzgerald, M.P. for County Clare, asked whether the duties on certain British goods imported into Ireland, which had originally been imposed for twenty years following the Act of Union, were to be continued. He admitted that the Chancellor of the Exchequer, Nicholas Vansittart, had already told him what he intended to do, but added: 'It is extremely important that by a statement made in his place the public in Ireland should be apprised of my right hon. friend's intentions.' In this way the public in Ireland learnt from Vansittart that he proposed to continue the duties for a period which he could not specify.[49]

Later in the same year a Member named Wilbraham asked for a denial of rumours which, he claimed, were widespread among 'the labouring population of Lancashire,' that the Government intended to seize the funds of the friendly societies and savings banks. Vansittart duly made the denial, saying: 'Even if the Treasury were base enough, they have not the power to misappropriate these funds.'[50]

Another occasion on which question and answer were used as a means of reassuring the public occurred as a result of the outbreak of cholera in 1832. In February John Wilson Croker, the essayist, who has been credited with first giving the name 'Conservative' to the Tory party, asked Charles Poulett Thomson, the Vice-President of the Board of Trade, whether there was any truth in the reports that cholera in 'the lower parts of the town' had since spread to the upper. He added: 'The best possible mode of preventing unnecessary alarms and of satisfying the public mind is to have no mystery whatever on the subject.'

Poulett Thomson confirmed that there had been cases of cholera at Rotherhithe and Limehouse, but said he had no information that the disease had spread further. Lord Althorp thereupon gave notice of his intention to bring in a Bill to give the Privy Council special powers for preventing the spread of cholera, and within a few days the Bill was passed.[51]

The only delay occurred over a difference of opinion as to whether a reference to the pleasure of the Almighty should be included in the preamble, which one Member proposed should read: 'Whereas it hath pleased Almighty God to visit the United Kingdom with the disease called the Cholera, or Spasmodic or Indian Cholera.' In the end the House of Lords decided this issue by adopting an Anglican compromise suggested by the Bishop of London, and the preamble began: 'It having pleased Divine Providence.'[52]

This use of the parliamentary question for purposes of widespread publicity was a new development in the practice. Another new development, of which many more examples were to be furnished later, and of which the first traces were apparent shortly before 1832, was the use of the question to promote sectional commercial interests.

In 1831 Thomas Courtenay, M.P. for Totnes, asked Lord Althorp whether he intended to persist in raising the duty on wines from the Cape of Good Hope. Althorp answered that he had received a deputation of merchants and others concerned with the Cape wine trade, and that after hearing their arguments, he had agreed for the next two years not to raise the duty to the same level as that on continental wines.[53]

In the same year Edward Ruthven, M.P. for Downpatrick, asked Sir Henry Parnell, the Secretary at War, whether it was intended to discourage horse-breeding in Ireland 'by withdrawing the King's

Plate from that country.' Parnell suggested rather scornfully that
Ruthven should address himself to 'some honourable gentleman
belonging to the Treasury.'[54]

The increasing impact of public opinion on parliamentary proceedings, while helping to shape the form of many questions, also
had important effects both on the amount of business which Parliament had to transact and on the work to be done in the departments
of state for which Ministers were responsible to Parliament. In particular, there was a rapid growth in the number of petitions. In the
five years from 1811 to 1815 4,498 petitions had been presented. The
corresponding figure for the years 1828 to 1832 inclusive was 23,283.

The discussion of petitions came to occupy an alarming proportion of the time of the House of Commons, as was inevitable so
long as there was no effective limitation of the period which could be
devoted to any particular subject. When major issues, such as
Catholic emancipation or the reform of Parliament, were being
considered, both Houses spent many hours discussing petitions,
while they had before them Bills concerned with the very subjects
with which the petitions dealt. The natural result was the adoption
of measures to limit discussion, and thus the first stage in a process
which was to lead eventually to severe restrictions on all forms of
parliamentary activity, including the asking of questions.

The problem of how to find time for everything Parliament was
required to do was discussed at some length in November 1830,
when Peel proposed certain changes in procedure. He said that he
was opposed to morning sessions, as Members did not get their
letters from the General Post Office until 9.30 a.m., and after dealing
with them they had to attend committees. Instead he put forward
a proposal, which had been made to him by Manners Sutton, that
the Speaker should take the Chair at 3 p.m., and public business
should begin without fail at 5.

Objections to this proposal were made on various grounds. One
Member said that if petitions were still to be received, it would be
impossible to begin public business at 5. Another claimed that the
cause of the difficulty lay in the number of subjects which gave rise
to petitions, adding: 'If the House would consent to parliamentary
reform, to the reduction of taxes and to the abolition of slavery, the
only question remaining would be how they should occupy their
time.'[55]

Two other practical suggestions, both of them more in line with present-day than with the current practice, were also made. One was that when a Member had a petition to present, which he considered required the attention of the Government, he should first communicate with the Minister to whose department the subject-matter of the petition belonged. The other was that there should be no full discussion on petitions when they were first presented.

In the end Peel's suggestion for meeting at 3 p.m. instead of at 4 was adopted; and although the next year an attempt by the Government to have Wednesdays added to Mondays and Fridays as days on which Government business took precedence did not succeed, the tendency to regulate the time of the House in the interests of the Government of the day, rather than in those of private Members, was beginning to become more evident.

Restrictions on the use of parliamentary time did not yet extend to questions. Private Members still enjoyed the fullest freedom in this activity, and Speaker Manners Sutton allowed a good deal of latitude in his interpretation of the rules of the House. Even the giving of notice was still an act of courtesy and not a rule. In 1823, for instance, the Marquis of Lansdowne asked Liverpool in the House of Lords whether any communication had been made to him about a treaty or convention for the military occupation of Switzerland by the Austrian Army. Liverpool answered: 'I had not even heard of the report to which the noble Marquis has alluded until within the last half-hour from the noble Marquis himself.'[56] On the same day Brougham asked Canning a similar question in the Commons, and Canning too denied any knowledge of the report.[57]

Individual Ministers did attempt to control the subject-matter of questions. In 1828 Peel denied the right of a Member to put a question about amendments to a Bill made in the House of Lords. In 1831 Palmerston, who had become Foreign Secretary the year before, answered a series of questions on events in Belgium, going through, in the words of Croker, 'a kind of political catechism with exceeding good humour.'[58] In the course of one of his replies he said: 'Whatever information the House of Commons may require in order to enable it to form an opinion of the policy of His Majesty's Government I shall always be ready to give. But if gentlemen expect that His Majesty's Ministers are here to serve no purposes but those of a newspaper, I can assure them that they will find themselves greatly disappointed.'[59]

There were also a number of Speaker's rulings on the manner in which questions should be asked. In 1831, after Sir Richard Vyvyan had indicated his intention of reading extracts from a letter in putting a question, Manners Sutton declared: 'When a Member goes out of the usual course for the purpose of asking a question, he is bound to confine himself to merely putting the question as a dry, simple query. Such, in this instance, would be the most convenient and least irregular.'[60]

Manners Sutton gave another ruling of a similar kind later in the same year. Henry Hunt, the Radical Member for Preston, whose political activities had in the past landed him in prison, prefaced a question by saying: 'A vast deal has been said in the public papers respecting the non-attendance of the Duchess of Kent and the Princess Victoria at the Coronation.' At this point Manners Sutton intervened to say: 'An hon. Member, in putting a question, must take care not to raise an argument on it. . . . Any explanation of facts is disorderly, inasmuch as it may create debate when there is no question before the House.'

Hunt pointed out, not unreasonably, that in the past explanations lasting as long as a quarter of an hour had been given, and added: 'I really do not know how to put the question I have to ask.' However, he succeeded in extracting from Althorp the information that there had been great misrepresentation in the press, and that the Duchess had written to King William, saying why she wished to be excused from appearing at his Coronation. 'These reasons,' Althorp said, 'appeared satisfactory to His Majesty, and His Majesty in consequence excused her attendance.'[61]

The House of Lords allowed even greater latitude to those who asked questions, with the result that Brougham, who, when he was appointed Lord Chancellor, was experienced in the ways of the Commons but not in those of the Lords, complained vigorously of the lack of discipline. 'The Speaker of this House,' he said, 'has no power to interfere in the order of your proceedings. . . . I regret that the Speaker has no further authority, for . . . I have seen in the course of the last session, as well as in this, more breaches of order and more irregularity than I have ever witnessed in any Parliament or, perhaps, in any public assembly whatever.'[62]

Such attempts as were made during Earl Grey's premiership to control the form of questions asked in the Lords were resented. In 1832 the Earl of Aberdeen, who had been Foreign Secretary under Wellington, complained of 'the new system of discipline' which he charged Grey with trying to impose. 'I have been a Member of your Lordship's House for twenty-five years,' he said, 'and I know that it has always been the practice to put questions and to ask for explanations from the members of the Government either with or without notice. . . . It is a matter of great convenience that in this House there should be such a practice. In the other House frequent opportunities occur for putting questions and calling for explanations when questions are before the House, such as on occasions of Committees of Supply. . . . In this House there are no such opportunities, and therefore it has been found convenient and useful that explanations should be called for on important subjects and frankly given, without its being necessary to resort to the formality of a motion.'

He went on to say that he had always given notice of questions he intended to ask, but that he had not always received the same courtesy when he had been in office. Grey denied that he had tried to introduce a new discipline, and admitted the general convenience of questions, but added : 'What I deprecate is the putting of questions not for the mere purpose of eliciting information, where explanation can be properly given, but merely as a pretence for declamation against the Government. . . . Against questions put with these improper views and in that improper spirit and temper I have protested and will protest.'[63]

Four months later the Marquis of Londonderry made a similar complaint to that expressed by Aberdeen, and cited two specific instances to show the value of questions. One was an occasion when he himself had 'fortunately gained some information for the public' on the subject of Belgium; the other was the extracting from Earl Grey of an expression of hope that the good sense of the people of England would put down political unions.[64]

The developments in the use of the parliamentary question between 1815 and 1832 clearly showed that Parliament, before it decided to reform itself, had already acquired many of the attributes of a popular assembly, even though the administrations which ruled for nearly the whole of the period could not in any sense of the term be described as popular Governments. The Members who were elected through the system of close corporations, rotten boroughs, and patronage were becoming increasingly responsive to public opinion. At the same time Parliament was already beginning to discover that the more it expressed the demands of the public, the more it would be called upon to do, and the less easily it would find time for the proper exercise of its functions. The seeds of a plant, which would later consistently obstruct and attempt to dislocate the work of Parliament, had already been sown by the admission of the Catholic Irish to membership; the growing number of petitions had already necessitated measures to limit the discussion of these expressions of popular opinion; and Governments, both Whig and Tory, had discovered that in order to carry out their programmes, they would have to make increasing demands on the time of the Commons.

But the subordination of the private Member to the exigencies of Government or Opposition, and the fitting of all parliamentary activities, including the asking of questions, into clearly defined compartments of time, remained as tasks to be carried out by those who were elected to the reformed Parliaments. So too did the necessary corollary to the execution of policies which would be increasingly responsive to popular opinion: the creation of an effective bureaucratic machine which could translate the demands made on Governments into action. This last need was little appreciated before 1832. A radical reformer such as Hume could, without being charged with inconsistency, expend equal energy in demanding cuts in Government departments and calling for complicated returns, as, for instance, of the number of hackney-coach and cabriolet licences which had been granted. And in 1824 the state of the Treasury's administration was such that a Member could describe its system of keeping accounts as so cumbrous and inefficient that it 'might almost disgrace a tribe of Indian savages.'[65]

An opportunity for summing up the work of the last years of the unreformed Parliaments was provided in 1832, when Manners Sutton announced his intention to retire from the office of Speaker. In seconding the vote of thanks, Goulburn declared: 'Hereafter, when any individual reviews the last fifteen years of the proceedings of Parliament, if he looks upon them as an impartial historian, I doubt not that he will record them as forming a period of our history when the rights of the House of Commons were best upheld with the least pretensions.'[66]

Outside Parliament, over great stretches of the country the years in question were the years of the darker industrial ages; nor is it easy to pick on a period of modern history when Britain was more consistently badly governed than it was between 1815 and 1830. Yet the restricted claim by Goulburn about the rights of the House of Commons was by no means an outrageous one. Among the chief reasons why this was so was the remarkable development in the exercise by Members of their right to ask questions of the Government.

VI

The Reformed Parliament (1832–1848)

WRITING to Sir Walter Scott shortly before the Reform Bill of 1832 had become law, John Wilson Croker, who really kept a vow he had made to end his parliamentary career if the Bill went through, had declared: 'If it be carried, England, no doubt, may still be great and happy; but it will be under a *different* form of constitution.'

This belief that a new political system had been created was fairly widespread. Earl Grey had defended the Reform Bill against its critics by saying: 'I am indeed convinced that the more the Bill is considered, the less it will be found to prejudice the real interests of the aristocracy.' But such warnings were generally overlooked. When Parliament met in 1833, Cobbett seemed to be symbolizing a new order of things by deciding to occupy Peel's seat on the front bench. As the seat was Peel's by courtesy and usage and not by right, Cobbett had to be allowed to remain where he was.

The physical appearance of Parliament and its Members after 1832 did not at first alter appreciably. Charles Dickens in *A Parliamentary Sketch* described the dress of a number of typical representatives of the people. He wrote of the 'stout man with the hoarse voice, in the blue coat, queer-crowned, broad-brimmed hat, with corduroy breeches, and great boots'; of the metropolition representative 'in the black coat with the velvet facings and cuffs, who wears his *D'Orsay* hat so rakishly'; and of the old-fashioned county Member with his 'loose, wide, brown coat, with capacious pockets on each side; the knee-breeches and boots, the immensely long waistcoat, and silver watch-chain dangling below it, the wide-brimmed brown hat, and the white handkerchief tied in a great bow, with straggling ends sticking out beyond his shirt-frill.' The picture which met the eye of the parliamentary reporter was closer to that of the late eighteenth century than to that of the sombre frock-coats and top-hats and the heavy beards and side-whiskers of forty years later. Dickens ended his sketch with a picture of an elderly peer drinking a huge tumbler of hot punch in Bellamy's kitchen, which served both Houses of Parliament, while his companion 'damns and drinks, and drinks and damns, and smokes.'

For more than eighteen months the reformed House of Commons continued to sit in its traditional chamber, which had originally been St. Stephen's chapel. Then on 16th October 1834 a fire, which was enthusiastically cheered by large crowds, burned the Houses of Parliament down. Temporary arrangements had to be made, and in spite of an assurance given in answer to a question in the House of Lords in 1835 that 'two years would be the utmost period required to complete the new building,'[1] these temporary arrangements lasted more than fifteen years. The Commons moved to the Court of Requests, and the Lords to the Painted Chamber. The Painted Chamber was so narrow that it had a constricting effect on the freedom and flow of debate. On one occasion, according to the testimony of Greville, Brougham, while speaking, overheard the Duke of Wellington mutter: 'Take care what you say next,' and promptly broke off.

When the new Houses of Parliament came to be built, it was generally felt, just as it was felt when another reconstruction had to take place in the twentieth century, that many of the features of the earlier building ought to be preserved. But the new Houses were not only built on a much more magnificent scale; they also incorporated a number of new features. One of the most significant of these, for the light it throws on Parliament's conception of its functions, was the provision of much better arrangements for the public reporting of debates.

A new relationship between Parliament and the press developed between 1832 and 1848. When a suggestion was made in the Commons in 1834 that arrangements might be made for providing authentic reports of the debates, Althorp opposed it on the grounds that newspaper reports already met most needs. The fidelity and accuracy of these reports were, he said, 'such as create surprise rather than disappointment.'[2] He added that full and faithful reports would not be to Members' advantage, as they would show up the impurity of their English and would be too long for the public to read. In 1844 Peel, answering a question from Macaulay about the occupation of Gwalior, said: 'For what I know of the subject I am indebted to the courtesy of the editor of *The Times. The Times* newspaper has the means of anticipating Government in the receipt of overland despatches.'[3] And Cobden declared that the best platform from which to address the country was the floor of the House of Commons.

The earlier distrust of parliamentary reporters vanished gradually. The debates on the Seduction and Prostitution Bill introduced in 1847 were, it is true, held in secret session in the Commons. In the Lords the Bishop of Norwich, when moving the third reading of the Bill, said it was 'not one for discussion.' Brougham objected to the passage of a Bill which could not be discussed; two other peers agreed with him, and the Bill was dropped.[4] Apart from this episode, no serious attempts to restrict the freedom of the press to report debates were made; and it was indicative of the changed relationship that shortly before the new House of Commons was completed Lord John Russell, as Prime Minister, and Peel, as leader of the Opposition, personally tested the acoustics in the reporters' gallery.

A less unanimous approval was given to the proposals, which were eventually adopted, for admitting ladies to hear debates, one Member in the Commons declaring, when the subject was discussed in 1836, that he hoped 'every honourable Member who is blessed with daughters will negative this idle and ridiculous proposition.'[5] A year earlier Brougham in the Lords had stated that he felt an 'absolute and entire devotion to the sex,' but he wished 'always to see them in their proper places.'[6]

The period of the occupation of temporary premises by Parliament lasted approximately as long as that between the passage of the Reform Bill of 1832 and the year 1848, when revolution swept across Europe and only narrowly missed Britain. It also nearly coincided with it in time. During those years between 1832 and 1848 changes of great importance in parliamentary practice and procedure occurred, although the changes were neither so startling nor so sudden as some of the advocates of the Reform Bill had hoped and most of its opponents had feared.

Joseph Hume, with his Radical's belief in the probability of progress and his Radical's disappointment at the slowness of the march, declared in 1836 that he was 'mortified to see that two sessions of the second reformed Parliament have elapsed with scarcely one-tenth of the benefits to the people which they have a right to expect, according to the fair promises made to them.'[7]

But more distant views, which had the benefit of retrospect, were to give a rather different picture of the work of the early reformed Parliaments. Gladstone in later life stated that 'as a whole our level of public principle and public action were at their zenith in the twenty years or so which succeeded the Reform Act of 1832.' He also said of the Reform Act that while for England it meant improvement, for Scotland 'it was political birth.' A modern critic of Parliament, Mr. Christopher Hollis, has made the interesting comment that between 1832 and 1867 Parliament was probably freer in its voting and debating than it has ever been before or since.

The increase of parliamentary business has been fairly steady during the last century and a half, although there have from time to time been years of exceptional pressure or relative quiescence. In the two decades following the 1832 Reform Act there developed, alongside the inevitable increase of work, a growing realization of the need to devise new methods of coping with it. Some of these methods were the restrictive ones of rules to curtail debate; others were to be of deeper constitutional importance, for they would involve the creation of new machines to assist the individual members of the Government in dealing with their steadily mounting work. These new machines, which between 1832 and 1848 remained largely in prototype, were the machines of bureaucracy and party.

All these developments resulting from the growth of the business of legislating for the country strongly influenced and were themselves considerably affected by the system of asking parliamentary questions.

The extent to which business was growing occupied the attention of the House of Commons frequently after 1832. In a debate on the subject of regulating business, which took place in 1833, C. W. Wynn, M.P. for Montgomeryshire, attributed the increasing length of speeches to the fact that reports of debates were now printed and constituents therefore had to be impressed.[8] The next year, on 8th July, a motion for giving a limited degree of precedence to

Government business as the session was already well advanced was debated. Hume opposed the motion, saying: 'If the House should adopt the resolution ... it would preclude the possibility of honourable Members bringing forward any new matter, however important, because the Bills which His Majesty's Government now have before the House will occupy every hour of the time which yet remains of the present session.'[9] The motion was withdrawn, but twelve days later a similar motion giving orders of the day precedence over notices of motions was carried.

There were still occasional interludes of relative idleness. On 7th February 1837 a Member could preface a question: 'As there is now no business before the House and seeing the noble Secretary for Ireland in his place. . . .'[10] But such opportunities occurred less and less often. In July 1843, Peel spoke of an increasing tendency to extend adjourned debates over four or five days and said he thought that in that session there had been 'more than the usual impediments in the way of the Government proceeding with its measures.'[11]

Three days later he had to announce the postponement of certain Bills because of lack of time. One of these was a Factory Bill, which would have served to reduce the hours of work of children and to provide them with some form of education. Lord Ashley spoke with understandable bitterness of his disappointment at the postponement of a measure to the study and preparation of which he had, as he explained, devoted some ten years.[12]

By 1848 the feeling that more effective steps must be taken to limit discussions had become so widely shared that a Committee of the House of Commons was appointed to inquire into the conduct of public business. In calling attention to the problem in April of that year, Lord Stanley, who later became fourteenth Earl of Derby, compared the manner in which Parliament had come to conduct its business with that prevailing twenty-five years earlier. Now, he declared, 'constituencies watch their representatives more narrowly, perhaps requiring them too frequently to submit their individual judgement to the wishes of their constituents. . . . Representatives have greater inducements to recommend themselves to the notice of their constituents by much greater activity in speaking—a result which does not tend to the advancement of the public business.'[13] The future Prime Minister clearly felt that Members of Parliament were already in danger of degenerating into delegates.

The measures which the House of Commons actually took to regulate its business in the two decades following the Reform Act were limited in scope. Parliament has always shown considerable corporate wisdom in declining to accept new measures of restraint until the need for them has become apparent. Ancient liberties are seldom restored, but they are not easily lost, and a temporary excess of business has rarely, if ever, led to a permanent restriction of freedom.

After the passage of the Reform Act, Governments, whether Tory or Whig in complexion, found themselves more and more obliged in the later months of the summer to demand precedence for their measures in order to be able to carry them through before the session ended early in August; yet it was not until 1861 that the Government was given automatic precedence on a third day in the week, in addition to the Mondays and Thursdays on which by then they could already claim precedence. A day seldom passed without the transaction of a large volume of business, or at least discussion in the Commons; yet until 1855 that House had to rely on the good health of the Speaker in order to be able to meet at all, for until then there was no Deputy Speaker who could immediately take the Speaker's place. The Select Committee of 1848 made a thorough analysis of the effects of the increase of business; yet the resolutions which Lord John Russell moved the next year on the basis of the Committee's report led to comparatively minor changes, such as the introduction of simplified arrangements whereby the House could resolve itself into Committee and the taking of first readings of Bills without amendment or debate.

There was, however, one major change in procedure, which was finally adopted in 1839. This was the prohibition of debates in the Commons on the presentation of petitions. The growth in the number of petitions had long made the discussion of more than a small fraction of them impossible, but debates, usually of a rather desultory nature, continued to take place on petitions in the first session of the reformed Parliament. On 9th July 1833, for instance, two petitions, one for the better observance of the Sabbath and one for the independence of Poland, were both debated at some length,[14] but in the same year a resolution limiting freedom of discussion to some extent was passed. This resolution was not enough to prevent debates on the flood of petitions presented in 1834 against the

sentences passed on the six agricultural labourers in Dorsetshire for
administering false oaths as members of a union, but three years
later the question of when and in what circumstances petitions could
be debated was again considered by the Commons.

On 12th December 1837 Joseph Hume presented a petition 'from
certain electors of Middlesex residing in the village of Hammer-
smith.' The petitioners complained of intimidation during elections
and advocated a secret ballot, and Hume spoke at some length.
Stratford Canning, who in the years between his two long stretches
of duty as Ambassador in Constantinople, was largely engaged with
parliamentary activities, thereupon appealed to the Chair. The
Speaker, James Abercromby, explained the rule which then prevailed. This was that Members, when presenting petitions, could
speak on them only in cases in which the character of an individual
was attacked and vindication was called for, or in which 'anything
is stated in the petition which requires the prompt vindication and
interference of the House.' Hume declared that this rule had been
'productive of serious detriment to the people of England' and
amounted to 'something very like a suppression of their complaints,
their wants and their wishes.'[15]

In 1839 the problem of the discussion of petitions finally came to
a head. The first petition presented in the session of that year
advocated the total repeal of the Corn Laws, and Speaker Abercromby admitted the possibility that the House might consider the
subject.[16] Two days later the Commons once again passed a resolution against debates on the presentation of petitions, a resolution
whose effect was to be permanent.[17]

The flood of petitions continued. The Convention of Industrious
Classes in 1839 drew up a petition with 1,200,000 signatures. There
were more than three million signatures to a petition presented in
1842, which began with a preamble against the Poor Laws, and
after listing other grievances demanded universal suffrage. And in
1848 the Chartists set about organizing what they intended to be the
greatest petition of all time, although its efficacy was limited by the
fact that among the signatures apparently appended to it were those
of 'Mr. Punch' and 'Victoria Rex.'

Attempts were also made from within the House of Commons to
revive the old system of discussion on the presentation of petitions.
In 1842 Robert Wallace, M.P. for Greenock, with the support of

Daniel O'Connell, moved for a return to the former practice, saying
the people did not wish to see their petitions 'lying in hundreds
upon the table and crammed into a bag, while not the slightest
attention has been paid to their contents.'[18] But the motion was
defeated by 237 votes to 50, and as a means of influencing immediately the decisions and discussion of the House of Commons the
petition was doomed.

In the House of Lords, on the other hand, the presentation of a
petition continued for some time to be an admissible prelude to a
debate. On 12th July 1842 Lord Wharncliffe presented a petition
in a rather unusual manner. The petitioners proposed that some of
the education grant should be spent for the advantage of the singing
classes which were organized by a certain Mr. Hullah in Exeter Hall.
Wharncliffe strongly supported the proposal himself. 'Should these
institutions,' he said, 'be enabled to continue their useful labours,
there can be no doubt that in a very short time a large proportion of
the lower classes in the metropolis will be withdrawn from the public
houses, to which they now resort for their evening's occupation and
amusement, and the vicious habits which at present degrade and
pauperize so many thousands of persons will be in great measure
abandoned.' He added that the choral meetings at Exeter Hall had
been highly praised by Mendelssohn.[19]

It was somewhat curious that Wharncliffe had adopted the method
of speaking on the presentation of a petition, for he was himself a
member of the Government, holding the office of Lord President of
the Council, an office which he filled with such success that even
Greville wrote of him: 'He really too does the business himself.'
Palmerston seized on this point ten days later, when he asked a
question in the House of Commons. He prefaced his question by
giving credit to Wharncliffe for his 'liberality of sentiment and
enlightened views,' but said that as Wharncliffe was a member of
the Government, the impression had been formed that a supplementary estimate would be added to the education grant. He asked
Peel what the Government's intentions were. Peel quite clearly did
not know. He answered that he was to have met Wharncliffe that
day but had been 'unavoidable prevented.'[20]

Three days later Peel answered Palmerston's question. He said
there would be a supplementary estimate for education of £10,000,
the money to be distributed according to a decision which the Privy

Council had reached after consulting with the Archbishops of Canterbury and York. Palmerston then asked whether any of the £10,000 would go to Exeter Hall. Peel answered quite uncompromisingly: 'No.'[21]

Although the greater elasticity in the procedure of the House of Lords still permitted the effective use of the petition, it was clear that in the House of Commons some other form would have to take its place. When Robert Wallace and Daniel O'Connell had made their protest against the neglect of petitions in 1842, Sir Robert Inglis, M.P. for Oxford University, produced the unanswerable argument. There had, he pointed out, been 16,801 petitions presented in the previous session of Parliament, and to adopt Wallace's proposal 'would necessarily involve not only 16,801 speeches but 16,801 replies.'[22] The logical successor to the presentation of the petition was clearly the asking of the parliamentary question.

The supersession of the debate on the petition by the parliamentary question was a gradual process. The number of questions of which notice was given in the session of 1847 still amounted to only 129, or an average of about one per day. It may therefore be said that the effects of the increase of business on the development of the parliamentary question between 1832 and 1848 are more clearly apparent to the modern historian than they were to the contemporary Member of Parliament, although it is significant that in 1848 the number of questions of which notice was given leapt to 222.

The relationship between the practice of asking questions of Ministers and the weaknesses of the administrative machinery, on the other hand, was a relatively clear one. Before 1848 the British machinery of government provided some justification for Bernard Shaw's assertion that in the nineteenth century there was 'an obstinate prejudice against the organization of a competent bureaucracy.' A Treasury minute of 1836 stated that it was desirable that nominees to posts in the Customs Office should know how to read and write and do simple arithmetic, and an even more damning indictment was to come in the next decade, when Charles Trevelyan and Sir Stafford Northcote produced their paper on *The Reorganization of the Permanent Civil Service*. In this they declared that the Civil Service was attracting 'the unambitious, and the indolent or incapable.' Those who entered the service after the age of twenty-five had generally failed in other jobs, so that 'the dregs of all other professions are attracted towards the Public Service as a secure asylum.'

One form of administrative weakness which questions revealed in the early reformed Parliament was the remarkable ignorance which members of the Government displayed of important actions which were being carried out in their name and on their behalf. This was most evident in the field of foreign affairs, in which any Government necessarily had to rely largely on the efficiency of individual ambassadors.

In 1833, for example, the Turkish Empire seemed in serious danger of collapse. Revolts had occurred in Bosnia, Albania, and Syria. The French had already occupied Algiers and the emergence of Greece as an independent kingdom had been formally ratified a year earlier. On 22nd April 1833 Thomas Attwood, the great champion of parliamentary reform, referred to rumours that Constantinople was already in possession of the Russians, and asked what steps His Majesty's Government had taken 'to prevent a result which would be disastrous to the best interests of Europe and inconsistent with the honour of England.' The reply which Lord Althorp, then Chancellor of the Exchequer, gave was that he knew nothing 'of Constantinople being in possession of the Russians.'[23]

It was not altogether unreasonable for Althorp to know nothing of the occupation of Constantinople, for it had not in fact taken place, but the chief reason for his ignorance became clear a fortnight later. Then Joseph Hume, in a long and argumentative question, asked: 'Who is the Ambassador from the Court of England to the Porte, and if there is any such person, why is he not at his post?' This time the answer was given by Palmerston. The last Ambassador, Sir Robert Gordon, had, he explained, returned home 'early in last year.' He was to have been succeeded by Sir Stratford Canning, but Canning had been sent 'on an important mission,' and Gordon's actual successor was Lord Ponsonby, an experienced diplomat, who had already arrived. When pressed on the subject, Palmerston said that Ponsonby would have arrived earlier but for the fact that the frigate which was to have conveyed him from Naples to Constantinople had been wind-bound. The period during which this frigate had been wind-bound in the then agreeable city of Naples was one month. Palmerston loyally concluded that during the year in which there had been no ambassador in Constantinople the secretary at the Embassy had acted 'with great judgement and discretion.'[24]

Five years later Stratford Canning himself asked a question in the Commons which again revealed the ignorance of members of the Government of what was happening in the field of foreign relations. On 24th July 1838 he asked Sir John Hobhouse for information about a report that an expedition of between five and six hundred men had sailed from Bombay to the Persian Gulf. Hobhouse at the time was President of the Board of Control, the name then given to the Government department responsible for the affairs of India, and now given to the department responsible for the affairs of lunatics. Hobhouse could give very little accurate information. After a rather irrelevant preamble in which he said that 'our commercial relations with that part of the world have become much more extensive than formerly,' he said the expedition had sailed on either the 2nd or the 5th of June 'in consequence of instructions from the Government at home and the Governor-General of India.'[25]

Even this information was not altogether correct, as was made clear three days later, when Stratford Canning asked another question. This time he addressed his question to Palmerston, who was then Foreign Secretary. Canning asked whether there was a secret treaty between Russia and Persia, whether the siege of Herat in Afghanistan undertaken by the Shah of Persia was being directed by the Russian envoy, and whether there was a possibility that British troops would be engaged in hostilities with Persia. Palmerston, after saying he had no knowledge of any secret treaty, then declared that the expedition from Bombay had been sent 'not by this Government but by the Governor-General of India.' Peel reasonably enough said this was no answer to the question and asked whether the expedition had sailed 'with hostile intentions against Persia.' Palmerston's only reply was to say that this question ought to have been addressed to Hobhouse. With curious forbearance the Opposition allowed the matter for the time being to be dropped.[26]

In fact, the defence of Herat was being largely directed by a British artillery officer named Eldred Pottinger and the Persians

eventually had to call off their siege of Herat, but until the British
Minister, Sir John McNeill, whose mission was in any case largely
financed by the East India Company, returned to England from
Persia the next year, the Government at home had very little knowledge of what was going on.

An even more remarkable admission of the Government's
ignorance of events in Asia which a parliamentary question elicited
was made in 1840. On 12th March a question was put to Lord John
Russell, then Secretary of State for the Colonies, whether there was
any truth in 'a report, very generally believed, that war has been
declared against China.' The wording of Russell's reply must have
served to tell the questioner just how much the Government knew.
'There has,' Russell said, 'been no official intelligence amounting to
what the honourable Member has stated, namely a declaration of
war against China. Instructions have been given to the Governor-
General of India to make some active preparations, and although no
intelligence of the nature alluded to has been received, I presume
that some directions given or some act done by the Governor-
General has given rise to the report of a declaration of war having
been made.' In answer to a supplementary question from Peel
Palmerston said he 'apprehended' that any communication with
the Government of China 'would be carried on in the name of this
country . . . and not of the East India Company.'[27]

In fact a war which was to have lasting and important consequences had already been under way for some time. Its purposes, as
revealed to Parliament one week after Russell had given his evasive
answer, were to obtain reparations for insults and injuries offered
to the British Superintendent in Canton, Captain Elliot, and other
British subjects; to obtain 'an indemnification' for British merchants
for the loss of their property; and to obtain security for the persons
and property of British subjects trading with China.

The trade in question was largely in opium, the value of the
trade in this commodity amounting to some £4,000,000 a year, and
the war led to the cession to the British of Hong Kong. But there
was considerable justification for Lord Ashburton's statement in
the House of Lords that the public had been 'left more in the dark
respecting the expedition to China than has ever been the case
respecting any expedition of equal importance and strength.'[28]
Even when the Duke of Wellington asked in the House of Lords on

7th May 1841 'whether the island of Hong Kong has been taken possession of by the treaty,' the reply of the Prime Minister, Lord Melbourne, was: 'I believe it has.'[29]

Difficulties of communication in days before the electric telegraph was invented, and the fact that India was still largely an autonomous territory ruled by Englishmen but not ruled from London, could to some extent explain the ignorance which successive Governments revealed of what was done in their name in distant countries. But comparable ignorance was also shown of what was happening at home. On 1st August 1845 Thomas Wakley, M.P. for Finsbury, who had already by that time gained a considerable reputation in the Commons for his speeches on medical subjects, asked a question about the employment of paupers in workhouses in the task of crushing bones. He said the paupers were in the habit of extracting the marrow from the bones and 'gnawing the meat which they sometimes found at their extremities.' The right to possess these bones, he added, often led to quarrels. Sir James Graham, the Home Secretary, answering, said he could not believe 'in the existence of such an abuse' and added: 'I shall institute an enquiry this very night.'[30] He made the enquiry and four days later informed the Commons that the Poor Law Commissioners had never heard of bone-crushing being carried on in workhouses.[31]

The next year Graham had a rather different story to tell. Captain George Pechell, M.P. for Brighton and a distinguished naval officer, called the attention of the House, not for the first time, to the case of a man in the workhouse at Eastbourne who had nearly died while being engaged in bone-crushing, and Graham then said: 'The occupation has become very general in the workhouses throughout England, for it appears that it has been adopted in upwards of 150 out of about 500 unions.'[32] Two months after this, on 5th March 1846 Ralph Etwall, M.P. for Andover, brought up the subject again. He produced documents to show that in the workhouse at Andover the paupers regularly ate the marrow from bones which had been 'decomposing and lying in heaps for months,' although only dry bones were supposed to be crushed there. This led Graham to announce that from 1st April 'the bone-crushing will throughout these unions entirely cease and never, I hope, be revived.' He prefaced this announcement by declaring that it was 'melancholy at the present juncture, and in the existing state of public affairs, that so much of the precious time of this House should have been occupied in a matter which, after all, is only . . . a workhouse squabble in the south of England.'[33]

The administration of the Poor Laws was, like the administration of the Army, one of those subjects on which Ministers of the Crown in the 1830s and 1840s had continual difficulty in answering questions asked in Parliament, because the control which they themselves exercised in these spheres was limited. The Poor Law Commissioners sanctioned by the Act of 1834, the so-called Three Kings of Somerset House, were not themselves answerable to Parliament, although their powers were in certain respects very nearly absolute, and attempts to exercise parliamentary control over details of Army administration, and particularly over the Commander-in-Chief, were vigorously resisted.

On 30th March 1836 Sir William Molesworth, the Radical Member for East Cornwall and a strong advocate of the abolition of flogging in the Army, put a question to Viscount Howick, the Secretary at War, about the appointment of Lord Brudenell to the lieutenant-colonelcy of the 11th Light Dragoons. Lord Brudenell, he pointed out, had been removed from the command of the 15th Hussars by a court-martial, which had declared his habit of having the conversation of officers taken down in the orderly room as 'a practice which cannot be considered otherwise than as revolting to every proper and honourable feeling of a gentleman.' Howick answered that such appointments were entirely the concern of the Commander-in-Chief, Lord Hill. He even admitted that he had said to Lord Hill: 'It is for your lordship to determine upon it; I have no means of judging whether the appointment is right or wrong.'[34]

This led Hume to ask scornfully whether the Secretary at War was 'merely a clerk to the Commander-in-Chief,' and the attack continued. On 3rd May Molesworth moved for referring to a Committee the conduct of the Commander-in-Chief in making the appointment, saying he did so 'upon the principle that some officer of the Crown ought to be directly responsible to this House for the administration of the military department of the State.' As Lord Brudenell was the officer who, nearly twenty years later, as the Earl of Cardigan, was to send the Light Brigade to its doom at

Balaclava, Molesworth might be thought to have had a better case, on many counts, than the Commons admitted. They defeated his motion by 322 votes to 42, largely on the grounds that it could be considered as a vote of censure on a much-liked Commander-in-Chief.[35]

Ignorance of fact and lack of effective control, where control was needed, were by no means the only forms of administrative weakness which questions asked between 1832 and 1848 revealed. A searching light was more than once thrown upon the system of patronage and appointment.

On 27th April 1838 the Earl of Winchilsea stated in the House of Lords that he had read in a newspaper that a legal adviser had been appointed to the Governor-General of Canada, the Earl of Durham, and asked whether the adviser, whose name was Turton, was the same man who had been at their lordships' bar three or four years earlier 'in a case of shameful adultery.' Although Winchilsea had read the newspaper report only that morning and could not have given very lengthy notice, the Prime Minister, Lord Melbourne, answered the question. He said arrangements had been made for a legal adviser to be appointed to help Lord Durham, but after reconsideration the decision had been changed and no appointment had been made.[36]

Three days later the Earl of Winchilsea raised the matter again. By this time he had learnt that Durham and Turton had gone out to Canada in the same ship, and he told the Lords: 'If I find the individual to whom I have alluded going out to Canada in a responsible position, going out in a public character now or with a promise that when he gets out there he will be placed in a situation of public trust and confidence . . . I will state it boldly to the noble Viscount that he has not acted with that candour which becomes him.' Melbourne answered even more emphatically than before that no appointment had been offered by the Government to Turton, and that if he had gone to Canada, he had gone 'without any prospect of an appointment and without any intention on the part of the Government or on the part of my noble friend, the Earl of Durham, to appoint him to any public situation whatever.'[37]

There the matter rested for a few months. But on 2nd July Lord Wharncliffe informed the House of Lords that the *Quebec Gazette* stated that Turton had been appointed Second Secretary to Lord

Durham. He added that he attached much less importance to the question of Turton's private life than he did to that of 'having answers given by Ministers of the Crown, when questions are put to them, which may be relied on.' Melbourne had no better defence than to say he believed the despatches from Lord Durham contained no mention of Turton's appointment, but Brougham then rushed, a little surprisingly, to Turton's defence. He admitted that Turton had been divorced by his wife for seducing her sister and conceded that seduction was 'a foul offence.' But he pointed out, Turton had not been guilty of incest, and he and the Bishop of London then wandered off into a somewhat irrelevant discussion about the propriety of marrying a dead wife's sister.[38]

The Earl of Winchilsea brought up the question of Turton's appointment more than once, and the next year, the Earl of Durham, who by then had returned to England, accepted full responsibility for it himself. After this Winchilsea made one final move. On 19th February 1839 he brought forward a motion for the laying on the Table of any correspondence between Her Majesty's Government and the Governor-General of Canada on the subject of Turton's appointment. A debate followed in which the Ministers, in spite of Durham's spirited defence of his actions, found themselves in a rather difficult situation. They were saved by Lord Brougham. He revealed two facts about Turton's qualifications. One was that he had been a successful Advocate-General in India. The other was that he and Durham had been at school together. After that the Earl of Winchilsea withdrew his motion and the matter, by common consent, was dropped.[39]

The appointment of Turton may have been justifiable, but the same could hardly be said of one appointment which was queried in the House of Commons in 1834. On 3rd March Daniel O'Connell, who then represented the City of Dublin, asked a question about the choice as a stipendiary magistrate in the colonies of a man named Lawrence Dundas, who had absconded after being charged with forgery and peculation in Ireland.

O'Connell had already discussed this appointment with Lord Stanley, the Secretary of State for the Colonies. Stanley had not known about Dundas's past, and O'Connell now asked at whose instance Dundas had been appointed and whether the Government intended to proceed against him. Lord Stanley told the House that

8

Dundas's appointment had been cancelled after O'Connell had discussed the matter with him, and he asked not to be forced into a breach of confidence by naming the person who had recommended him. He added that the Government did not intend to take the matter further as the people who had been defrauded could bring actions themselves. O'Connell seemed rather surprised by this last answer. Dundas, he pointed out, had 'forged receipts of the payment of tolls on Wexford bridge,' and he had 'in various ways put £6,000 or £8,000 at least of the public money into his own pocket.'[40]

Less than a fortnight later O'Connell showed the goodness of his heart. He told the House of Commons of a letter he had had from Dundas. In this Dundas had declared that he had made good all the deficiencies, that he had not been charged with any crime, although it was true he had resigned his post as Chief Constable of Wexford, and that he needed a job in the colonies, 'having a large family to provide for.' O'Connell expressed the view that Dundas ought at least to have a chance of proving his innocence. As a further argument in favour of taking this course he cited the evidence of a correspondent who had informed him that the frauds committed in the county by Dundas 'in connection with the police force were carried on in all the other counties of Ireland.'[41]

The quality of their civil servants being so variable, their information about happenings abroad being so scanty and delayed, and their control over certain branches of the administration being so tenuous, it is remarkable, and even surprising, that so many Ministers of the Crown were able in the early years of the reformed Parliament to give detailed answers to questions asked at short notice.

Palmerston was a master of the unprepared answer to the unexpected question. Gladstone quickly revealed an equal capacity when he assumed office as President of the Board of Trade. In 1844, for instance, he could answer with no hesitation a question asked without notice about the number of members to be appointed to a railway committee who were themselves directors of railways. Similarly Lord John Russell, when asked a question on the subject of whether the Dean of Manchester was to retain the living of St. Paul's, Covent Garden, began by saying that he had had only an hour's notice of the Member's intention to ask a question on the subject and then went on to answer it in detail.[42]

Palmerston, Gladstone, and Russell were all men of extraordinary capacity, but not even they could continue to support the steadily increasing burden of government without the help of improved machinery in the forms of a bureaucracy outside Parliament and a party within. Resistance to the creation of an efficient bureaucracy lasted until the decade of the fifties; party organization was already gathering strength in the forties. The formation of cohesive political parties was eventually to determine the scope and utility of parliamentary questions to an extent which can hardly be overstated.

At the time of the passing of the Reform Act there was still a fairly widespread feeling that a political party whose activities were carried on outside parliamentary circles was a dangerous and probably a subversive institution. The very legality of political organizations operating in the country at large was questioned in both the House of Lords and the House of Commons in 1833.

On 17th June the Earl of Winchilsea asked in the Lords whether the Government intended to bring forward any measures that session 'for the suppression of political unions.' Earl Grey, the Prime Minister, admitted that political unions were 'totally inconsistent with good government,' as they were 'established solely for the purpose of effecting a control over the Houses of Parliament.' But he said he did not consider it either necessary or desirable to suppress them. The Marquis of Londonderry accused the Government of actually approving of these unions, whereupon Lord Seymour stated: 'Had it not been for the institution of Conservative clubs organized by those very parties who so loudly decry political unions, there would now be scarcely a political union of any kind in existence throughout the country.'[43]

Ten days later in the House of Commons George Finch, M.P. for Stamford, moved that 'certain voluntary associations, denominated political unions, are subversive of the authority of the Crown, unconstitutional and illegal, and that His Majesty's Ministers will be fully justified in enforcing the law of the land for their suppression.' He went on to assert that 'all political power which is not established by law is an unconstitutional power,' and that 'the only political union should be the British Parliament.' Lord Althorp, the

Chancellor of the Exchequer, gave it as his opinion that political unions were not illegal unless organized on a military principle, and Finch's motion was defeated by 78 votes to 8.[44]

One reason why these so-called 'political unions' were considered so dangerous was that they might be expected to advocate policies to which the overwhelming majority of Members of Parliament were opposed. The Bishop of Exeter gave expression to one particular fear when he asked in the House of Lords on 20th January 1840 whether the Government had taken any steps to halt the progress of 'the system of Socialists' in the country. The Home Secretary, the Marquis of Normanby, answered that no such steps had been taken.[45]

The Bishop brought the subject up again on several occasions in the course of the next few months. By his diligence he succeeded in obtaining the resignation of the Superintendent-Registrar of Birmingham because he held the post of Vice-President of the Social Society, and he persuaded the House of Lords to carry a motion for an address to the Queen asking 'that inquiries should be made into the diffusion of blasphemous and immoral publications, especially as to the tenets and proceedings of a society established under the name of Socialists.'[46]

In spite of these demands for suppression, party organization outside Parliament gained steadily in strength, and it received indirect encouragement from one provision of the Reform Act of 1832. This placed on those who had the right to vote the responsibility of ensuring that their names were on the electoral register. The registration fee was one shilling in England and two shillings in Scotland. The importance of an organization to remind voters of their rights and obligations became increasingly apparent.

Inside Parliament, party alignments, though suddenly confused by the manner in which the Corn Laws were repealed, also tended to become steadily more definite. An older and a newer view of Members' responsibilities to party were expressed in 1841, when Disraeli contended that Melbourne ought to resign after the evident defeat of his party at election time. Melbourne did not agree, his opinion being that it was not right 'to judge what the conduct of the Members may be by their declarations at the hustings.'

When Peel agreed, as a Conservative, to introduce the measure which led to the repeal of the Corn Laws—an action on his part which the Whig Melbourne called 'damned dishonest' and the Conservative Aberdeen 'very noble'—he split the Conservatives in a manner which that party has never allowed to be repeated. Conservatives for the most part had to decide whether they were Peelites or not, and the confusion was such that for a number of years the world did not know whether such an eminent figure as Gladstone was still a Conservative or had become a Liberal, for the good reason that he did not know himself.

But the very need for the majority of Conservative Members to make a decision in this matter was at least a reflexion of the growing strength of party. An obstinate Radical such as Joseph Hume could declare as late as 1848 that 'party has been the bane of the country,'[47] but a more realistic appreciation of what was happening was made by Disraeli when he declared on 30th August in the same year: 'I say, you can have no parliamentary government if you have no party government, and therefore, when gentlemen denounce party government, they strike at that scheme of government which in my opinion has made this country great and which, I hope, will keep it great.'[48]

The natural corollary to the growth of party was the emergence, in an age in which Members of Parliament cherished their independence, of what was known as 'the private Member.' For the first century after it was introduced the parliamentary question might have been considered primarily a weapon to be used by leading members of the Opposition. In the second half of the nineteenth century it was to become more and more the weapon of the private Member.

Commenting in 1840 on changes which had taken place in the course of thirty years, Lord John Russell declared: 'When I first entered Parliament, it was not usual for Governments to undertake generally all subjects of legislation. Since the Reform Bill it has been thought convenient that the Government should propose changes in the laws.'

This development, which could have occurred only when Governments enjoyed relatively strong party allegiances, meant that the range of subjects on which private Members were expected to initiate measures gradually narrowed. The trend was already apparent in the first fifteen years of the Reformed Parliament. The effective measures introduced by private Members were tending to become either those which commercial or other sectional interests demanded, or else measures which, while embraced by the popular contemporary catchword 'reform,' were concerned with some particular abuse or grievance. Questions asked during the period revealed this tendency repeatedly.

On 6th May 1836, for example, Dr. Bowring, M.P. for the Clyde Boroughs, asked the Chancellor of the Exchequer, Thomas Spring Rice, whether he knew of 'a process which has been lately introduced into this country,' for the manufacture of sugar from beetroot. If the experiments were successful, it might, Dr. Bowring suggested, 'be necessary, as has been the case with the recent cultivation of tobacco, to pluck up the beetroot by the roots.' Spring Rice, a politician of whom Lord Melbourne complained that he was too much given to detail and possessed of no broad vision, answered that he had heard of this form of experiment and that 'the result has been a most signal failure.'[49]

The dealers in sugar were not satisfied with this reply, and less than a year later the President of the Board of Trade, Poulett Thomson, announced, in answer to a question, that as he had heard of preparations to manufacture sugar from beetroot 'on an extensive scale,' he would introduce a Bill, 'not for the purpose of checking the manufacture, but to prevent its being carried on without paying any duty at all, while other sugar is burdened with a duty.'[50]

The Government's action caused hardship among individuals. In 1840 Daniel O'Connell presented a petition from a man named Hercules Bradshaw, who claimed to have lost £16,000 because he had been allowed to manufacture beet sugar 'without any intimation of the intention to impose such a duty being previously conveyed to him.'[51] O'Connell even moved that a committee should be set up to inquire into the particular case of Hercules Bradshaw's difficulties, but the motion was defeated by twenty votes, and the claims of those who dealt in sugar manufactured by more traditional processes were upheld.[52]

In the same year Viscount Sandon, M.P. for Liverpool, asked a question in the Commons about a trade agreement with Naples. He did so, as he said himself, 'on the part of persons interested in the trade in sulphur.'[53] Five years later the claims of another important commercial interest were advanced, when Sir Charles Lemon, M.P.

for West Cornwall, asked the Vice-President of the Board of Trade
whether the Government intended to introduce a Bill 'to prevent
excessive trading for oysters during the breeding season.' Sir George
Clark replied that the Government did not intend to do so immediately, but he agreed that the subject was 'worthy of the consideration of the Government.'[54]

Questions asked in the Commons with persistence by Radicals
and Irish Members did much towards helping to remove one
grievance about which there were strong feelings in certain parts of
Ireland. On 4th March 1835 William Finn, M.P. for Kilkenny,
asked whether His Majesty's Government had, as reported in the
papers, received addresses 'from those illegal and unconstitutional
bodies, the Orange Societies in Ireland.' Peel gave a rather evasive
answer, saying the question would be better addressed to the Chief
Secretary for Ireland.[55]

Before long the Government found they had to deal with others
beside ill-organized Irish Members in the matter. On 4th August in
the same year Hume moved for an address to the King praying him
to direct his royal attention to the nature and extent of Orange
lodges existing in the Army. He estimated that there were 1,500
Orange lodges, of which 229 were to be found in Antrim alone, and
that they were secret societies of a kind which Army officers and
other ranks were prohibited from joining by orders made in 1822
and 1829. Hume's motion was carried, and King William IV returned an answer that he would 'discourage and prevent any
attempts to introduce secret societies' into the ranks of the Army.[56]

This answer was still too evasive to satisfy Hume. On 8th February the next year he again asked a question on the subject, and on
23rd February he raised his sights even higher. He moved for an
address to the King asking him to remove judges, lords lieutenant,
chief constables, and even police officers who attended Orange lodge
meetings. In support of his case he brought forward evidence to
show that magistrates and jurors had been influenced by the lodges
to fail in their duties; he described the activities of armed bands
which roamed across the countryside; and told of a procession of
more than 4,000 Orangemen, headed by Members of Parliament,
who marched into a town with bands playing *The Protestant Boys*.
He even went so far as to implicate the King's brother, the Duke of
Cumberland, and Wellington's former general, the Marquis of

Londonderry. With some effect he read a letter from the Marquis of
Londonderry which complained of 'the present state of liberal Whig
feeling ... and the very refractory and insubordinate state of the
pitmen.'

Hume was now addressing a Whig Government, and Russell
succeeded in having an amendment to Hume's motion carried.
This limited Parliament to praying His Majesty 'to take such
measures as His Majesty may deem advisable for the effectual
discouragement of Orange lodges.'[57]

Three days later both Houses of Parliament learnt what the result
of this prayer had been. Russell himself and the Member for County
Cavan both informed the Commons that steps had been taken by
the Duke of Cumberland for the dissolution of Orange lodges. A
similar announcement was made in the House of Lords by the Duke
of Cumberland himself. Lord Melbourne gracefully concluded the
dispute by saying the honourable attitude adopted by the gentlemen
belonging to these societies would put an end to them 'without any
further interference on the part either of His Majesty's Government
or of Parliament.'[58]

The suppression of the Orange lodges was a spectacular success
achieved by the combination of English Radicals and Irish Catholics.
Less spectacular but perhaps no less important measures of reform
came as consequences of questions asked by Members acting, not as
representatives of extreme sections of the House of Commons, but
rather as individuals concerned with a particular problem.

On 5th February 1838 Viscount Ebrington, M.P. for North
Devonshire, asked a question to which a recent disaster at sea had
given rise. This was whether the Government had 'any legislative
measures in contemplation for the purpose of securing passengers
against the risks to which they are constantly exposed on board
steam-boats as at present conducted.'

The answer was given by Poulett Thomson. He said the Government had not yet had time to investigate the causes of the particular
disaster referred to, the loss of the steamer *Killarney*, but he added:
'It is unquestionably of the greatest importance to ascertain whether
in regard to steam-boats generally some restrictions cannot be made
as to the quantity of livestock shipped on board these vessels,
similar to those which exist in regard to other passenger-boats.'[59]

Five years later a select committee was appointed 'to enquire into the shipwreck of British vessels and preserving the lives and property of shipwrecked persons'; and the way was open for the long series of legislative measures designed to ensure the safety of ships and seamen, with so many of which the name of Samuel Plimsoll was later to be associated.

Two other questions, which could be considered early forerunners of later important measures, pointed to the needs for a Court of Criminal Appeal and a properly organized fire brigade. On 2nd December 1847 William Ewart, M.P. for Dumfries, mentioned two instances in which convicted persons were later discovered to be innocent. One was that of Mary Ann Turford, who had been sentenced to six months in prison for stealing a watch; the other was that of Thomas Whalley, whose sentence had been transportation for fifteen years.

Ewart asked whether it was the intention of the Government 'to institute a Court of Criminal Appeal.' Sir George Grey, the Home Secretary, answered that he did not consider it 'a very convenient move to bring such an important subject forward in the shape of a question.' He emphasized the difficulties in the way of such a reform, but went on: 'I do not say that there are not cases in which such a court of appeal might exercise a useful jurisdiction.' Another advantage of the reform, which was not in fact to take place for sixty years, would be, he said, that it would relieve the Home Office of the duty of dealing with compensation for wrongful convictions, a duty of which it would gladly be rid.[60]

The question about precautions against fire was asked on 2nd June 1845 in connection with a fire which had broken out in Dover Street. The Home Secretary was then Sir James Graham, and he informed the Commons that he had considered a policy of taking precautions against fire 'in the police arrangements of the metropolis.' He also said that the Commissioner of Woods and Forests had enquired what was being done in this matter in Paris, Vienna, and the United States. His own view was that responsibility ought not to rest with the police, but that 'as in Paris a separate establishment should be created, the duty of which should be to take precautions against fire.'[61]

The increasing use of the parliamentary question as a means of promoting measures not provided for in the legislative programmes of Governments, added to the general growth of business, led inevitably after a time to the taking of steps to control the use, and possible abuse, of questions. The first indications of an increasing control were already apparent before 1848. By 1835 questions had become so far recognized as a regular part of business that notices of them began to be printed on the order paper, although it was not until 1849 that a special position on the paper was assigned to questions.

The principal measure of control over questions between 1832 and 1848 took the form of refusals on the part of Ministers to answer certain kinds of questions, some of these refusals being later accepted as precedents. There were also a number of Speaker's rulings.

In 1841 Lord John Russell firmly refused to answer a question about an action taken by a member of the Royal Family. This refusal was itself indicative of a growing desire on the part of responsible statesmen to keep the Crown out of politics.

On 29th January he was asked whether a letter reported to have been sent by Prince Albert's secretary to the Loyal Repeal Association of Ireland, thanking that body for a congratulatory address on the birth of the Princess Royal, was or was not authentic. Russell's answer was evasive, and the Member, whose name was Captain Polhill, said he would repeat the question four days later.

Russell thereupon stated that if notice were given, he would answer any question on an act done by the advice of Her Majesty's Ministers. 'But I will not,' he said, 'undertake to be so prepared in reference to any act done by Prince Albert.' When Polhill did repeat his question later, Russell said he had not 'thought it necessary to make any enquiry on the subject.'[62]

Refusals to answer questions also extended to the advice offered to the Crown in certain specified fields, such as the conferring of honours and the prerogative of mercy. On 13th April 1842 William Smith O'Brien, the Irish revolutionary, who was later to be transported to Tasmania, asked whether the Lord Mayor of Dublin, as well as the Lord Mayor of London, would have an honour conferred on him on the occasion of the birth of an heir to the Throne. Peel replied: 'I must positively decline answering any such questions as to the advice which I deem it right to give to the Crown on the disposal of civil honours.'[63]

Two years later, on 19th April, John Bright, then M.P. for

Stockport, put a question to the Home Secretary, Sir James Graham, about the case of a woman named Mary Furley, who, 'being at the time in a state of the most appalling destitution,' had thrown herself into some water, with her child in her arms. She herself was rescued, but her child was drowned. She was tried for murder and convicted, and in passing sentence of death, the judge threw out no hope of a commutation of her sentence. Graham replied that it was not consistent with his duty to enter into a discussion on the subject.[64]

Graham elaborated his views on the propriety of answering questions about recommendations to mercy the next year. On 4th August 1845 a question was asked about a case in which a man named William Mays had been convicted of the crime of assaulting a gamekeeper. Graham replied: 'It is not by any means convenient that I, as Secretary of State, should be called upon to state the advice which I am prepared to offer to the Sovereign with respect to the exercise of the royal prerogative.' Somewhat illogically he then went on to explain why he intended to recommend a free pardon in this case.[65]

Precedents were also established for refusing to disclose future budgetary policy by answering questions. On 6th February 1843 Thomas Milner Gibson, M.P. for Manchester, asked Peel whether the Government intended to maintain 'the present prohibitory duty on foreign sugar.' Peel answered: 'Without intending anything like disrespect to the honourable Member, I must decline answering his question. To do so would be inconsistent with my duty, for I might be asked a similar question with respect to every other article upon which duty exists.'[66]

Several years later Sir Charles Wood, when Chancellor of the Exchequer, took advantage of this precedent. Answering a question about the Government's financial proposals for the year 1848, he said: 'This year, most unquestionably, it will be necessary to renew the income tax. But I must say it is exceedingly inconvenient at the present moment to state what are the views of the Government with respect to the taxation of the country.'[67]

A question about opinions expressed at a meeting of the railway department of the Board of Trade,[68] and a question based on a speculation in a newspaper that Prince Albert was to be given the title of King Consort, were both declared by Ministers of the Crown in 1845 to be improper.[69] One year earlier an even more decided refusal had been given in answer to a question about matters occurring outside Parliament for which the Government, it was claimed, was not responsible.

On 21st June 1844 William Christie, M.P. for Weymouth and Melcombe Regis, referred in a question to the fact that the Solicitor-General, Sir Frederick Thesiger, who later became Lord Chancellor, had obtained leave to bring in a Bill for the disfranchisement of Sudbury, where there had been wholesale bribery at the last election. Christie then asked about Thesiger's own election at Abingdon. Thesiger, he claimed, while being carried in a procession, led by a brass band, to the Crown and Thistle Inn, had scattered what was known as 'scramble money' amounting to £50 among the crowd.

Thesiger replied: 'A very inconvenient and, as it appears to me, irregular practice has been introduced into this House of putting questions to Members, not in relation to any business before the House or to any Bills with which Members are charged, but with regard to matters wholly foreign to such topics and relating to occurrences in a very different place and which have no connection with the business before the House, however much they may excite the curiosity of honourable Members.' He refused 'most decidedly' to answer Christie's question.[70]

Thesiger was fully entitled to refuse an answer, as Christie admitted, but his opinion that the question was an improper one was, in this instance, based on an assumption very much open to dispute.

Exception was also taken by more than one Minister to the growing habit of having lengthy questions, which contained doubtful statements, printed in the order paper and thereby circulated. Peel objected to one such question asked in 1842, which referred to the 'general stagnation of trade and want of employment among the working classes,' and which advocated the substitution of a silver for a gold standard.[71]

Another question, to which strong exception was taken on the grounds that it was not only argumentative, but without the benefit of privilege, would have been libellous, was asked four years later. In this case the question was not printed before it was asked. On 11th May 1846 John Collett, M.P. for Athlone, asked a question based on a long statement alleging some highly improper practices in Hampshire.

According to his story, a man named Silvester had been approached by a police constable and asked whether he wanted a job. Silvester said he did, and the policeman then told him to take a hare and a pheasant to a fisherman named Bridger and his wife and then lay information, for which he would receive £5. Silvester refused the offer, saying he would rather go into the workhouse.

According to the report appearing in the *Hampshire Independent*, on which Collett had based his question, the name of Sir T. C. Heywood of Holywell House was mentioned in the conversation between the policeman and Silvester. Collett also pointed out that one of the magistrates by whom the Bridger case had been tried was Sir Charles Taylor, who had sat in Parliament for over thirty years.

Sir James Graham, the Home Secretary, said he could not give an answer at once, and he expressed the hope that the question would not be put on the paper. If it were, he pointed out, Collett's allegation would be 'circulated about the country for several days before it could be answered.'[72]

A week later Collett brought the subject up again, now saying that Mrs. Bridger had been trapped into buying game and had been sentenced by Sir Charles Taylor to imprisonment with hard labour. Graham answered that the enquiries he had made led him to believe there was no truth in the story of the trap set by a policeman, and that Silvester was 'a convicted felon, having been found guilty of horse-stealing.'[73]

But by this time feeling on both sides had become too strong for the matter to be dropped. On 21st May Collett was asked by Grantley Berkeley, M.P. for West Gloucestershire, whether he had sent an affidavit with charges against Sir Charles Taylor to the Home Secretary. Collett said he had, and Berkeley declared: 'If the charge is untrue, the Member who brought it forward, unsupported by evidence, is not fit to sit in the House.' Graham added that if Collett believed the story he had heard, his proper course was 'to become prosecutor and proceed against Sir C. Taylor at law.'[74]

Collett did not follow this suggestion. Instead he asked some weeks later whether Sir Charles Taylor still continued 'in the commission of the peace for the county of Southampton.' When Graham answered that he did and that the Crown did not intend to pursue the matter further, it became clear that the feeling of the House was strongly in favour of the Government. Another Member named Collett protested that he was already suffering from the fact that his constituents were confusing the two of them, and several Members made it clear that they considered the Member of Athlone had abused his privilege of asking questions.[75]

At a time when parliamentary questions were controlled by usage rather than resolution, it was natural that Speaker's rulings on the subject should consist of explanations of what the usage was and what constituted an irregular departure from that usage. One ruling, which was repeated more than once, concerned the irregularity of indulging in arguments when putting questions.

On 5th July 1836, for instance, John Walter, M.P. for Berkshire, in putting a question, made a rambling statement about a placard he had seen in the window of a country post office, inviting young women and widows of good character between the ages of fifteen and thirty to emigrate to Van Diemen's Land. He was interrupted by Speaker Abercromby, who said: 'It is quite competent for honourable Members to put a question, but not to follow it up by reasons and explanations.'[76]

Walter had therefore to confine himself to asking whether the placard had been circulated with the permission of the Under-Secretary of State for the Colonies. Sir George Grey said he believed it was not an official notice, and he confirmed this three days later, when in answer to a further question on emigration he said the placard was issued by, a voluntary committee of gentlemen,' who had acted under regulations sanctioned by the Government.[77]

The Speaker's ruling in this case effectively served the purpose of preventing a discussion on the merits of emigration without a specific motion on the subject, and the unwillingness of the House to have such a discussion was shown soon afterwards. On 11th July Wakley moved for an address to the King praying for the withdrawal of the placard. 'Two-thirds of the emigrants,' he said, 'are irrevocably and finally consigned to prostitution' and he quoted a Hobart newspaper, which stated: 'When we find that the heads of these young females are filled with such notions as that "Van Diemen's Land is a splendid little spot, filled with pretty white cottages, each with single men, of all ranks and callings, waiting for wives," we cannot hold scathless the authors of such delusion.'

When Wakley had finished, the Speaker asked who seconded the motion. There was a silence, and then Wakley announced: 'I second the motion.' Daniel O'Connell commented: 'Oh, Mr. Wakley,' and the subject was promptly dropped.

A question about the proceedings of a select committee which had not yet reported to the House was ruled out of order by Speaker Shaw Lefevre in 1848, and the rule against reference to an earlier debate in the same session, which applied to discussions in the Commons generally, was also pointed out by the same Speaker.

On 12th July 1847 William Mackinnon, M.P. for Berkshire, asked another member, Ralph Osborne, M.P. for Wycombe, a question about a speech he had made in a debate in which, according to the report, he had 'traduced a Portuguese nobleman.' Speaker Shaw Lefevre at once pointed out that Mackinnon could not allude to a debate which had taken place in that session, but Osborne suggested that he might be allowed to answer. The Speaker's ruling was: 'If the honourable gentleman wishes to explain anything in his former speech having reference to an individual, he can do so, but not by way of answer to a question from another honourable Member.'

Osborne then went on to explain why he had described the Portuguese nobleman as a defaulter. It was because he had been engaged in an extensive trade in Britain and through the conduct of his partner had become bankrupt. He had later, Osborne admitted, come into some property, paid off his liabilities, and now had 'the good fortune to be the Minister of Finance in the Portuguese Government.'[79]

Speakers' rulings on questions between 1832 and 1848 were, in fact, limited in scope, and in the House of Lords there was even less control over the recognized privilege. Most of the discussions about the procedure of asking questions which took place in the House of Lords were concerned with the problem of whether notice ought to be given.

On 14th July 1834 Lord Melbourne announced in answer to a question asked in the House of Lords that he had accepted the task of forming an administration, subject to the conditions that he should have the co-operation of Althorp and the sanction and approval of Grey.[80] Eleven days later the Earl of Winchilsea concluded a lengthy speech by asking a question about the policy Melbourne intended to pursue and the measures he would take 'in the present awful state of the country.'

Melbourne answered that his general policy would be that of the last Government, which Grey had led, and then went on to say: 'The noble Earl said that he had given notice of his questions. That is a novel thing in parliamentary practice, and I cannot exactly see the utility of it. When a notice of a motion is given, the objects and purport of the notice can generally be gathered by the nature of the notice, but it is quite a different thing as regards a notice to this effect—"I shall tomorrow ask questions as to foreign policy and domestic policy." Is there any possibility of collecting from such a notice the precise nature of the questions that may be asked?'[81]

Melbourne, in fact, seems to have been somewhat confused on the subject of the procedure of asking questions. Less than a year later the Marquis of Londonderry put three questions to him about relations with Spain, to which he replied that he could not give the answers until the next day, as he had had no notice.[82] From more than one of his answers it was clear that the practice of asking questions was not one which he welcomed.

Brougham, on the other hand, had strong views on the practice and continued to insist on his right to ask questions without notice long after most other Members of the Upper House had recognized the advantages which the giving of notice afforded.

On 27th February 1838 he addressed a question to Melbourne about a certain Julia Newman, whom, he said, 'I ought to call a gentlewoman if she had not degraded herself by crime.' Miss Newman had been sentenced to fourteen years' transportation for robbery, but had been committed to Bethlem, where the matron had decided she was not insane. In putting his question, Brougham said: 'Between seven and eight o'clock this morning I sent a note to the noble Viscount couched in as respectful terms as I could employ, intimating my intention of putting a question this evening.' He added: 'By giving a formal notice I by no means intend to express disapprobation of the opposite course, namely the bringing forward such a motion or the putting such a question as the present without any notice at all.'

Melbourne produced evidence of conflicting opinions on the state of Miss Newman's mind, and said that the practice of giving notice 'tends more than any other, not merely to my convenience, which is nothing, but to a full, fair and satisfactory discussion of any topic that may be brought under the consideration of this House.'[83]

The principal differences between the practices of the two Houses in the asking and answering of questions were procedural ones, the differences themselves reflecting the greater freedom of discussion allowed in the House of Lords as a consequence of its much smaller volume of business. There was, however, one other difference, which was not procedural. In the House of Lords questions could still be put to bishops about disciplinary measures to be taken against individual clergymen.

On 11th March 1844 Lord Lilford asked the Bishop of Peterborough whether the Rev. Herbert Marsh was still allowed to perform his clerical duties. The Bishop admitted that Marsh had had 'a criminal connexion,' which 'took place at Paris,' but this particular offence had been committed more than four years before it had come to the Bishop's knowledge. The Church Discipline Act, the Bishop explained, 'does not permit me to take any cognizance of a case which has occurred more than two years back.'

But the Bishop was able to give the House an assurance that all Marsh's duties in his parish had been performed for some time by a curate, Marsh himself 'residing sometimes at Peterborough and sometimes in this great metropolis.'[84]

In 1867 Bagehot wrote: 'Since the Reform Act the House of Lords has become a revising and suspending House.' So far as legislation was concerned, this may have been substantially true, and for many years after the passing of the Act of 1832 the House of Lords was careful to avoid a recurrence of the direct clash and the constitutional crisis which its opposition to the Reform Bill had caused. But for the announcement by Ministers of the Crown of statements of major importance the House of Lords was still considered in the eighteen-thirties and eighteen-forties as appropriate a chamber as the House of Commons. Not only did Melbourne explain in answer to a question in the House of Lords the conditions on which he was prepared to form an administration, but on 26th January 1846 an even more eagerly awaited statement was made in answer to a question put in the Upper House.

9

On that day the Duke of Richmond asked the Duke of Wellington whether he had received 'Her Majesty's permission to state to your Lordships' house those reasons which induced the Government to resign office and afterwards to re-accept office.' The Duke of Wellington answered that that permission had been given, and went on to say: 'When the accounts were received from Ireland and from different parts of Great Britain in the course of the last autumn of the state of the potato crop, and of the inconveniences which were likely to result from it, my right honourable friend at the head of the Government felt it to be his duty to call his colleagues together.'

Peel, the Duke went on, 'stated to his colleagues certain propositions. . . . One of the measures was that Her Majesty's servants should recommend to Her Majesty by an Order in Council to suspend the operation of the existing Corn Laws, so as to open the ports for the admission of foreign corn duty free.'

He described the strong differences of opinion within the Cabinet; how he himself tried unsuccessfully to reconcile these differences; how Peel advised the Queen that another administration should be formed; and how that attempt too failed. After that the Queen asked Peel to remain in office until efforts to form a new administration were successful, and Peel in turn asked the Duke to stand by him.

Then came the Duke's explanation of the reasons which had prompted him to make his final and supremely important decision. 'I was of opinion,' he said, 'that the formation of a Government in which Her Majesty could have confidence was of much greater importance than the opinions of any individual on the Corn Laws or any other law.'[85]

With this unequivocal expression of a political philosophy the triumph of the doctrine of free trade was ceded beyond the possibility of doubt.

VII

Free and Vigorous Growth (1848–1867)

IN 1861 the report was published of a Select Committee on the Business of the House of Commons, The chairman of the committee was Sir James Graham, and its members included Palmerston, Bright, and Disraeli. Among those who gave evidence was Thomas Erskine May, the Clerk to the House, whose name was to become almost synonymous with the rules of parliamentary procedure. One question the committee put to May was:

'Is not the habit of asking questions comparatively a modern practice?'

May replied:

'Undoubtedly it has greatly increased during the last ten years.'

The next question was:

'The practice has increased, but the practice existed many years ago, did it not?'

'Yes,' May answered, 'but it was exercised with comparative rarity, and in no case were the notices printed.'

May was right in fixing at some ten years earlier the point at which a great increase in the practice of asking questions began. Between 1848 and the second important extension of the franchise in 1867 was indeed the period in which the practice flourished most vigorously and most freely. The controls and restrictions remained minimal; the number of questions asked rose sharply and their scope was greatly extended; the machinery for providing the answers steadily improved; and a tendency developed towards making the question a substitute for a formal motion. This tendency was ultimately, but not until some years later, to lead to new and stringent rules for restricting the liberty of questioning.

The public did not cease to use the petition. In fact during the five years from 1868 to 1872, inclusive, the number of petitions totalled 101,573, compared with 70,072 thirty years earlier and 23,283 forty years earlier. But as a parliamentary device the petition had already by 1848 been superseded by the question, and after 1848 more and more Members of Parliament came into a full realization of the effective use to which the question could be put.

Resistance continued in some quarters to what was still regarded as a relatively new practice. In 1853, for instance, an unusual proposal was put forward for rearranging the parliamentary calendar. This was that Parliament should sit in the winter instead of in the summer, and its advocate, Henry Drummond, M.P. for West Surrey, a fervent believer in the immediate approach of the end of the world, gave as one of his reasons the manner in which summer days were wasted in asking and answering questions.

'A Member,' he said, 'reads a paragraph in a newspaper and asks a question on the subject—one about a dispute with a cabman and another about the soldiers getting wet at the encampment at Chobham. There is a great loss of time in answering questions of this kind.' He admitted one objection to his proposal might be: 'Oh, what will become of the foxhunting?' But, he went on, 'I do not believe there are many hunters left in the House. In my opinion we ought to return to a commonsense view of the subject and live in the country in pleasant weather and in town in winter.'[1]

Drummond's suggestion for transforming parliamentary habits in this way was not adopted. But his opinions on questions found an echo four years later in an answer given by a Minister of the Crown. On 7th August 1857 A. S. C. Stratford, M.P. for Northamptonshire, asked whether the new chimney-pots on Somerset House were 'found to answer.' Sir Benjamin Hall, First Commissioner of Works, prefaced his reply by saying: 'Certainly very singular questions are asked in this House, but I never expected that we should descend to such trifling matters as the chimney-pots of Somerset House.'[2]

In 1857 it was not altogether surprising that a Minister of the Crown should have given such a scornful answer to a question of this kind. But in the years which followed Members of Parliament tended to ask more and more detailed questions about matters of administration, and after the Northcote-Trevelyan reforms had been introduced, the Civil Service became steadily more efficient in supplying Ministers with the answers.

The establishment of the Civil Service Commission by Order in Council on 21st May 1855 did not transform the public service into an efficient body overnight. The growth of an efficient service was indeed a gradual one. But the setting up of the Commission was a landmark of the greatest importance, and the complaints against the service as a whole, which Members of Parliament had so often voiced before that date, diminished with remarkable abruptness after it.

In 1850, for instance, Sir Benjamin Hall, as M.P. for Marylebone, himself asked a question about 'a young lady of interesting appearance and prepossessing manners,' who had 'the honour of holding office of registrar of one of the ecclesiastical courts.'

He went on to say: 'I do not wish to impugn the morality of the dignitary who appointed this young lady; indeed she has held the office ever since she was five years of age.' But he had heard that few, if any, of the returns ordered by the House a month earlier from the prepossessing registrar had been sent in, and he wanted to know whether they were likely to be available soon.[3]

Two years later, on 7th June 1852, Viscount Duncan, M.P. for Bath, asked a question based on a remarkable report which he had read in *The Times*. This was that a cheque drawn by the Poor Law Board and signed by its President, Sir John Trollope, and its Secretary, Lord Courtenay, for £149 had been dishonoured at the Bank of England, and that Glyn and Company, who had presented the cheque, had been told that there were not sufficient funds to meet it.

Trollope answered the question himself. The mistake, he said, had arisen from 'mere inadvertence on the part of the accountant who transacts the monetary business of the Poor Law Board,' and who had failed to make the necessary application to the Treasury. The accountant, Trollope said in extenuation, was 'a very old and valuable servant of the public, having been in the public service for about eighteen years without ever making a similar mistake.'[4]

After 1855 not only did Parliament cease to hear such astounding revelations of how the administration of the country was carried on and such lame attempts to justify or excuse it; but within a few years Members had begun to take up a new attitude towards the position and rights of public servants.

By 1865 questions came to be asked by more than one Member with the object of obtaining a half-holiday on Saturday in the Civil Service, and Palmerston announced in answer to one of these questions that a commission would be set up to consider the problem.[5]

The next year Myles O'Reilly, M.P. for County Longford, brought the subject up again, and H. C. E. Childers, Secretary to the Treasury, announced the Government's decision. This was that the existing arrangements, whereby heads of departments granted as many clerks as possible a half-holiday on Saturday, would remain in force.

Childers then went on to compare the working hours of civil servants with those of clerks in other offices. In the Department of Inland Revenue the clerks worked from 10 a.m. to 4 p.m. and had a leave allowance ranging from 28 to 40 days. The same hours were kept in the Customs Office and Post Office, where the leave allowance was 32 days or one month. A big railway company, on the other hand, employed clerks from 9 to 5, with a half-hour break for refreshment, and granted them 14 days' holiday. The hours at the Bank of England were from 9 to 4 for five days of the week and 8 to 3 on Saturdays, one hour being allowed for dinner and the holiday period being 18 days. A shipping company employed its clerks from 10 to 4 and sometimes till a later hour when they were busy. The hours on Saturday were from 10 to 2, and the holiday allowance was three weeks.

In conclusion Childers declared: 'I do not think the Civil Service as a whole is overworked.'[6] None of the Members was sufficiently critical of the service to suggest it was underworked.

One field in which the reorganized Civil Service was able, when questions were asked, to provide detailed and valuable information of a kind not available to Ministers of the Crown in earlier decades was that of foreign affairs. The principal reason for this was not so much the improvement in the quality of the service as the use of the electric telegraph.

In particular, news from distant countries, where in the past the nation's representatives had had to wait months before receiving enquiries or instructions from the Government at home, could now be made available promptly.

Before 1850 information from a territory as distant as California still tended to be scanty. On 27th February 1849, Palmerston was asked whether the Government had appointed a consul at San Francisco or elsewhere in California. He answered that this question had been put to him 'privately by a number of persons, some of whom are no doubt interested in their own prosperity.' No consul, he said, would be appointed in the immediate future as there was no Government with which a consul could communicate. 'Under present circumstances,' he concluded, 'I fear a consul, like others, would have nothing to do but to pick up the gold and communicate with the gold-finders.'[7]

Even as late as 1856 the Government at home was liable to be caught by surprise by happenings in the United States of America. On 5th June in that year questions were asked in both the House of Lords and the House of Commons about a newspaper report that John Crampton, Her Majesty's Minister in Washington, had been summarily dismissed from the country to which he was accredited. In the House of Commons Palmerston replied: 'Indirectly Her Majesty's Government have received intimation of the fact ... that Mr. Crampton has received his passports and has quitted Washington for Toronto. Nothing from him has been received as yet.'[8]

Four days later he again stated that no definite news had been received from Crampton, and it was not until 13th June that both Houses learnt that Crampton and the three British consuls at Cincinnati, Philadelphia, and New York were 'considered as representatives unacceptable to the Government of the United States.' Palmerston, in giving his answer, added: 'Until the Government have had an opportunity of giving full consideration to all the circumstances connected with the case it cannot be expected that I shall say anything further.'[9]

On 16th June the House of Commons discussed the rather tense situation which had been created, and Palmerston, after announcing that the United States wished to maintain diplomatic relations through the Minister in London, declared characteristically: 'This country was never in a better position to carry on war, so if war were forced upon us, that very strength and that very preparation of which we may boast is also a reason why we may, without derogation from our dignity, act with calmness, with moderation and with due deliberation.'[10]

Palmerston's critics were not satisfied. A further debate took place a fortnight later when S. H. Moore, M.P. for Mayo, produced powerful evidence to show that Crampton and the consuls had been recruiting in the United States for the British Foreign Legion and that they had done so with the support of the Foreign Secretary, the Earl of Clarendon, although this was contrary to United States law.

Sir Richard Bethell, the Attorney-General, was put up to defend the Government's policy. He declared that the recruiting had not actually taken place on United States territory, and the next day the Government won what amounted to a vote of confidence in its policy by a majority of 274 over 80.[11]

In contrast with these happenings in America was the story of how successive Governments were held accountable for happenings in the Crimea and how they met the challenge. During the Crimean War a British Government was for the first time subjected to a persistent barrage of questions about its conduct of military and naval operations, and after telegraphic communication with the Crimea was established, the answers, though seldom satisfactory, were increasingly informative.

More than one important statement of Government policy in the matter of Anglo-Russian relations was elicited by questions before war was actually declared. On 8th August 1853 the Foreign Secretary, the Earl of Clarendon, said in answer to a question in the House of Lords: 'I should be very sorry if there existed the slightest misapprehension, even for a single day, with respect to my meaning with regard to the Russian occupation of the Danubian provinces. I have no hesitation now in informing my noble friend, without waiting for further discussion, that we look to the immediate and complete evacuation of the Danubian provinces as a *sine qua non* of any agreement whatever.'[12]

This was unequivocal, and six months later diplomatic relations with Russia were broken off. Then on 13th March 1854 a question was asked for which Lord Aberdeen's Government was much less well prepared. The question was put by Fitzstephen French, M.P. for Roscommon, to the First Lord of the Admiralty, Sir James Graham.

The evening before, Graham and Admiral Sir Charles Napier had been among those present at a dinner at the Reform Club, to which the press had been admitted. Fitzstephen French's question concerned a speech made by Graham in which he was reported to have announced that he had given Napier liberty to declare war on entering the Baltic.

Graham began his answer by saying: 'I am not disposed to admit the right of the honourable gentleman to put a question with respect to what happened after dinner at the Reform Club.' The words 'after dinner' were greeted with loud laughter, and Graham then attempted some sort of explanation. He said that Napier, who had spoken earlier at the dinner, had declared that he had hoped before entering the Baltic he would have authority to declare war. 'I stated,' Graham went on 'that when he entered the Baltic I hoped there would be no difficulty on his part in declaring war. But I have to state to the House that at present no declaration of war has taken place.'

After this admission John Bright, not surprisingly, moved the adjournment of the House. 'The right honourable gentleman,' he said, 'complained that he is asked about something that happened after dinner, and the House put an interpretation on that which I am quite sure was not justified by the state of the right honourable gentleman at the time.'

With growing scorn he described how Napier's bellicose utterances had been greeted with cries of 'Bravo, Charley!' and attacked members of the Government in general, and Palmerston in particular, for being present on such an occasion. Then, with his habitual oratorical splendour, he declared: 'The reckless levity that was displayed was in my opinion discreditable in the last degree to the great and responsible statesmen of a civilized and Christian nation.'[13] A fortnight later Britain and Russia were at war.

Within a month of the outbreak of war Graham was ingenuously informing the House of Commons in answer to a question: 'We have sent to Turkey since 8th February 830 officers, 21,119 men and 2,259 horses. We have sent in addition to this force 2,300 tons of provisions and commissariat stores and also 8,300 tons of advance stores. For this purpose we have employed 93 transports.'[14]

Graham's sense of military security was clearly no more developed than the sense of discretion which he displayed when dining at the Reform Club. But before long he showed signs of realizing the disadvantages of trying to answer questions about the conduct of the war in too great detail. Within a fortnight of informing the world, through the medium of the British press, of the exact strength of the British military contribution, he said in answer to a question: 'I do not think it would be possible to conduct a war if the Government were called upon to lay before the House the requisitions they might have received from the admirals on foreign stations with respect to what is necessary for the forces.'[15]

This greater sense of caution on the part of Ministers, of which there was to be increasing evidence as the war went on, did not prevent Parliament from demanding and getting a constant supply of information about the way in which the war was being mismanaged.

For this Members were in the first instance indebted to *The Times*, which had not only employed as a war correspondent a man of such ability as William Howard Russell, but also had means of communication which for a long time were superior to those of the Government. Russell's despatches provided excellent ammunition for parliamentary questions.

On 28th April 1854 Digby Seymour, M.P. for Poole, asked whether *The Times* had been accurate in reporting that the troops landed at Gallipoli had been provided with no medical stores, no medical staff and no proper quarters. Sidney Herbert, the Secretary at War, who was at first understandably reluctant to believe the scandals of which Miss Nightingale was later to make him thoroughly aware, answered: 'I apprehend it will be found that their wants have been fully and carefully attended to in this respect.'[16]

A week later Lord Lovaine, M.P. for North Northumberland, asked how 'the person who reported to *The Times* newspaper the condition of the troops landed at Gallipoli' obtained a passage from England. Bernal Osborne, Secretary to the Admiralty, answered: 'In consequence of his position, acquirements and general knowledge I have no doubt he did get a passage, but who gave it the Board of Admiralty is not aware.' He added that Russell 'would be from his position and education an excellent companion on board ship.'[17]

Questions about press correspondents did serve, according to Sidney Herbert's admission, to lead to an order forbidding the issue of rations to them from the Commissariat,[18] but as the war progressed Russell's reports began to be treated by the Government with less and less levity.

Mistakes were soon freely admitted. On 21st December 1854 the Duke of Newcastle, who was in charge of the War Office, said in answer to a question in the House of Lords: 'There have evidently been cases of neglect and want of foresight and attention to matters of real importance to the welfare of the Army and the Fleet.' He also admitted 'a want of organization in the port of Balaclava,' and said: 'I have felt it my duty to call on Lord Raglan to make immediate enquiry into this alleged gross neglect.'[19]

A month later Earl Grey asked for verification of a newspaper report that 'ships had been chartered from this country to bring home the 12th and 91st regiments from the Cape, and that no order to that effect having been given to the officer in command at the Cape, he had refused to allow the regiments to be embarked.' The Duke of Newcastle had to admit the report was substantially true.[20]

Three days after that Craven Berkeley, M.P. for Cheltenham, asked a question in the House of Commons about the charge of the Light Brigade. He described it as the 'melancholy disaster which occurred at the battle of Balaclava.' Sidney Herbert took exception to the term 'melancholy disaster,' but announced his intention of moving for an address to the Queen, praying 'that an enquiry should be instituted into the conduct of Lord Lucan for ordering the charge of light cavalry under circumstances which precluded the possibility of success.'[21]

No Government could survive the admission of such a catalogue of blunders and the public indignation they aroused. On the very day on which Berkeley asked his question about the charge of the Light Brigade Lord Aberdeen's Government was overwhelmingly defeated on a motion for a select committee to enquire into the general conduct of the war. The British public had found, as they were to find again, that the Government which had committed them to a war was unfit to conduct it, and Palmerston returned to the office of Prime Minister at the age of seventy.

Towards the end of April 1855, nearly three months after Lord Aberdeen's administration fell, telegraphic communication between Balaclava and London was at last established by the Government. Before that date the Government was continually behindhand with the news even of such matters as the losses of ships. When a question was asked in May 1854 about the reported loss of the paddle-steamer

Tiger, the Duke of Newcastle answered: 'The only information which has been received either by the Government or by anybody else, so far as we can ascertain, was by a telegraphic message which was received yesterday by a mercantile house in the City and the contents of which subsequently appeared in the newspapers.'[22] In December of the same year Graham said in answer to another question: 'The Government have received no official information with respect to the loss of the *Prince*, and the only information which has reached us was . . . by means of a letter written by one of the survivors and which was published in *The Times* newspaper.'[23]

By May 1855 the situation was changed. The ciphers used in messages transmitted by electric telegraph were still such that Palmerston informed the House of Commons that, for reasons of security, it would not be possible to give the exact words of despatches.[24] But Parliament did begin to receive up-to-date and reasonably accurate news about the progress and even the conclusion of the war.

On 3rd March 1856 Disraeli, after apologizing for putting a question without notice, asked for confirmation of a report that the preliminaries of peace had been signed in Paris. Palmerston was able to give the answer. 'No treaty,' he said, 'in the ordinary form signed by the plenipotentiaries and ratified by the Sovereigns has been signed, but substantially the preliminaries of peace have been signed.'

Disraeli promptly put the further question: 'When?'

'Some day last week,' Palmerston answered jauntily. 'I forget the exact day, but very recently.'[25]

The great improvement in communications was no doubt the chief reason why answers to parliamentary questions on foreign affairs became fuller, more accurate and more up-to-date in the eighteen-fifties and eighteen-sixties. But the personality of the man who was Prime Minister with one short interval from 1855 to 1865, and who had for so long been in charge of the Foreign Office, was an important contributory factor. Palmerston seldom missed an opportunity afforded by a question of making a forthright declaration on British foreign policy; and parliamentary and public opinion in the later years of his long career became much more concerned with foreign affairs generally, and with the protection of British subjects and interests abroad in particular, than had been the case in the eighteen-forties.

Palmerston's readiness to make categorical pronouncements about British foreign policy was illustrated when Francis Berkeley, M.P. for Bristol and Craven Berkeley's elder brother, asked on 7th July 1857 whether Her Majesty's Government would 'use its influence with His Highness the Sultan in support of an application which has been made by the Viceroy of Egypt for the sanction of the Sublime Porte to the construction of a ship canal across the isthmus of Suez, for which a concession has been granted by the Viceroy of Egypt to M. Ferdinand de Lesseps, which has received the approbation of the principal cities, ports and commercial towns of the United Kingdom.'

Palmerston replied:

'Sir, Her Majesty's Government certainly cannot undertake to use their influence with the Sultan to induce him to give permission for the construction of this canal, because for the last fifteen years Her Majesty's Government have used all the influence they possess at Constantinople and in Egypt to prevent that scheme from being carried into execution. It is an undertaking which, I believe, in point of commercial character, may be deemed to rank among the many bubble schemes that from time to time have been palmed upon gullible capitalists. I have been informed on what I believe to be reliable authority that it is physically impracticable except at an expense which would be far too great to warrant any expectation of any returns. . . . However, that is not the ground upon which the Government have opposed the scheme. Private individuals are left to take care of their own interest, and if they embark in impracticable undertakings, they must pay the penalty of so doing. But the scheme is founded in hostility to the interests of this country—opposed to the standing policy of England in regard to the connection of Egypt with Turkey, a policy that has been consecrated by the late war and issue of that war, the Treaty of Paris.'[26]

Nine months later, when Palmerston was no longer in office, Disraeli in his turn had to answer a question about the proposed Suez Canal. In one respect he was of the same mind as Palmerston. 'My own opinion,' he said, 'is that the project for executing a canal across the isthmus of Suez is a most futile idea, totally impossible to be carried out.' But he went on to say that unlike Palmerston he had not made up his mind about the political aspect of the problem.[27]

Statesmen of such eminence might differ in their conceptions of what the essential principles of British foreign policy might be, but of the increasing interest felt by Parliament in the eighteen-sixties in these principles there could be little doubt. In March 1864 a statesman so different from Palmerston in temperament and policy as the Earl of Shaftesbury, and one whose chief political concerns had for so long been the welfare of the oppressed classes and the strength of the Anglican Church, could declare in preface to a question: 'Never have I known the people of this country more profoundly stirred than at present, never have I known greater anxiety displayed than in the contemplation of the struggle between the little and gallant kingdom of Denmark and the two great, over-grown German powers—50 million against 3 million.'[28]

Some three months later Palmerston himself almost echoed Shaftesbury's words when he said in making a statement about the Danish war: 'There never was an occasion probably on which a Minister of the Crown had to make a statement . . . to this House of Parliament, and through it to the public, on which the feelings of the country, the aspirations and, I may say, the anxieties of the country were more deeply engaged.'[29]

These were balanced and sober statements. The assumptions expressed in them may be open to doubt, and Palmerston's pro-nouncement must be viewed in the light of the fact that he was about to justify a declaration of neutrality, but both statesmen reflected the mood of the time. Even clearer light on the growth of this mood is thrown by the contrasting outcome of questions asked and answers given on the treatment of British nationals abroad, first in 1852 and then in 1857.

On 10th February 1852 Chisholm Anstey, M.P. for Youghal, asked a question about some British subjects who had been expelled from Hungary. This was rather more than eighteen months after Palmerston had shocked many of his supporters by nearly engaging Britain in a war in order to support the claims of the money-lender Don Pacifico, and had then saved the Government by perhaps his greatest parliamentary performance. The British subjects with whom Anstey was concerned included a number of Protestant clergymen, some of whom had lived in Hungary for ten years. When he put his question, Lord John Russell, who answered, could give him no information.[30]

Four months later Anstey moved a resolution calling for 'prompt and earnest measures on the part of Her Majesty's Government' on behalf of the English clergymen. Soon after he did so it was discovered that less than forty members were present, and the House was counted out.[31]

The affair of 1857 led to a very different result. In December of that year two questions were put to Palmerston in the course of a week about two British engineers named Park and Watt, who had been imprisoned in Naples. In answering the second question Palmerston took the opportunity of stating:

'Of course it is well known that Neapolitan prisons are really a disgrace to a civilized country, and that the treatment to which prisoners are subjected is more fitting a barbarous age than the present time. However, the engineers have not been subjected to anything like torture except so far as the suffering from being handcuffed and strapped, when no such security was necessary, may be somewhat of that description.'[32]

Park and Watt had served on board the coastal steamer *Cagliari*, the command of which had been taken over by force sixty miles from Naples by some armed Sicilians who were on board. The *Cagliari* then made for the island of Ponza, where the garrison was overpowered and some prisoners were released. There was evidence, which was by no means negligible, that Park and Watt knew something of the plot, and the Neapolitan Government decided to put them on trial.

When the subject was discussed in the House of Lords in February 1858 the Earl of Clarendon, the Foreign Secretary, agreed that the affair had 'justly excited very great interest throughout this country.'[33] In that same month a new Government, headed by Lord Derby, came into power, and on 15th March Disraeli, who was then Chancellor of the Exchequer and Leader of the House of Commons, declared: 'When we accepted office, the case of the *Cagliari* was with one exception the first that engaged our attention.'[34]

A week later Disraeli said in answer to a question that Watt had been released, and that the trial of Park, who was now 'well lodged in a room looking upon the sea,' had begun.[35] By this time the Government had taken the unusual course of laying before the

House the opinion of the law officers of the Crown. Their opinion was that the arrest of the two men was illegal, and after considering it, the Government decided to demand compensation.

Park was released soon after Watt, and on 11th June 1858 the Foreign Secretary, the Earl of Malmesbury, was able to inform the House of Lords: 'The King of Naples has agreed to pay Her Majesty's Government the sum of £3,000 as compensation to the engineers.' He then announced the astonishing news that the King of Naples 'has, without any condition whatever, given up the ship *Cagliari* and the whole of her crew into the hands of Her Majesty's Government.'[36] It was not without reason that A. W. Kinglake, the author of *Eothen* and M.P. for Bridgewater, commenting on the affair in the House of Commons, pointed out that the release of Park and Watt had followed with remarkable speed on the transmission to Naples by electric telegraph of statements made in the British Parliament.[37]

Just as questions asked on foreign affairs increased greatly in both range and number between 1848 and 1867, so too did questions asked about India. Improvements in communications also brought about much more satisfactory answers than had been given by Governments in the past, a change which was itself indicative of a strengthening of control from the centre.

On 18th March 1853 Lord Derby declared in the House of Lords: 'Indian affairs are now beginning to excite great general interest in the public mind.'[38] There was little doubt that he was right. A fortnight earlier Lord John Russell had announced, in answer to a question asked in the House of Commons, that the Government intended to introduce a bill during that session 'for the government of India,'[39] and the announcement let loose something of a flood of questions and of heated debates on the subject.

A week after Russell's announcement John Bright, under pretext of asking a question on the motion for the adjournment of the House—a question which had in any case been already answered by Russell's statement—indulged in an hour's oratory on the subject of the misgovernment of India. He described the President of the Board of Control as 'the absolute ruler of India, so far as any individual in this country can be so,' and then pointed out that the holder of that office had been changed four times in a year. All four appointments he regarded as bad ones, and Lord Broughton, formerly Sir John Hobhouse, he described as 'one of the most contented and somnolent of statesmen that have ever filled that or any other office.' He declared that in a comparable period Manchester, which he represented, had spent twice as much on 'bridges, canals, banks, roads or similar works' as India, and summed up the policy of the leading statesmen of the day by saying: 'Whigs, Derbyites, Peelites and Russellites seem all of opinion that India is a bore, and the sooner her affairs are dismissed the better.'[40]

In 1853 it was still possible for the President of the Board of Control to give evasive answers about the actions of the Governor-General without questions being pressed home too strongly. On 23rd June of that year J. G. Phillimore, M.P. for Leamington, asked 'whether it is the intention of Her Majesty's Government to sanction the confiscation of the Nizam's dominions which the Governor-General of India has declared his intention to enforce.' Sir Charles Wood answered blandly: 'Not having heard from Lord Dalhousie what his intentions are or what he proposes to do, it would be premature to give an answer at present to the question of the honourable gentleman.'[41]

By 1857 the situation had changed. Question after question revealed the concern naturally felt about the Indian mutiny, and communications were already appreciably better. By that time the despatches from India, which came by two mails a month, were opened at Suez. A résumé was sent by electric telegraph via Trieste, and the full despatches then followed by sea.

It was a question asked in the House of Commons the next year which led to the first public revelation of a direct conflict between the Government at home and the Governor-General on the spot. On 6th May 1858 John Bright referred to a proclamation issued by the Governor-General, Lord Canning, in which, in Bright's words, he proposed 'to confiscate the soil of the Kingdom of Oude generally, leaving it to be disposed of hereafter as the Governor-General thinks fit.' Bright asked whether this proclamation was 'in accordance with instructions sent out by the Government in England.'

The immediate answer was given by the Secretary to the Board of Control, H. J. Baillie, who said that this was not so. Then in answer to a further question from Bright, Disraeli, who was

10

Chancellor of the Exchequer, made the remarkable statement: 'We
sent a despatch to the Governor-General of India disapproving the
policy which he indicated in every sense.'[42]

Such was the excitement caused by this statement that on the
same day Earl Granville took the unusual course of saying in the
House of Lords that it had come to his knowledge that Disraeli had
made this pronouncement 'in another place,' and asking the Earl of
Ellenborough, the President of the Board of Control, and himself a
most distinguished former Governor-General of India, for an
explanation. Ellenborough added confusion to the excitement by
replying: 'Of what has taken place "in another place" I know
nothing. No communication has taken place between me and the
right honourable gentleman or the other members of the Government as to the answer which has been given on the subject.'[43]

After this admission Ellenborough's position was clearly un-
tenable. Four days passed, and the House of Lords received some
explanation of the prevailing muddle. It learnt that Canning had
written a private letter, conveying his intention of making a proclamation on the subject of Oude, to Ellenborough's predecessor,
Vernon Smith, and Vernon Smith had not passed the letter on to
Ellenborough.[44]

The next day Ellenborough went very much further. He told the
House of Lords that before the publication of the Oude proclamation he had sent a letter to Canning, 'written in anticipation of the
capture of Lucknow and to be published as soon as we were in
possession of Lucknow, in which I directed that the Government of
India, having exhibited their strength . . . should temper justice with
generosity, should proclaim an amnesty, disarm the people and
wherever the amnesty was proclaimed should establish as soon as
possible the ordinary administration of the laws.'

Ellenborough's letter was published, and he himself accepted full
responsibility for its publication. He had known, he said, that the
moment news of Canning's proclamation was received 'questions
would be put in Parliament, both in this and the other House, to
which answers must be given, which answers could not be satisfactory without the production of this letter, which therefore we
could not resist.'

Ellenborough went on to say that he did not wish to cause any
confusion between the two issues, which were now causing so much

stir, that of Canning's proclamation and that of his own action in publishing his letter. Of the second issue he said: 'I am resolved, so far as I can effect it, that this question shall be treated on its own merits, and determined as I am that to the last moment of my life everything I do shall be to promote the peace and welfare of India I have today tendered to Her Majesty my resignation, and it has been accepted.'[45]

Even in resigning office Ellenborough chose to disregard his colleagues, for the Queen received his resignation before Lord Derby, the Prime Minister, had heard of it, an action which Disraeli was to describe as 'not unconstitutional but unusual.'[46]

The affairs of Oude were once again, as they had done in Sheridan's day, to provoke the House of Commons into long and heated debate. Three days after Ellenborough had resigned, Edward Cardwell, M.P. for Oxford City, initiated a debate which was to occupy four nights. He began by saying: 'Sir, I rise to invite the judgment of the House upon what I believe to be one of the most remarkable series of occurrences that has been witnessed in the history of British administration.'

Referring to Disraeli's answer to the supplementary question which Bright had asked on 6th May, he said: 'Has anyone forgotten the electric effect which that statement produced within the walls of this House?' The direct result of what had been said had been Ellenborough's resignation; and of the Government's condemnation of the Governor-General's actions, Cardwell said: 'Such a course on the part of the Government must tend in the present circumstances of India to produce the most prejudicial effect by weakening the authority of the Governor-General and encouraging the further resistance of those who are in arms against us.'

The Government's position was in every way a difficult one. Not only had it disowned the action of the Governor-General at a time of dangerous conflict, but it had already committed itself to a policy of supreme importance, that of transferring the effective control of India from the East India Company to the Crown. At that moment some indication of what the new regime would mean for the people of India was called for, and at the same time the disavowal of Canning's proclamation had to be justified.

The Solicitor-General, Sir H. M. Cairns, realizing the need for a convincing expression of general policy, did his best to provide one.

'Let us tell the people of India,' he said, 'that we are not ashamed to confess that we offer them mercy and justice and not spoliation; that the war which we wage against them is a war consistent with mercy and justice, and not made for the sake of plunder; and that no faction and no injustice will tempt the House of Commons, even for a moment, to lay themselves open to the suspicion that the dynasty we are about to introduce into India is to be a dynasty of reckless, ruthless and indiscriminate confiscation.'

The Government's critics were by no means silenced by this eloquent appeal. On the one side were those who complained that Lord Canning had not received the support he deserved, and on the other those, of whom Bright was the chief spokesman, who disapproved of the Government's general policy in India on almost every ground except its condemnation of Canning's proclamation.

When his turn came to join in the debate, Bright explained how he had come to ask his now famous question. He indignantly denied suggestions that the question had been arranged between himself and the Secretary to the Board of Control, H. J. Baillie, for an arranged question was still regarded as a reprehensible subterfuge. He admitted having spoken to Baillie when he had first learnt, through the Honorary Secretary of the India Reform Society, that a proclamation was being prepared, and said he had given warning that he would ask a question if Canning ever issued the proclamation. But that had happened three weeks earlier. He had first learnt that the proclamation had been issued by reading of it in *The Times* of 6th May, and he had asked his question the same day. 'Both question and answer,' he said, 'are before the House and the country.'

The justification of the Government's repudiation of Canning's proclamation was left to Disraeli, and he faced the task courageously. 'If,' he said, 'the relations between Her Majesty's Government and the Governor-General of India should be cordial, they should also be sincere; and if it is supposed for a moment that I or those with whom I act are prepared in any way to retract the opinions which we have expressed with regard to the policy of confiscation which Lord Canning, under evil influence, unhappily adopted, but which, I hope, and have some reason to believe, he has by this time relinquished, the House will indeed have misinterpreted what I have said.'

The immediate outcome of this tremendous debate was somewhat of an anticlimax. Cardwell's original motion was simply withdrawn, a compromise which led Bright, although he agreed with it, to say: 'We seem to have arrived at a conclusion which will, I think, excite the amusement and perhaps the ridicule of the public.'[47]

But later results provided clear proof that the Government, having declared a policy, had also succeeded in enforcing it. On 11th June Ellenborough's successor at the Board of Control, Lord Stanley, a future Foreign Secretary and the son of a Prime Minister, was able to answer a question in the House of Lords by saying that a new proclamation had been issued to the people of Oude, which was 'considerably modified.' He concluded: 'I hope and have reason to believe that the policy actually pursued in Oude has been a policy of conciliation and justice.'[48]

Less than two months later the royal assent was given to a Bill for transferring to the direct authority of the Queen 'the Government of Her Indian Dominions,' and the Government at home became answerable to Parliament for all actions in India carried out by its servants.

Concurrently with their extension over wider and wider fields of public interest, there was between 1848 and 1867 a steady growth in the efficacy of questions as a means of bringing about desirable reforms or voicing popular demands. Questions which led Governments to reconsider their policy, and in some cases to make important changes in the law, were asked on subjects ranging from Cleopatra's Needle to assaults on females, from vaccination to communication between railway passengers and guards, from the working conditions of women to the increasingly evident need for a Court of Criminal Appeal.

Cleopatra's Needle was the subject of a question asked by the Marquis of Westmeath in the House of Lords in June 1851. He wanted to know what steps had been taken to have it brought to England and received an extremely evasive answer.[49] Eighteen months later another question was put by Joseph Hume, and Disraeli then announced that an agreement had been reached between Her Majesty's Government and the proprietors of the Crystal Palace. This provided that the obelisk would be brought to England at the expense of the latter, and that if the Crystal Palace on its new site in Sydenham did not prove as popular as was expected, the Government would have the right to take possession of it on payment.[50] In fact the obelisk was brought to London more than twenty-five years later, and then at private expense.

The subject of assaults on females was raised by Henry Fitzroy, M.P. for Lewes, who had himself brought in a bill, which afterwards became the Aggravated Assaults Act, and which increased the punishments for offences of this nature. Before long he found that the provisions of the act for which he was largely responsible were being applied much more rigorously than he had foreseen, and in June 1858 he asked a question about a particular case.

This was a sentence of six months' imprisonment on 'a carpenter of the name of Croft . . . for kissing the daughter of the Reverend H. C. Collins of Farringdon Rectory, Devon, on landing from a steamer between Poole and Swansea.' The Home Secretary, Spencer Walpole, said his attention had not previously been called to this case. But he promised to look into any facts which Fitzroy might supply and consider whether the law needed amendment, adding, significantly, 'as may very possibly be the case.'[51]

The transporting of Cleopatra's Needle and even the unhappy fate of Croft the carpenter were subjects of limited interest in comparison with those of the dangers of railway travel and the still unconcluded battle against smallpox.

On 12th July 1864 Alexander Baillie Cochrane, M.P. for Hamilton, asked the President of the Board of Trade whether it would be possible to compel railway companies 'to introduce into the carriages some mode of communicating with the guards.' Thomas Milner Gibson, answering, said he did not intend to introduce a Bill for this purpose. This answer was found unsatisfactory, and the House was told of the fate of a certain Thomas Briggs of Clapton, who three days earlier had been 'murderously assailed, plundered and thrown from a first-class railway carriage on the North London Railway.'[52]

On 14th July Baillie Cochrane repeated his question, and Milner Gibson then admitted: 'The recent outrages and murder clearly show that the obtaining of this communication is much to be desired.' But he also spoke of difficulties in the way of legislation.[53]

Nearly a year later Sir Lawrence Palk, M.P. for South Devonshire, raised the subject again on the motion for going into Committee of

Supply. He informed the House; 'On the continental railways the guards are able to pass along the sides of the carriages and are able to see what is going on in each compartment at all times of day and night, and to communicate readily with the engine-drivers. I know no reason why the same system should not be adopted in England.' Milner Gibson admitted the need for some form of communication between guard and engine-driver and said that this was already to be found on some lines, although by no means on all.[54]

The principal railway companies set up a committee of their own to examine questions of communication, and on 23rd February 1866 Milner Gibson informed the House of Commons that he had seen the chairman of this committee and 'pressed upon him the necessity of doing something.'[55] The next year the Railways (Guards' and Passengers' Communication) Bill became law. Four years later the provisions of this Act were to be strengthened by those of the Regulation of Railways Act, which made proper means of communication between passengers and those in charge of trains obligatory.

Another Act which became law during the session of 1867 was one 'to consolidate and amend the laws relating to vaccination.' The Act of 1840 had provided facilities for vaccination for everyone at public cost, and by the Act of 1853 an obligation was placed on parents to have their children vaccinated within four months of birth. But this obligation continued to be widely evaded, and as late as 1864 the report of the Epidemiological Society showed that on an average 3,240 people in the country died from smallpox every year.

A question asked by Lord Lyttelton, who was constantly concerned with problems of popular education, in the House of Lords in the same year initiated a series of discussions in Parliament on the best means of enforcing vaccination, which led eventually to effective legislation.[56] The most important provision incorporated in the Act of 1867 was one imposing on registrars of births the duty of informing parents of their obligations. Public vaccinators were obliged to send the registrars certificates of successful vaccination, and self-interest and duty were made to serve a common end by an arrangement whereby registrars were to be paid 3d. for each certificate recorded and vaccinators a fee varying from 1s. 6d. to 2s. 6d.

Even swifter legislative action followed the asking of a question on 23rd June 1863. On that day John Bagwell, M.P. for Clonmel, asked the Home Secretary, Sir George Grey, whether his attention had been called to an inquest on a woman named Mary Anne Walkley. This woman had been employed by a certain Mrs. Isaacson, who traded under the name of Madame Elise, court dressmaker, of 170, Regent Street. Mary Walkley was said to have died of apoplexy, but the coroner's jury, while agreeing with this opinion, had found that her death had been 'accelerated by long hours of work in overcrowded apartments and by sleeping in an ill-ventilated bedroom.' Sir George Grey, who was aware of the jury's finding, spoke of the difficulty of establishing 'a general system of registration and inspection of these workrooms, many of which form portions of private houses.'[57]

Two days later a further question was asked by another Irish Member. This was Robert Dawson, M.P. for County Londonderry, who, after referring to the Walkley case, asked if it would not be 'desirable and humane to introduce legislation for the purpose of limiting and defining the hours of labour in millinery and other establishments where females are employed.' Sir George Grey again spoke of difficulties, but this time he added that if Dawson brought in a Bill he would 'willingly acquiesce in its introduction.' In the next session of Parliament an Act was passed 'for extending to women and children employed in various trades the regulations applicable to factories in general.'

The readiness of both Conservative and Liberal Governments in the eighteen-sixties to introduce social reforms when attention was called to the need for them by questions put by responsible Members of Parliament is, in retrospect, striking. But one reform, for which there had long been a demand, continued to be resisted although a question asked in 1866 led to a re-examination of an old problem. This problem was whether justice demanded the establishment of a Court of Criminal Appeal.

On 24th July 1866 Roger Eykyn, M.P. for Windsor, asked the Home Secretary whether the Government intended to take any action about a case in which a man named Neville Maskelyne Toomer had been sentenced at Abingdon to fifteen years' imprisonment, in spite of strong medical evidence in his favour. Toomer was an ironmonger's assistant, and he had been convicted of rape. The

Home Secretary, Spencer Walpole, answered the question cautiously. 'It is,' he said, 'usual at the Home Office, and with great propriety, to wait until the convict or some person on his behalf applies to have his case taken into consideration.'[59] This had not yet happened.

A fortnight later Walpole said, in answer to another question, that he had asked the judge who had tried Toomer to send him a copy of his notes,[60] and the prorogation of Parliament prevented the House of Commons from discussing the subject again until the next year.

On 1st April 1867 Sir Robert Collier, M.P. for Plymouth and a future member of the Judicial Committee of the Privy Council, asked Walpole if he would lay a copy of the judge's notes on the table. Walpole refused to do so, saying the notes were of a confidential nature and contained matters affecting the character of third parties. He also called attention to the legal and constitutional problems which arose through the lack of a Court of Criminal Appeal. 'There is,' he said, 'no precedent for the production of such papers, and to establish one will virtually be an interference with the prerogative of the Crown and will make the House a Court of Appeal in criminal cases.'

Nevertheless, he gave the House an account of some of the facts of the case, facts of which they were to hear a more colourful version later. Toomer, it appeared, had been convicted after being prosecuted by Miss Partridge, the woman whom he was supposed to have raped. Toomer claimed that Miss Partridge 'had been living with him on familiar terms,' and the jury, although finding him guilty, had said there were 'extenuating circumstances.' When asked to explain what they meant, they said that Miss Partridge had been 'indiscreet.'

Walpole then explained that he could have recommended a pardon only if he had decided that Miss Partridge had been guilty of perjury. The Home Office had told Toomer that he was at liberty to prosecute Miss Partridge for perjury, but this was going to be difficult. The testimony of two witnesses was needed before there could be a conviction on such a charge, and in any case Toomer, being a convicted felon, had forfeited his property to the Crown.[61]

Four days later Sir Robert Collier brought the subject up again on a formal motion, and this time he told the House the story of

Toomer's relations with Miss Partridge in some detail. Toomer, it seemed, had advertised for a governess to teach his daughter music. Miss Partridge had applied for the post and Toomer had asked her to send him her photograph. She had done so and had been engaged as a governess, but on arriving at Toomer's house she had discovered that Toomer had no daughter.

Nevertheless, Miss Partridge remained in Toomer's house for several weeks. Then one day, according to her testimony, Toomer kissed her and asked her to marry him. 'The prosecutrix also stated,' Collier went on, 'that on one occasion Toomer dragged her through the passage into a back room, undressed her, put her in bed, remained with her all night and finally effected his purpose.'

Miss Partridge remained in bed, took breakfast that morning, and the next day walked and took tea with Toomer. She had been in the habit of sharing a bedroom with one of Toomer's servants, but a few nights after the first episode took place she decided to sleep alone and left the door unlocked. Toomer came in and again spent the night with her.

All these facts Collier had taken from Miss Partridge's own testimony; the medical evidence had been in Toomer's favour; and Toomer claimed that Miss Partridge had been disappointed because she had not received a gift of £20 which she had expected. Nevertheless, the jury, after being out for several hours and at first disagreeing, had returned a verdict of guilty.

Walpole stood by his earlier pronouncements. He admitted the sentence had been too severe, but said the facts did not warrant a free pardon, and he was supported by both the Attorney-General, Sir John Rolt, and the Solicitor-General, Sir John Karslake. But no answer was returned to one statement which Collier had made in his speech.

'It behoves the House,' he had said, 'to investigate the manner in which the tribunal of appeal in the Home Office is worked—not from idle curiosity, but with a view to practical legislation. If many cases occur such as this ... it will be for the House to consider whether it cannot devise some better tribunal of appeal.'[62]

Spencer Walpole took no steps towards adopting this suggestion. A little more than a month after Parliament had vindicated his attitude towards the case of Toomer and Miss Partridge he resigned his office. In announcing Walpole's resignation, Disraeli explained that the sole reason was 'the state of his health brought about by pressure of public business on a nature which every member of this House must know is only too sensitive.'[63] The establishment of a Court of Criminal Appeal was delayed until 1902.

One respect in which there was greater freedom of questioning in the eighteen-fifties and eighteen-sixties than at other periods was that the House of Commons came in practice to sanction, for a short time, two distinct types of parliamentary questions. Both developed out of the earlier, comparatively unregulated practice.

One type of question was that which is still asked today. This type was defined by Thomas Erskine May in the *Manual of Rules and Orders of the House of Commons*, which he prepared in 1854 under the direction of the Speaker. Rule 152 read: 'Before the public business is entered upon, questions are permitted to be put to Ministers of the Crown relating to public affairs; and to other Members, relating to any Bill, motion or other public matter connected with the business of the House, in which such Members may be concerned.'

This was not only a regulation of the nature of permissible questions, but also of the time at which they might be asked. The phrase 'time for questions' had already begun to be used. In May 1849, for instance, Baillie Cochrane began a question addressed to Palmerston: 'Seeing the noble Lord the Secretary of State for Foreign Affairs now in his place, which is a rare sight at the time for questions. . . .'[64]

The other type of question was that which was asked after a motion had been made for the adjournment of the House or that the Speaker should leave the Chair. Questions asked on these occasions differed from the parliamentary question asked today, and from the questions put at the beginning of the day's proceedings, in one important respect. They were asked when a formal motion was before the House. Nevertheless, they continued for some time to be regarded as 'questions,' to be referred to as such, and to be used for much the same objects as questions asked when there was no motion.

One inconvenience of this method of questioning was that in certain respects the ordinary rules of debate applied when it was adopted. For instance, no matter how many questions were put to him, a Minister could rise to answer only once. In May 1853, on a motion for going into Committee of Ways and Means, Palmerston, who was then Home Secretary, was asked a number of questions about the discovery of a large quantity of gunpowder in the house of William Hale, who had invented a rocket for use in war. It was suggested that the gunpowder was kept there for Kossuth, who might eventually use it for fomenting a revolution in Hungary. After Palmerston had answered these questions, Cobden rose to ask him another, but he was interrupted by the Speaker, Shaw Lefevre, who pointed out that Palmerston was not allowed to speak again on this subject.

Cobden thereupon commented, reasonably enough: 'I suppose, Sir, you are the authority, without appeal, on all points of order, but if it be the rule of this House that the Minister for the Home Department can only be allowed to answer one question on such an occasion . . . I think it would be well to consider whether it might not be well to relax it in order to promote the despatch of business.'[65] Shaw Lefevre was himself fully aware of the incovenience of the system, and before the Select Committee on Public Business of 1854 he said that one effect of it was that 'the House is obliged to listen to *ex parte* statements which cannot be answered.'

The occasion on which the largest and most varied collection of questions tended to be put was when the motion for the adjournment of the House over the week-end was made on a Friday. This use of the adjournment motion became general after 1848, and in May 1851 Shaw Lefevre commented: 'With respect to the motion being in practice of late made an opportunity for Members asking questions, the honourable Members will see that it is not a very regular practice.'[66]

Nevertheless, the practice persisted until in 1860 one Member calculated that 85 hours had been spent during the session in the discussion of questions asked on the motion for the adjournment. The next year Lord John Russell commented that on one Friday evening he had had to answer almost as many questions 'as are contained in what on the other side of the Tweed is called *The Shorter Catechism.*'[67]

Various proposals were made for overcoming the inconveniences which the new practice had created. On 25th March 1859 Bright declared: 'It appears to me that the House is falling into a most

absurd practice every Friday evening. . . . On the other evenings of
the week Ministers rise several times to answer questions which are
put to them. But on the Friday they can rise but once, and the
consequence is that the questions put to them and their replies to
those questions present, when reported in the public prints, a most
disjointed appearance.'

He suggested that on Fridays Ministers should answer each
question in order, but the Speaker, Evelyn Denison, replied that if
they were to allow 'any honourable Member to speak two or three
times on the motion for the adjournment . . . the inconvenience of
the present system, which is very great, would be considerably
increased.'[68]

Nearly a year later Andrew Stewart, M.P. for Cambridge, moved
a resolution 'that it would tend to the regularity of the debate on
the motion for adjournment on Fridays if the Clerk were instructed
to place in their order on the paper, one after another, all questions
to be addressed to each particular Member of the Government; and
if Mr. Speaker were to call on hon. Members in such order, and the
Members of the Government to reply, so that each subject might be
closed before a different one taken up.' Disraeli opposed this
suggestion, saying there was already a danger of questions asked on
Fridays developing into debates, and that this danger would be
increased if Stewart's resolution were approved. 'We have,' he said,
'on Friday evenings a sort of conversazione which it is for the public
advantage should be tolerated.'[69]

The Home Secretary, Sir George Lewis, supported Disraeli, and
Stewart withdrew his resolution. But the time spent on questions
asked on Fridays increased. In March 1860, 25 minutes were devoted
to a question about India, 45 minutes to a question about the Irish
poor, and 30 minutes to a question about the French annexation of
Savoy. On three consecutive Fridays the motion for adjournment
was finally accepted at 7 p.m., 8 p.m., and 8.30 p.m., and as the
session neared its end, the feeling grew that some new regulation
was needed.

On 24th August 1860 Thomas Duncombe, M.P. for Finsbury,
moved that 'on the question of adjournment from Friday to
Monday all discussions shall be confined to questions relating to the
intended business of the following week or to matters of public
urgency demanding immediate attention.' The effect of this, he

said, would be 'to go back to the old system that prevailed in the
House. It is only during these last few years that the present system
with regard to questions on the motion for the adjournment till
Monday has come into practice. . . . It originated from the late
Speaker, who gave permission to Members to raise all kinds of
questions on the motion for the adjournment.' Sir George Lewis
agreed that 'a perfect farrago of questions are put on the most
miscellaneous subjects and great confusion arises from the fact that
two or three questions are sometimes put to the same Minister.'
But he deprecated the proposal to limit questions in general to the
subject of the next week's business, and he considered the term
'public urgency' too vague.[70]

Duncombe was in one respect a pioneer, whose path would
eventually be followed, when he suggested that a duty should be
imposed on the Speaker of deciding what was and what was not a
matter of urgent public importance. But his proposals for controlling
the flow of questions on Fridays was not adopted. Instead, the
House of Commons approved a motion made by Palmerston on
3rd May 1861 that Mondays, Wednesdays, Thursdays, and Fridays
should be days on which Government orders would have precedence, but that the motion for going into Committee of Supply or
Committee of Ways and Means should stand as the first order on
Fridays. On this motion opportunities for raising a variety of
subjects would be provided, but as Sir James Graham, who had
been chairman of the Select Committee on Public Business of 1861,
explained, 'these discussions which are now irregular on the motion
for the adjournment will then be conducted in a perfectly regular
manner.'[71]

The Commons then adopted as a Standing Order the resolution
of the Committee of 1861 that 'the House at its rising on Friday do
stand adjourned to the following Monday without question put.'
From that time onwards the distinction between the question asked
at the beginning of the day's proceedings and the general discussion
on the motion that the Speaker should leave the Chair became a
clear one, and these general discussions soon ceased to be regarded
as forms of the parliamentary question.

Another method of extending a question into a debate was
tolerated rather longer. This was the practice of moving the adjourn-

ment of the House when an answer to a question asked at the normal question time was considered unsatisfactory. The practice was adopted occasionally before 1848, and, within narrow limits rigorously controlled by the Speaker, it is still permitted today.

After 1848 the motion for the adjournment of the House was made more and more frequently. The motion itself was, of course, a mere formality, because it was regularly withdrawn once its mover considered the discussion had been carried far enough. But from time to time objections were raised to the practice. Disraeli, in particular, protested against a motion for the adjournment after a question had been asked on foreign affairs, saying it must lead to a debate. This, he said, would culminate in Palmerston 'indulging again in those instructive and inspiriting attacks on foreign countries and foreign ministers, which, though they may be very amusing, certainly do not tend to a conciliatory course of diplomacy.'[72]

The expedient was also used often enough to engage the serious attention of the Select Committee on Public Business of 1861. The conclusion the Committee reached was embodied in its fifty-sixth recommendation, which declared:

'A practice has arisen of putting questions to Ministers on notice, when no Motion is before the House; and these questions, and the answers to them, are confined within narrow limits, intended to be precautions against irregular debate. There is convenience in this course; but to prevent this license (*sic*) degenerating into abuse, it is most important that both the questions and answers should be as concise as possible, and not sustained by reasoning, which might give rise to debate. Recourse on these occasions has been sometimes had to the expedient of moving the Adjournment of the House for the express purpose of opening debate. This proceeding is to be regarded with the greatest jealousy. It is in reality an abuse of one of the forms of the House, with the avowed intent of virtually breaking its essential rules. Your Committee have come to the conclusion that this evil has not reached the point where special interference by a new Standing Order would be expedient. They are satisfied still to rely on the forbearance of Members in the use of forms which respect for ancient usage leaves unaltered; and the marked disapprobation of a large majority of the House may check the growth of so objectionable a practice.'

The conflict between the persistence of individual Members and the disapprobation of a large majority did not reach its climax until after 1867. Before then the committee's recommendation of watchfulness combined with tolerance received general approval. The disinclination to tamper with rules and restrict the liberties of individuals was as strongly felt as ever, and pressure of business did not yet demand extreme measures.

The eighteen-fifties and eighteen-sixties were not, indeed, decades in which political strife was at its keenest, and a graph indicating the increase of parliamentary business over the past century and a half would probably show a horizontal rather than a vertical trend between 1848 and 1867.

It may or may not have been significant that the day immediately preceding that on which the Commons met for the first time in their new chamber, in 1850, had been Derby Day, and therefore no business had been transacted. But the tradition of adjourning for Derby Day continued to be observed year after year, and even the great debate on Oude in 1853 was interrupted for a whole day for this purpose. As late as 1st May 1863, indeed, the House of Commons transacted no business for another reason, which was simply that less than forty Members were present.

Although the general tolerance exercised meant that between 1848 and 1867 remarkably few controls were imposed by order of the House on questions, and even on the discussions to which questions might lead, the part played by Speakers in calling attention to the usages of the House grew in importance. One reason for this was acceptance of the practice of giving notice of questions and therefore of bringing them to the Speaker's attention before they were printed.

Interference by Speakers who corrected the form of a question was sometimes resented. In 1855 Owen Stanley, M.P. for Chester, even claimed that it was a breach of privilege, but was told by Shaw Lefevre: 'If the honourable Member proposes to put a notice upon the paper which is irregular, of course the part which is irregular will be left out. It is very irregular that any matter should appear in print in the shape of an argument, and in fact all notices of questions should be made as short as possible.'[73]

From time to time questions in an irregular form slipped past the Speaker and the clerks. On 25th August 1860 James White, M.P.

for Brighton, after referring to the action of the House of Lords in opposing a Bill for the abolition of the duty on paper, asked 'whether as a precedent has been established for the revision by the House of Lords of the provision annually made by this House for the service of the Crown, it will be in future expedient to obtain the concurrence of the House of Lords before any proposal for the remission of taxation is put to this House.' The Speaker, Evelyn Denison, intervened to say: 'If the second part of this notice had been brought to me while in the House, I should have asked the honourable Member whether it was his serious intention to put the question or whether it was intended in an ironical sense; and if so, I should have informed him that to discuss any matter in this House in an ironical sense is unparliamentary and out of order.'[74]

Gradually control over the wording of questions became tighter. On 12th February 1861 Sir John Trelawny, M.P. for Tavistock, asked the Home Secretary whether he had been informed of a recent decision in the county court at Rochdale, when the judge had 'non-suited a plaintiff on account of the inability of the witness to affirm her belief in God or in a future state of rewards and punishments.'

The case had been one in which a daughter had sued her mother for the value of a piano, and the irreligious daughter had been the only witness on her own behalf. Sir George Lewis, answering, explained that the law permitted any oath which was binding, adding, with a curious confusion of religion and nationality, 'so that a Mahomedan, a Hindu, or a Chinese may be sworn according to the ceremonies which are binding on his conscience.' A special form of affirmation was permitted to members of the Society of Friends, but the law assumed the existence of some religious belief.

Trelawny, in this case, was allowed to ask his question, and he received a full answer, but by the Speaker's direction his question had had to be altered from its original form. The words 'belief in a future state of rewards and punishments' had been substituted for 'belief in certain speculative propositions.' This original version, Speaker Denison declared, 'appeared to me not to be becoming words so applied.'[75]

A further challenge to the right of the Speaker—a right which came in fact to be exercised by the clerks—to exclude argumentative statements about religious beliefs was made as late as 1867.

11

George Whalley, M.P. for Peterborough, who seldom missed an opportunity of attacking Catholicism in general and Jesuits in particular, called attention to a rather salacious pamphlet entitled *The Confessional Unmasked*, which was finding its way into schools.

In framing his question, Whalley had said of the practice of confession that it had been 'of late years adopted by many clergymen of the Church of England.' This sentence had been excluded on the grounds that it involved a matter of opinion and might be considered an imputation on the Anglican clergy, and Whalley objected to its exclusion. Speaker Denison then told the House: 'It is continually the duty and the practice of the clerks at the table to amend and alter in some degree the notices that are given.' Disraeli strongly vindicated the clerks, admitting that his own questions had sometimes been altered, and the subject was quickly dropped.[76]

For the rest, between 1848 and 1867 Speakers' rulings on questions were far from restrictive, and although individual Ministers sometimes chose not to answer particular questions, few important precedents for refusing answers were established.

In 1856 Palmerston rather bad-temperedly protested against 'the practice that has been growing up of late . . . of asking the Government what is their intention on this, that or the other matter.' He had been asked what the Government proposed to do about disbanding the foreign or German legion, which then numbered some 15,000 men, and his reply was that what the Government proposed to do would be 'found perfectly consistent with law and propriety.' What they in fact did was to enable large numbers of the Germans to settle in South Africa.

Palmerston's answer provoked J. A. Roebuck, one of the most persistent of the critics of Lord Aberdeen's Government during the Crimean War, to complain, not unreasonably, that it amounted to telling Members that if they asked questions before a decision was taken they were asking too early, and if they asked after it had been taken they were too late.[77]

In 1857 James Wilson, Secretary to the Treasury, who had himself once lost a fortune by unsuccessful speculation in indigo, refused to answer a question about contracts given to the Royal Mail Steam Packet Company and the Australian Royal Mail Company on the grounds that it was 'founded on no public motives and only bearing on the interests of private companies.'[78] Yet the next year the same Member put the same question to the same Minister and received a full answer.[79]

Nearly all the other refusals by Ministers to answer were justified for reasons which were already accepted as valid: for example, because comment could not be made on a matter *sub judice*, because an answer would necessitate disclosing the opinions of the law officers of the Crown, or, in the later stages of the Crimean War, because an informative answer would be of direct help to the enemy. But in 1857 Sir Charles Wood, as First Lord of the Admiralty, did make an important claim of privilege.

He had been asked by Sir Charles Napier, who was then M.P. for Southwark, why Commodore Keppel had been recalled from the Chinese seas, in spite of his acquittal by a court-martial after losing a ship. In refusing to answer Wood said: 'I think it most inexpedient that the House should interfere with the appointments of officers by the executive.'[80]

Interventions by the Speaker after a question had been put were provoked in nearly all cases by Members who, in asking a question without notice or altering a question of which notice had been given, indulged in argument or expressions of opinion. But one important rule which had been accepted by the House was enunciated with finality by Speaker Shaw Lefevre, when he stated in 1849: 'It is against the rules of Parliament to put questions to individual Members not connected with the business of the House.'[81]

This immunity from questioning about activities which might be held to be private did not apply to Ministers of the Crown, and the distinction which the House made by this ruling between private Members and Ministers was clearly shown in a sensational manner in 1864.

On 29th February of that year William Cox, M.P. for Finsbury, put a question to James Stansfeld, M.P. for Halifax. It did not relate to anything which Stansfeld had said or done in Parliament or to the department with which Stansfeld was connected. It concerned an action which Stansfeld was alleged to have taken in a purely private capacity, and Cox himself described the question as a 'personal' one. Yet the question was admissible simply because Stansfeld held office as a Junior Lord of the Admiralty.

Cox's question referred to a statement made by the French Crown Prosecutor at the trial of a man named Greco and others for the attempted assassination of the Emperor Napoleon III. The prosecutor's statement was that Greco had been told that if he needed money he should apply to Mr. Flower at 35, Thurloe Square, Brompton. This, it was pointed out, was the address of an English brewer and Member of Parliament called Stansfeld, who, according to the prosecution, had acted as banker for some other conspirators who had attempted to assassinate the Emperor in 1857.

Stansfeld vigorously denied the charge. He disclaimed any knowledge of Mr. Flower and also refuted a suggestion which had been made that Giuseppe Mazzini, the Italian patriot, might be implicated in the conspiracy.[82] But his denials were not considered altogether satisfactory, and on 17th March Sir Henry Stracey, M.P. for Great Yarmouth, brought the subject before the attention of the Commons again. It was immediately given the precedence accorded to a matter of privilege.

Stracey began by saying of Stansfeld that he had 'not the honour of his personal acquaintance' and then went on to refer to trials held in 1857 and 1858, in both of which the name of 'le brasseur Stansfeld' had been bandied about. From this he proceeded to discredit Mazzini. Stansfeld had declared that Mazzini was incapable of assassination, and Stracey therefore read a letter written by Mazzini himself, in which he described how he had given money and help in obtaining a passport to a young man who had informed him of his intention to assassinate 'Charles Albert, the traitor of 1821.' Stracey concluded by suggesting that Mr. Flower or Fiore was really Mazzini himself. When Stansfeld admitted that letters for Mazzini, even under the name of Fiore, were received at his house, the case against him clearly became stronger.

Palmerston defended Stansfeld staunchly. He said that he had fully answered the only charge against him, that of having any cognizance of a plot against the Emperor's life, and when a vote was taken, Stansfeld's supporters were in the majority.[83] But the vote was a close one, 171 against 161, and Stansfeld immediately offered to resign.

The next day Palmerston again came to Stansfeld's defence. In answer to a question he made it clear that he himself had dissuaded Stansfeld from resigning. A motion for the adjournment of the

House was made, and the discussion became general. One member described it as a painful subject, and the next speaker, Ralph Bernal Osborne, a peripatetic politician who was at the time M.P. for Liskeard, added: 'Well, it is a painful subject, but somehow or other I recollect in the course of my parliamentary experience that there is nothing in which this House so much delights, nothing which will attract such a numerous attendance of Members, as a purely personal and painful subject.'[84]

The interest of the House was too great for either the Government's or Stansfeld's comfort. After an interval of a little more than two weeks Stansfeld announced his resignation, saying he realized he had become 'a source of difficulty and a cause of embarrassment to the Government.' He thanked Palmerston for his defence and said of Mazzini: 'I have long had a very deep general sympathy with that which has been the object of his life—the unity and independence of Italy.' He continued to deny any knowledge of the conspiracy against the life of the Emperor Napoleon.[85]

In the Lords, as in the Commons, the period between 1848 and 1867 was one in which questions became more and more a regular part of the proceedings, and in the Upper House too there were few restrictions on the liberties of individual peers. The ease with which these liberties could be abused was shown in a somewhat curious fashion in 1858 by the eccentric Earl of Kingston.

On 3rd June of that year the Earl of St. Germans drew their Lordships' attention to 'a very inconvenient practice on the part of the Earl of Kingston in placing notices of questions upon your Lordships' paper which he does not ask and without naming a day on which he will ask them.'

Most of these questions served in one way or another to discredit particular individuals. Going through the list, the Earl of St. Germans pointed out: 'One relates to a Customs House officer of Liverpool; another to the appointment of Mr. Sullivan to Lima; another "whether the resignation of General Ashburnham, Commander-in-Chief of the Chinese expedition, was a voluntary act of that officer; or if not from what sources were the expenses of his return to this country defrayed." Another was "whether the whole course and conduct of Rajah Brooke in the East has not been such as to desecrate the name of England for humanity and justice." '

The Earl of Malmesbury, the Foreign Secretary, replied. He had to admit there was nothing in the existing rules to prevent the Earl of Kingston from acting in this way. Lord Redesdale said that in the past it had been the invariable practice when asking a question to state the day on which it would be asked. Lord Campbell pointed out that the notice paper was 'sent all over the kingdom to every public library' and might thus become 'the vehicle for disseminating the most atrocious libels.'[86] But it was clear that some special measure would have to be devised for curbing the Earl of Kingston.

On 7th June Kingston, who had nine questions down in his name, announced that he would postpone them 'to a future evening.' This gave Earl Grey an opportunity of defending one of the people whom Kingston had been defaming, Rajah Brooke. The Earl of Wicklow went further and said: 'The questions of the noble Earl have been on the paper for four nights. On one occasion the noble Earl was sitting opposite when the clerk called upon him, but he merely shook his head and refused to put the questions.' He concluded by expressing the hope that some measures would be taken 'for the protection of the public against such a practice.'

Several unsuccessful appeals were made to Kingston either to ask his questions or to withdraw his notice of them, and in the end a partial solution, applicable only to this particular case, was found. The House resolved 'that the said questions have been sufficiently answered and ought not to be renewed.'[87] It was tacitly assumed that no other peer was likely to conduct himself in the same manner as the Earl of Kingston.

This practice of giving notice of questions, which the Earl of Kingston had abused, grew steadily in the two decades after 1848, and in 1866 a Committee of the House went so far as to recommend that it should in most cases become obligatory. The House of Lords was in fact the first to adopt the practice of circulating notices for a whole week at a time instead of daily, a practice which the Commons did not adopt until 1865. The recommendation of the Lords' Committee of 1866 was a further step towards bringing the procedure of the two Houses in the asking and answering of questions more into line.

After 1867 this trend was to be gradually reversed. Whereas the Lords were to retain their freedom to enter into general discussions when questions were asked, the Commons eventually came to accept more and more restrictions affecting different parts of their procedure. These restrictions were the outcome, firstly of a new climate which prevailed in the Commons after the second extension of the franchise in 1867, and secondly of the emergence of the extraordinary figure of Charles Stewart Parnell.

VIII

The Irish and the Closure (1867–1881)

THE Representation of the People Act of 1867 was put through by a Conservative Government, in spite of the defection of three Ministers, and against the tradition that extensions of the franchise were a Liberal prerogative. It was also a much more sweeping measure than the one which the Liberals had planned and unsuccessfully promoted, for it added more than a million voters to the registers. An amendment moved by John Stuart Mill for allowing women to vote had been defeated, as had Mill's proposal for some sort of proportional representation, but the vote was now given for the first time to large numbers of working men in the industrial towns. Forty-two new boroughs were created, and the cities of Birmingham, Manchester, Leeds, and Liverpool each gained the privilege of being represented by three Members. For a comparable extension of the franchise country districts had to wait until 1884.

This transformation of the electorate, amounting as it did to the introduction of democracy in urban districts, soon had a pronounced effect on proceedings in the House of Commons. Governments and individual Members came to concern themselves with new fields of activity, and these new concerns were soon reflected in the putting of questions on subjects which Parliament in the past had seldom considered.

One new and extremely fruitful field for questions was that of popular education. The main crop of these questions came after the passing of the Education Act of 1870 associated with the name of W. E. Forster. This act provided for the setting up of elected school boards, and the activities of these boards and the inspectors of schools came under continual parliamentary scrutiny.

On 26th June 1873, for example, George Hunt, M.P. for North

Northamptonshire, asked Forster a question about an inspector in Wiltshire, who had refused to allow elementary school children to sing 'God Save the Queen' on the grounds that it was contrary to the provisions of the 1870 Act. Forster admitted that the ban had been imposed by the inspector but added: 'I need not say that he, like every other inspector, would from feelings of loyalty have had great pleasure in hearing the anthem sung, but he thought its singing under the circumstances contrary to the Act.'

The circumstances were that the children had been called upon to sing the national anthem during the hours set aside for secular as opposed to religious instruction. On the question whether the inspector's interpretation of the act was correct Forster commented: 'The opinion of the department . . . is that it is not so, and we have informed the inspector that he laboured under a mistake.'[1]

Nearly four years later, on 26th March 1877, Alderman John Barran, M.P. for Leeds, asked a question based on a report in the *Leeds Mercury* that a little girl had been dismissed from a school receiving a Government grant at Boston Spa 'for omitting to curtsey to the clergyman's wife in the street.'[2] He did not at first get a very satisfactory answer, and on 20th April he repeated his question.

The answer was then given by Viscount Sandon, the Vice-President of the Council, who said that the reports on the reasons for the girl's expulsion were contradictory, but that he had informed the managers of the school that 'expulsion should not be used as a punishment unless the misconduct of the child is of such a character as to make its association with the other children injurious to them.' This was not considered to apply to the girl who had failed to curtsey, but there were other schools within easy reach of her home, and Sandon had not thought it right to force the school which had expelled her to choose between taking her back and losing the Government grant. He expressed the hope that when the opinion of his department on expulsion had become known there would be no recurrence of such cases.[3]

The thirst for knowledge of the details of educational administration shown by Members, and the capacity of the Government's machine to provide the answers, were shown by a question put as early as 1871, when Forster was asked when the parishes of Headbourn Worthy, Otterbourne, and Colden Common would receive replies to their applications for grants towards building schools. He was able to answer the question in the most complete detail.[4]

Searching enquiries on educational matters were not confined to the administration of the 1870 Act. On 10th March 1871 William Wheelhouse, M.P. for Leeds, asked whether it would be possible 'for the Government to provide for and secure the education generally of blind and deaf-mute children,'[5] and three years later a question was even asked about happenings at a public school.

The question in this case was addressed to the Home Secretary, Richard Assheton Cross, and was put by Michael Bass, M.P. for Derby. A boy named Loxdale had, according to newspaper reports, been flogged by the headmaster of Shrewsbury school with eighty-eight strokes. The matter had been considered by the governors, who had decided that the punishment was not excessive, although they had asked the headmaster not to do it again. Cross answered that he knew no more of the matter than he had read in *The Times*, but suggested that the M.P. for Denbigh, G. Osborne Morgan, who was a governor of the school, might want to say something. Morgan admitted that five of the governors, including the Bishop of Manchester, had indeed decided that the punishment was neither excessive nor improper. He added that he himself had resigned from the governing body in consequence.[6]

Even the universities were not immune from questions about the management of their affairs. On 18th July 1878 Dr. Charles Cameron, M.P. for Glasgow, asked the Chancellor of the Exchequer 'whether it is a fact that during the past twelve years the Regius Professor of Medicine at Oxford has not delivered any course of lectures on medicine and that the Clinical Professor of Medicine has not given any course of clinical instruction.' Both these chairs were held by the same man, of whom Sir Stafford Northcote said in reply: 'The University are entirely satisfied with the manner in which Dr. Acland performs his duties.'[7]

The administration of the Poor Laws was another subject on which many questions were asked, and in contrast with the days of the Poor Law Commissioners, Ministers were now able to give full and accurate, though not necessarily satisfactory, answers.

On 11th March 1870 John Talbot, M.P. for West Kent, asked 'whether it is true that the carriage used for fever patients in the

Westminster Union is usually drawn by paupers; whether on a recent occasion the men who had drawn a patient in this carriage to the special Fever Hospital in Hampstead were found by the medical officer there in a state of complete exhaustion; and whether the Poor Law Board have any means of putting a stop to such a practice.'

George Goschen, who was then Chief Commissioner of the Poor Law Board, answered. 'I was,' he said, 'at first under the impression that the carriage in which the fever patients are so drawn was an ordinary carriage with a pole or shaft, and that the paupers were harnessed to it like beasts of burden. But it turns out upon enquiry that the vehicle is merely a sort of hand ambulance, like a water-cart for an invalid, but with a covering or top to it. The paupers receive sixpence a day for their labour, and there are always more volunteers for the service than are required, the fact being that they regard the day's outing and the sixpence as a rather welcome relief to the monotony of workhouse life. . . . The foreman who accompanied the three paupers on the occasion referred to asserts that he was not aware that the men were exhausted, although they asked for some beer when they arrived.'

This was not the whole of Goschen's answer. He went on to explain that the guardians at Westminster had informed him they were considering whether to provide a new ambulance, which would be drawn by horses, and he added, as an admission of the value of a question on such a subject: 'Of course, in the present, as in many other cases, publicity really means prohibition.'[8]

Two questions asked in 1873, one concerning the actions of a relieving officer and the other a sentence passed in a magistrates' court, also directed public attention to the administration of the Poor Laws. The first question implied that a child at St. Germans in Norfolk had died because the relieving officer of the parish had refused to allow proper medical attention on the grounds that the child's father was a member of the Labourers' Union. The relieving officer denied this, saying his grounds for refusal were that the father was quite able to pay for a doctor; the guardians supported the relieving officer; and the President of the Local Government Board said he did not therefore think he could interfere.[9]

The second question related to a sentence of one month's imprisonment passed by the Halstead magistrates on a man named

Samuel Mays for leaving his wife and family as a charge on the parish while he himself was in Durham looking for work. Henry Austin Bruce, the Home Secretary, said in answer that Mays had found work in Durham at a wage of one pound a week, and that out of this he had sent his family in all the sum of £1 16s. 0d.

'The offence,' Bruce went on, 'of leaving a wife and children chargeable to the poor rate is punishable by three months' imprisonment. The magistrates sentenced him to one month's imprisonment, observing that the prisoner was quite right to go away if he could better himself, but if he did so, he was bound to make arrangement for the support of his family in his absence.' Bruce's conclusion, which in the existing state of the law could be considered justified, was: 'It is not easy to decide these cases satisfactorily.'[10]

The Post Office was another department of the Government whose work gave rise to numerous questions. In the eighteen-seventies, most of these questions were concerned with the operations of the telegraph service, which had been taken over from private enterprise; but other new developments in communications also attracted attention.

On 13th May 1869 Charles Hambro, M.P. for Weymouth, asked the Postmaster-General 'if it is a fact that in certain parts of Wales the Post Office mails are now conveyed on velocipedes instead of on horses, and if this change has been found to add to the efficiency and economy of the service.' The Marquis of Hartington, who had accepted the office of Postmaster-General in preference to that of Lord Lieutenant of Ireland, denied that there was any intention of introducing a change in the general system of delivery. But he added: 'An experiment has been tried or will shortly be tried to ascertain whether in certain rural districts these machines can be used by post messengers on roads which are not very hilly or are otherwise adapted for the purpose.'

He went on in the manner which has come to be known as dead-pan: 'As the practice of riding or driving upon velocipedes does not form part of the examination of the Civil Service Commissioners, I think it will be necessary to allow the use of these machines to be optional.'[11]

In the mid-nineteenth century a competent bureaucracy came into existence for a variety of reasons, one of the reasons being that the movement in favour of radical reform had imposed more and more tasks on Governments. After 1867, when democracy began to be established as the British form of government, the demands made on the State increased steadily, and in time the bureaucracy was to become very large, very powerful and, eventually, propelled by a momentum of its own.

This growth of the power of the bureaucracy was a gradual one, and only its first beginnings were apparent before the last quarter of the nineteenth century. But even before 1881 Members of Parliament had begun to show increasing interest in the executive actions of the entrenched servants of the public.

One of the traditional functions of Members of Parliament had been to act as a counterweight to the executive when the executive had been identified with the Crown. In the eighteen-seventies there was a temporary revival of opposition to the Crown. The Queen's evasion of her duties caused public comment, and republican sentiments were expressed by figures as considerable as Joseph Chamberlain, the future imperialist, and Sir Charles Dilke, who was actually to hold the office of Under-Secretary of State for Foreign Affairs and would certainly have held much greater office but for his notorious refusal to deny a charge of adultery.

In a public speech at Newcastle-on-Tyne in 1872 Dilke attacked royal extravagance, as exemplified in the filling of such posts as those of the Women of the Bedchamber and the Clerk of the Closet, and suggested that the Duke of St. Albans, who received £1,500 a year as Hereditary Grand Falconer, should become 'Hereditary Grand Pigeon-Shooter in Ordinary at nothing at all a year.' A question was put to Dilke in the House of Commons asking him to justify and explain the republican speeches he had made, but it was disallowed. Dilke was not a Minister, and the question did not relate to 'any Bill, motion or other public matter connected with the business of the House.'[12]

Four years before Dilke's public outbursts, on 22nd May 1868, D. J. Rearden, M.P. for Athlone, had given notice of his intention to ask Disraeli 'whether it be true that the Queen has been compelled through delicate health to retire from England during the remainder of this session, and if so whether it is the intention of Her Majesty's Government ... to advise Her Majesty to abdicate.'

There were loud cries of protest when he gave his notice, and the Speaker, Evelyn Denison, ruled: 'The House has anticipated my decision by the expression—the indignant expression—of feeling with regard to the terms employed in the notice of the honourable Member. No doubt questions may be addressed by a Member of this House to the confidential advisers of the Crown as to any matter relating to the discharge of public duties by the Sovereign. But these questions must be addressed in respectful and parliamentary terms. The question of the honourable Member is not couched in such terms and cannot be put.'[13]

The Speaker's action, and the support he received from the overwhelming majority of the House of Commons, showed that in spite of Queen Victoria's temporary unpopularity, in spite of her outrageous political partisanship during the years when Disraeli and Gladstone were leaders of the Conservative and Liberal parties, the ancient belief that it was the personal actions of the Sovereign which Members of Parliament were expected to control was no longer generally held.

Instead watchfulness had to be exercised over the executive as embodied in a new form, the form of a bureaucracy presided over by Ministers of the Crown; although it was not until the twentieth century that the bureaucracy came to function on important issues in practice—although never in theory—largely independently of the Ministers.

The mistakes of the bureaucracy were exposed by questions when they occurred, and were looked for, even when they had not occurred, to an extent which was sometimes embarrassing to Ministers.

On 28th June 1870, for instance, a question put to W. E. Baxter, Secretary to the Admiralty, drew forth the statement that 'owing to a very strange mistake in the pension branch of the Admiralty a person who was discharged from the service by the Duke of Somerset in October 1861 received on 13th June 1870 a sum of £2,233 9s. od. as the commutation of a supposed pension, no such pension ever having been granted.' Baxter added: 'The Treasury and the Admiralty have instituted a thorough investigation into the circumstances of this extraordinary case.'[14]

This was a fair admission, but an indication of the testiness some Ministers were to show when the actions of their subordinates were too closely scrutinized was given by H. A. Bruce, when answering a question about police discipline in 1871.

The question concerned a policeman, who had been suspended for drinking in a public house with the mother of a prisoner on whose behalf he had given evidence. Bruce, who was then Home Secretary, appealed to the questioner, Roger Eykyn, M.P. for Windsor, to reconsider whether 'the discipline of the force can be preserved if questions of this kind are raised, and whether the time of the House is properly occupied in listening to them.'[15]

Some nine months later, on 25th March 1872, Bruce was again called upon to justify police action, and again doubts were expressed about the propriety of putting questions in the House on the subject. In this case the question was about the search of the premises of a cigar merchant in the Haymarket, named John Goodered, who was suspected of selling liquor illegally, and whose wife had been sick at the time the search was carried out. The questioner, John Yorke, M.P. for East Gloucestershire, referred in particular to the action of the police in 'causing a female searcher to search for brandy in the pocket of the wife of a clergyman who was with the sick person at the time.'

Bruce on this occasion justified the action of the police at some length, declaring that the clergyman's wife 'was, it was said, a constant visitor with her husband both at this house and at other houses of a similar nature and had assisted in the concealment of these liquors.' There was a heated argument about what and what might not be discussed with propriety, at the end of which the Speaker, Henry Brand, remarked: 'I am bound to state that the House of Commons in these enquiries condescends to very minute particulars.'[16]

This condescension to minute particulars, although it formed an ever-present threat, did not in fact unearth many scandals in the actions of the bureaucracy, for the Civil Service grew steadily in competence. The final elimination of privilege in 1870, when competitive tests for entry into the service were made compulsory by Order in Council, served to complete the establishment of the type of service which Sir Charles Trevelyan had foreseen, a service which, so long as it was not burdened with tasks for which its structure was not devised, could confidently encounter most forms of criticism and questioning.

The scandals in administration which questions revealed between 1867 and 1881 were rather in the administration of justice in the courts than in the actions of the executive servants of the Crown. On 13th July 1875, for example, Charles Ritchie, M.P. for Tower Hamlets, asked a question about a thirteen-year-old girl, Sarah Chandler of Spalding in Lincolnshire, 'who on a visit to her aunt at the almshouses in the town had plucked a flower from a geranium.' For this she had been sentenced to fourteen days in prison and four years in a reformatory. Richard Assheton Cross, the sympathetic and much-liked Home Secretary, answered that he had immediately discharged the girl from custody and expressed his entire disapproval to the magistrates.[17]

Less than a month later another question was put to Cross about a servant girl named Annie Divine, who had been sentenced to forfeit wages amounting to £3 10s. od. for unlawfully leaving her master's service. The reason she had given for leaving had been that 'her bed had been removed from a loft in which she had previously slept and put into her master's room at the foot of his bed, and she felt shame to undress before him.' This time Cross explained that he had no power to act, but he agreed that if the facts had been stated correctly he would again disapprove of the magistrates' judgement.[18]

With the growth in the efficiency of the machinery of government, the part played by individual Members of Parliament in initiating legislation after first asking questions gradually became less important. Samuel Plimsoll did, it is true, ask a number of pertinent questions to support the campaign for improving the conditions of merchant seamen which he conducted with unyielding vigour and a frequent disregard of the niceties of parliamentary behaviour. So too did a number of other Members who helped him to achieve his considerable successes.

Questions asked in the Commons also pointed the way to future changes in the divorce laws and the law on the subject of criminal assault. On 15th May 1876 Lt.-Col. Egerton Leigh, M.P. for Mid-Cheshire, asked the Attorney-General 'whether it is true that a woman, should her husband commit adultery, is not allowed to marry again, a husband not being prevented marrying again should his wife commit adultery; and whether, should such be the case, a Bill will be brought in to remedy the injustice to women.'

Sir John Holker, the Attorney-General, answered: 'By the law as it stands, a husband is enabled to obtain a divorce if his wife commits adultery, but a wife cannot obtain a divorce on that ground. She must go further and prove cruelty and desertion as well as adultery.'

Colonel Leigh did not succeed at once in persuading the Government that a reform was needed. Sir John Holker declared: 'I do not admit that the law as it stands works any injustice to the woman, and therefore I do not admit that a Bill on the subject is necessary.'[19] A more immediate success was, on the other hand, achieved after attention had been called by a question to an extraordinary case which came before the courts in 1880.

The case was one of an indecent assault on a girl of seven. The assault had been committed by a man named Broadley, and when the case was tried at the Leicestershire Quarter Sessions it was stated in Broadley's defence that the child had consented. The chairman decided that consent by a child of seven could not be admitted, but when the case came before the Court of Appeal, the court ruled that the chairman's decision was wrong. The sentence of twelve months' imprisonment with hard labour, which had been passed on Broadley, was therefore quashed.

On 10th June 1880 Peter Taylor, M.P. for Leicester, put a question on this case to the Attorney-General, Sir Henry James, who had to admit: 'There is no rule of law which fixes the age below which consent cannot be given.'

James went on to say: 'It would be well that on the first opportunity the Government should consider whether there should not be some fixed rule of law in relation to the age at which consent could be pleaded in assaults of this character.'[20] In the same session of Parliament, which ended less than three months after Taylor had asked his question, an Act was passed 'to amend the criminal law as to indecent assaults on young persons.'

An undertaking to consider whether regulations might be changed to allow children's games to be played in Hyde Park was also made when a question was asked about the prosecution of a boy for 'playing at rounders or baseball.'[21]

12

But the slow and long decline in the power of the individual Member of Parliament to bring about changes in the law had already begun. After the introduction of democracy in 1867, not only was the power of the bureaucracy steadily strengthened, but so, inevitably, with the need for better organization, was the power of the political party.

In the second half of the eighteen-seventies party divisions and antagonisms became much wider and stronger than they had been a decade earlier. So long as Lord Derby, who in any case preferred Homer to politics, continued to lead the Conservative party, and so long as Gladstone, in his premature and misleading phase of semi-retirement, could retain the state of mind which led him to note in his diary in 1875 : 'My prospective work is not parliamentary'—the political scene continued to be relatively peaceful. But with the revival and heightening of the personal conflict between Gladstone and Disraeli, and with the tremendous growth of party organization which the Act of 1867 and the introduction of the secret ballot in 1872 precipitated, politics became steadily more controversial and even violent.

The growth of the power of party soon began to alarm certain Members of Parliament. On 11th June 1877 Sir George Bowyer, M.P. for County Wexford, even asked the Attorney-General whether the Federation of Liberal Associations, of which Joseph Chamberlain was president, could be considered a traitorous conspiracy within the meaning of the Act of 1799. Sir John Holker answered: 'It is a matter of great difficulty.' But he made it clear that the Government had no intention of testing the legality of the federation in the courts.[22]

Party divisions, after the introduction of democracy, came to represent more and more faithfully a split within the public opinion of the country on foreign and colonial affairs. This split was between the elements which may, in simplified terms, be described as the Conservative imperialists and the Liberal noncomformists. In the eighteen-seventies the cause of one side or the other in this dispute was advanced more and more belligerently in Parliament, by means of questions as well as in debate.

A number of questions asked in 1873 illustrated the kind of issue on which one party came to feel more and more strongly, and which its leaders, and indeed the leaders of the other party, had to treat with circumspection.

These questions concerned the continued existence of licensed gambling-houses in Hong-Kong, although in 1871 an order had been made forbidding the licensing of new gambling-houses any-where in the colonies. In May 1873 Edward Knatchbull-Hugessen, the Liberal Under-Secretary for the Colonies, announced in answer to one of the questions on the subject, that when the order had been made in 1871 the only colonies in which there had still been licensed gambling-houses had been Hong-Kong and Heligoland, and that the licences in both these colonies had since been withdrawn.[23]

Six years later, when British troops were engaged in fighting both Afghans and Zulus, the strength of feeling on colonial issues had become such that a Member of Parliament could speak of Her Majesty's Government 'insulting and trampling' these peoples 'under foot.'[24]

The only war which occurred in Western Europe between 1867 and 1881, the Franco-Prussian War of 1870, did not cause a split in Britain along party lines between sympathizers with the one side and the other. Consequently the Government in power when the war broke out was not greatly harassed by questions on the subject.

An answer to a question about possible German aggression was, however, given by Disraeli on 12th April 1875, which ought perhaps to have been better remembered than it was. He had been asked by Owen Lewis, M.P. for Carlow, whether 'a menacing note' had been sent by the Prussian to the Belgian Government, and in answering he described the note as one 'of remonstrance' rather than menace. But he added that Great Britain was one of the powers guaranteeing the neutrality and independence of Belgium, and he concluded his answer by saying: 'If the independence and neutrality of Belgium were really threatened, we should do our duty to our Sovereign and not be afraid to meet Parliament.'[25]

The readily combustible moral indignation of the British people in the eighteen-seventies may not have been fired by the Franco-Prussian War. But less than ten years later the country was to be seriously split over an issue of foreign politics which was generally regarded as a moral issue. The immediate causes of this split were the war between Russia and Turkey and the news of the Turkish atrocities in Bulgaria.

The ferment the news of the atrocities aroused in Britain was perhaps without precedent: Gladstone's pamphlet on the subject, in spite of the verbosity and obscurity of his literary style, sold 200,000 copies within a month. The political bitterness engendered and expressed in Parliament was intense; and of the many weapons used by the Liberal opposition to the supposedly pro-Turkish policy of Disraeli, by no means the least effective was that of the parliamentary question.

Questions on the Turkish atrocities were mainly directed to two ends. One was to emphasize their horrible nature and thereby discredit the Conservative Government indirectly. The other was to show that the Government had been incompetent because it had based its faulty judgement on inadequate information.

On 19th March 1877 Walter James, M.P. for Gateshead, asked the Under-Secretary of State for Foreign Affairs a question about reports of outrages by the irregular troops known as Bashi Bazouks at Karatzova in Salonika, and in particular whether it was true 'that the male population were severely beaten, the women outraged and the community plundered of its entire movable property.' Robert Bourke, the somewhat easy-going spokesman for the Foreign Office in the Commons, had to admit that the Government had had no reports of outrages in the area mentioned.[26]

This failure to obtain reports had been the subject of a supplementary question put by Gladstone nearly a month earlier, when he had asked: 'Is it not the case that the Consul at Adrianople was unfortunately not in full possession of the power of bodily locomotion and was consequently not able to pay visits to the disturbed districts?'[27]

Gladstone received no satisfaction to his question about the unfortunate British Vice-Consul at Adrianople, Mr. Dupuis, and five days later, on 27th February, he reverted to the subject. 'Perhaps,' he said, 'the Government will be kind enough to ascertain whether the statement is correct, which I believe has been pretty freely made in and out of the House, that Mr. Dupuis was paralytic and totally incapable of visiting the district.' Sir Stafford Northcote, Chancellor of the Exchequer and Leader of the House, went no further than to say that he would make enquiries;[28] yet a month later the House was to hear of a journey made by Dupuis to a place ten hours distant from Adrianople in order to investigate outrages.[29]

On the other side of the House of Commons questions were asked, reasonably enough, about reports of the hanging of Polish doctors, who were Austrian subjects, by the Russians when they reached Sofia.[30] But the effective pressure by questions was directed against those whose support was given to the masters of the Bashi Bazouks.

The extent of this pressure was such that in March 1877 Sir Stafford Northcote, never the most urbane, and seldom the most skilful, of Ministers when questions were put to him, complained of questions on Turkey being 'made not the vehicles for asking for information but for conveying in an indirect form attacks or imputations on the Government which it would be far better should be made in direct debate or discussion.'[31]

The campaign against the Conservative Government on the moral issue associated with Turkish mercenary troops had extraordinary results. Gladstone was able to make an electrifyingly successful tour of Midlothian, and the Liberal Party acquired a clear moral ascendancy, which might have made its position unchallengeable for many years to come but for two crippling weaknesses which it had already begun to show. One was that it had failed, as it was to continue to fail, to marry old Whig happily to new Radical. The other was that it produced a logical policy for Ireland.

The effects, first of the extension of the franchise and then of the introduction of the secret ballot, on the representation of English, Scottish and Welsh constituencies was considerable. But on the selection and conduct of Irish Members they were even further-reaching.

Before 1872 Irish Members had made no serious attempts to obstruct the workings of the British Parliament. English Members had repeatedly complained that an excessive amount of time was spent on the discussion of Irish affairs. But apart from one or two brief skirmishes in the eighteen-fifties they had had no grounds for suggesting that the Irish Members were exceeding their rights or abusing their privilege of representing the interests of their nation.

After 1872 a new type of Irish Member, animated by a new spirit, emerged. The session of 1874 had been barely opened when Isaac

Butt, M.P. for Limerick, a man who, though for long the acknowledged leader of the Irish Party, was in many ways the embodiment
of moderation, moved an amendment to the Queen's Speech, which
began: 'We also think it right humbly to represent to Your Majesty
that dissatisfaction prevails very extensively in Ireland with the
existing system of Government.'[32]

This hardly disputable assertion was negatived on a vote by a
majority of 314 against 50, and signs of fight were soon shown by,
among other methods, a steadily swelling flood of questions on
Irish affairs. Within a year Henry Lopes, Conservative Member for
Frome, was saying of the Liberal Party that it was 'allied to a
disreputable Irish band, whose catchword in the House is Home
Rule and repeal of the union.'

Alexander Sullivan, M.P. for County Louth, a journalist, who
made a point of informing the House of Commons that he was not a
gentleman, put a question to Lopes about this statement,[33] and when
he could not obtain satisfaction in this way, raised the subject as a
matter of privilege.

In doing so he said that when the vote by secret ballot had been
adopted, 'many old gentlemen went out declaring that there was an
end to the constitution, that we were beginning to Americanize our
institutions . . . and that in the House of Commons the business of
the country would be conducted in language which would not be
tolerated in polite society.' He agreed that working men's candidates
had been elected, but said it was not from them that offensive
language had come.[34]

On 24th April 1877 a motion for the appointment of a select
committee to examine demands for an Irish Parliament to control
the internal affairs of Ireland was defeated by the comparatively
small majority of 417 against 350, for already many English
Members had come to realize that the House of Commons in Westminster was not necessarily the best place for the detailed examination of Irish internal problems. One reason for the rapid spread of
this belief was that just over two years earlier Parnell had first taken
his seat after successfully contesting a by-election in Meath.

Parnell soon allied himself with Joseph Biggar, the ugly but
courageous Member for Cavan, and by July 1877 they had become
so successful in using for purposes of obstruction the liberties
enjoyed by Members of Parliament under the existing rules of

procedure that a question was put to him about a speech he had made in London. In this he was recorded as having said that he and Biggar had been at work for two months, that the English Members would already be glad to be rid of them, and that if they only had ten men with them they could put a stop to all Parliament's work. This particular question was disallowed on the grounds that it did not relate to any Bill or motion before the House.[35]

A number of other Irish politicians did not agree with Parnell's and Biggar's methods. John O'Leary, the distinguished Fenian journalist, declared: 'I have not yet been able to see how Ireland is to be freed by keeping the Speaker of the English House of Commons out of bed.'

But the pleasure which their methods could afford soon became apparent even to others who were less seriously minded than Parnell himself. On 6th August 1878 Major Purcell O'Gorman, M.P. for Waterford, was called to order by the Speaker and asked to apologize for continually interrupting a speech by calling out, 'Hear! Hear!'

O'Gorman's defence was a novel one. 'I have a right,' he said, 'to cheer if I think proper, or to say "Oh! Oh!" at every comma, at every colon, at every semi-colon spoken in the language of this House. I have done nothing wrong. If I did do anything wrong, I am an Irish gentleman and know how to apologize for it. But I have done nothing wrong and will not apologize.' After a debate on the subject of his behaviour he was directed to withdraw for 'disorderly conduct and disrespectful behaviour towards the Chair.'[36]

By the time O'Gorman's colourful essay in obstruction occurred, the House of Commons had learnt that obstruction, when directed by as purposeful, as uncompromising and as commanding a character as Parnell, was not only a serious political weapon, but that it was threatening to bring the traditional parliamentary procedure into ridicule and disruption. In 1877 the debate on the South Africa Bill was stretched out to twenty-six hours; in the same year Parnell replaced Butt as president of the Home Rule Federation; in 1878 a select committee, which included Parnell among its members, was appointed to consider how public business could best be expedited; and when Isaac Butt died in May 1879, power such as no other Member of Parliament had ever acquired in four years of parliamentary life, without once holding office, rested with the man of

whom Sir Winston Churchill, in frequently quoted words, declared:
'In a nation preternaturally eloquent he could scarcely jerk out his
most familiar thoughts.'

The manner in which Parnell's power was used, and the lengths
to which Parliament was prepared to go to combat it, form the
story of the great parliamentary crisis which was resolved in 1881.
When the crisis was past, new forms of procedure had been adopted
whose consequences were to be felt long after the country now
known as Eire had ceased to send representatives to Westminster;
permanent encroachments on freedom of debate had been accepted
as necessary; and precedents of the greatest importance for the
steady erosion of the rights of Members of the House of Commons
to express themselves in any way at any time on any subject had
been established.

In contrast with the House of Commons, the House of Lords
retained its liberties almost untrammelled both in the debating of
motions and in the asking and answering of questions.

The chief procedural problem relating to questions with which
the Upper House was concerned continued to be that of the giving
of notice.

On 25th November 1867 Earl Granville referred to a 'recommendation made by the committee of last year that no question
should be put without public notice having been given upon the
paper.' He then said he hoped he was not acting irregularly by putting
a question without notice, because he did not want to initiate a
debate; whereupon he began a lengthy criticism of the Government
for its policy towards Abyssinia.[37]

A question put in this manner and on this subject was in fact
almost certain to lead to a debate. Less than a week before Earl
Granville asked his question, the Speech from the Throne at the
opening of Parliament had declared: 'The Sovereign of Abyssinia,
in violation of all international law, continues to hold in captivity
several of my subjects, some of whom have been especially credited
to him by myself, and his persistent disregard of friendly representa-
tions has left me no alternative but that of making a peremptory
demand for the liberation of my subjects and supporting it by an
adequate force. I have accordingly directed an expedition to be sent
for that purpose alone.'

One of the subjects held in captivity was Captain Cameron, whom the British Government had appointed British Consul, although how far the Sovereign of Abyssinia regarded him as such seemed open to doubt. Lord Stanley, the Foreign Secretary, when questioned on this point, said: 'I should imagine, Sir, that King Theodore's acquaintance with the duties and office of a British Consul was of a very vague character. I do not suppose he has even heard of an exequatur. There is, however, no doubt that Consul Cameron had been recognized by King Theodore in his capacity of representative of the British Government.'[38]

This recognition had not prevented King Theodore from writing a letter about Cameron in which he declared: 'So I said to him, "You are not the servant of my friend the Queen, as you had represented yourself to be," and by the power of God I imprisoned him.'

The other men arrested with Cameron were Dr. Blane of the medical staff of the Indian Government, Lieutenant Prideaux of the Bombay Staff Corps, and Mr. Rassam, the Assistant Resident at Aden, to whom Austen Henry Layard, the Under Secretary for Foreign Affairs, paid a warm tribute in answer to a question in the House of Commons by saying: 'Mr. Rassam is a gentleman by birth and education. He is a brother of Her Majesty's Vice-Consul at Mosul. I have had great experience of Easterns, and I never knew an Eastern so thoroughly unselfish, honest, upright and able as Mr. Rassam.'[39]

The expedition was a triumphant success, and when it had achieved its object, Disraeli felt able to declare: 'As a feat of arms it would be difficult, probably impossible, to find its parallel for completeness and precision.' The march of four hundred miles into unknown territory resembled, Disraeli declared, 'more than any other event in history that I can compare it with, the advance of Cortez into Mexico. But there is this fortunate difference between the Abyssinia expedition and the great invasion of Cortez—that we did not enter Abyssinia to despoil the innocent but in a spirit of justice, humanity, religion and civilization, and that we are about now to vacate the country in a manner which will prove to the world the purity of our purpose.'[40]

After the many expressions of congratulation and the conferring of honours had come to an end, Parliament heard little about Abyssinia. But some four years after Disraeli had delivered his panegyric, Robert Lowe, in answer to a question, revealed an interesting consequence of the campaign. This was that Her Majesty's Government now found itself *in loco parentis* to the son of the dead King Theodore, Prince Alamayon.

The boy had fallen into the hands of a certain Captain Speedy, who had taken part in the expedition. Speedy cared for him as well as he could, but when he himself was posted to Penang, he decided to hand the boy over to the Government. Lowe described the prince as 'an exceedingly bright, tractable child,' but lacking any elementary education and unable to read or write. The decision the Government therefore took was to send him to live in the family of the headmaster of Cheltenham College, who was asked to report from time to time on his progress.[41]

When Granville asked his question in November 1867, however, the success and the wisdom of the Abyssinian expedition had been open to doubt. In prefacing his question he had quoted the Foreign Secretary, Lord Stanley, as saying: 'It would be madness to throw a British army into an unknown country, in a tropical climate, far from the sea, very far from its reserves and supplies, without a full previous investigation as to the means of moving, feeding and keeping them in health.'

In these circumstances Granville's determination to put his question without notice was indicative of the reluctance which many Members of the House of Lords showed to adopt the new procedure. In declining to enter into any discussion on the Abyssinian expedition, Lord Derby pointed out that Granville had himself been a member of the committee which had made the recommendation about the giving of public notice.[42]

Four months after this exchange between Granville and Derby, the House of Lords, on 31st March 1868, debated the report of the select committee of the previous year. The opinion expressed by most peers who spoke was that questions asked without notice should be allowed, but that they should not be permitted to develop into debates. The Earl of Malmesbury, the Lord Privy Seal, undertook to draft a resolution which should embody this opinion.

Malmesbury's motion, which he made two days later, was 'that it is expedient that notice of an intention to ask a question should be given in the minutes except in cases which admit of no delay.' At the suggestion of the Lord Chancellor, Lord Cairns, this motion was modified to read 'that it is desirable where it is intended to make a statement or raise a discussion on asking a question that notice of the question should be given in the Orders of the Day and Notices.' In this form the motion was carried.[43]

Even this limited restriction on the freedom to ask questions continued to be resented. On 27th May 1870 the Earl of Carnarvon asked a question based on reports that numbers of armed Fenians had crossed the borders of Canada from the United States, the purpose of his question being to suggest that the Government would be wise to reconsider its decision to withdraw certain regiments from Canada.

The question was put to Earl Granville, who was then Secretary of State for the Colonies, but before he could answer, Lord Lyveden rose to say that Carnarvon was 'not simply asking a question of urgency,' but was 'entering on a question of policy,' and that he was acting irregularly in doing so without notice.

In spite of this intercession, Granville answered the question at length, and a future Prime Minister, the Marquis of Salisbury, then spoke of 'the somewhat futile object of bringing our proceedings more into conformity with those of the House of Commons.' He went on: 'If we are not able at any moment in cases of urgency to bring up any subject we think fit, we are in a position very inferior to that of the other House, where by moving the adjournment a Member may bring forward any matter deemed urgent. I, for one, do not intend to observe the rule.'[44]

Some four months later, on 15th July 1870, a sense of urgency and military operations again caused a question to be asked without notice in the House of Lords. The Earl of Malmesbury led up to the question by saying: 'Although under an order of your lordships I have no right to put to my noble friend opposite the Secretary for Foreign Affairs, without giving notice, any question with regard to the complications now existing between France and Prussia, yet I think your lordships will allow me to do so at a moment of such very great anxiety as the present.'

He then said that the 'public journals' had announced that France had declared war against Prussia and asked for confirmation of the news. Granville was unable to give him official confirmation, because Her Majesty's Government had not been notified that a state of war existed. 'But,' he added, 'I have no reason to doubt the truth of the commercial telegrams and Reuter's despatch.'[45]

In contrasting the rules of the House of Lords in 1870 with those of the House of Commons, Lord Salisbury was drawing attention to important differences which already existed and which were to increase greatly in extent during the next two decades. But whereas he suggested that in one respect the Commons enjoyed greater freedom of debate, the coming changes were all to be in the opposite direction, and even the particular liberty he referred to was soon to be whittled away.

Party antagonism, the representation of the more varied interests of wider sections of the community, and the tactics of deliberate obstruction combined to make it more and more difficult for the House of Commons to transact its business in the time available, and for individual Members to take the floor as and when they chose.

Already in the eighteen-seventies the ballot for motions made by private Members had become such a hazardous method of obtaining a hearing that Members were combining to shorten the odds. On 19th June 1876 Speaker Brand called attention to this irregularity and said: 'If two or more Members of the House holding the same opinion on some specific motion combine together to ballot for precedency ... such a practice is an evasion of the rules of the House.'[46]

By 1877 the habit of extending debates well beyond midnight had become so common and so inconvenient that on 13th February the Commons resolved that except for a money Bill no opposed business would be taken after 12.30 a.m. But even this sensible arrangement gave rise to complaints that it limited the opportunities enjoyed by private Members to bring forward measures.

On 27th July in the same year Sir Stafford Northcote successfully moved the first of a number of important resolutions designed to counter deliberate obstruction. One method adopted by the most belligerent Irish group had been to move every few minutes during a debate in Committee of the Whole House that the Chairman do report progress or that the Chairman do leave the Chair. Northcote's resolution was designed both to make obstruction by this method irregular and to facilitate the suspension of obstructive Members.[47]

When a newly elected House of Commons met in 1880, it became clear at once that the prospect for Gladstone's Government of carrying through controversial measures speedily was a bleak one. Even during the traditional exchange of courtesies accompanying the re-election of the Speaker, an Irish Member, Frank O'Donnell, M.P. for Dungarvan, said that in supporting the choice of Henry Brand, he spoke 'as a member of that third party in the House whose concurrence will probably be found to be more and more advisable in most matters of importance as session is added to session.'[48]

The threat was clear, and it was not surprisingly over a measure concerned with the maintenance of order in Ireland that the great crisis in the procedure of the House of Commons arose and was resolved. The measure was the Protection of Person and Property (Ireland) Bill.

At nine a.m. on 2nd February 1881 Speaker Brand returned to the House and took the Chair in place of the Deputy Speaker, Lyon Playfair. He then said:

'The motion for leave to bring in the Protection of Person and Property (Ireland) Bill has now been under discussion for about five days. The present sitting, having commenced on Monday last at four o'clock, has continued until this Wednesday morning, a period of forty-one hours, the House having been frequently occupied with discussions upon repeated dilatory motions for adjournment. However prolonged and tedious these discussions, the motions have been supported by small minorities in opposition to the general sense of the House.

'A crisis has arisen which demands the prompt interposition of the Chair and of the House. The usual rules have proved powerless to ensure orderly and effective debate.... A new and exceptional course is imperatively demanded, and I am satisfied that I shall best carry out the will of the House and may rely upon its support if I decline to call upon any more Members to speak and at once proceed to put the question from the Chair....

'Further measures for ensuring orderly debate I must leave to the judgement of the House. But I may add that it will be necessary for the House itself to assume more effectual control over its debates or to entrust greater authority to the Chair.'

The question was put and carried by 164 votes against 19. The closure had been adopted, and the dignity and efficacy of Parliament had been preserved.[49] But once resort had been had to the device of the closure to break the power of Parnell and his followers, all subsequent devices to curtail debate, which are regularly adopted by all Governments today and are equally regularly denounced by all oppositions as dictatorial, were logical and consequential developments.

With so many methods adopted between 1867 and 1881 to expedite business and limit debate, it was not surprising that new restrictions should also be placed on the right to put questions. The importance and value of the system of questioning were no longer disputed. Disraeli was voicing a common belief when in 1868 he described the asking of a question as the exercise by a Member of Parliament of 'one of his most important privileges.'[50]

But the very growth of the system began to cause anxiety, for the number of questions asked continued to mount steadily, although the increase between 1870 and 1880 was nothing like so rapid as it was between 1880 and 1885.

On 12th April 1870 R. B. Osborne, M.P. for Waterford, declared: 'The country has got a new House of Commons now, and I am amazed at the thirst for information manifested by it. Formerly there used to be three or four questions put on the paper by gentlemen connected with large places, but now there is scarcely a Member for the most insignificant borough who does not ask questions on matters of all kinds—one has even got up his enthusiasm on the subject of policeman's hats. An hour and a half are taken up every night by this thirst for information.'[51]

The next year, when the Commons debated a motion made by Gladstone for the appointment of a select committee on public business, Charles Newdegate also made a protest against what he considered abuses of the privilege of asking questions.

'There has been carelessness,' he said, 'on the part of the great body of the House on the subject of questions put before the commencement of the regular business of the House. . . . One of the objects of the Committee of 1861 was the limitation of the enormous number of questions on Fridays on going into Committee of Supply, but it seems to me that now this excess of questions prevails whenever the House meets. The House has virtually no control over the questions which are asked. I have heard questions put which are most unworthy of the attention of the House, and yet the House has no opportunity of expressing its opinion either for or against these questions.'[52]

These were individual judgements, and the House did not register any formal approval of them. Indeed, when a group of Conservatives formed themselves into what was temporarily known as the Fourth Party and became in the words of Sir Winston Churchill, the son of one of them, 'the most formidable and effective force for the purposes of opposition in the history of the House of Commons,' a new impetus was given to the multiplying of questions. In 1880 Lord Hartington stated that in four months John Eldon Gorst had spoken 105 times and asked 18 questions, Sir Henry Wolff had spoken 68 times and asked 34 questions, and Lord Randolph Churchill had spoken 74 times and asked 21 questions.

The Select Committee on Public Business of 1878 asked Sir Thomas Erskine May for his views on ways in which the number of questions might be limited. 'The only limit,' he answered, 'of which it is susceptible is that the question should be regular and fit to be put, and that is already secured. There is considerable vigilance exercised over the form of questions. Beyond that, I am not aware that any limitation could well be applied.'

The limitations which were in fact applied were on the nature of questions and the extent to which the asking of a question might be permitted to develop into a debate. The practice of moving the adjournment of the House, when a question had been asked, in order that the subject of the question might be debated had become more and more frequent after the abandonment of what Disraeli called the Friday 'conversazione.' Already in 1869 the Speaker, Evelyn Denison, felt obliged to say: 'Unless the privilege is exercised with forbearance, the result will be fatal to the successful conduct of public business.'[53]

The advisability of altering the rules so as to preclude unnecessary motions for the adjournment was carefully considered by a select committee soon afterwards, but it was decided to make no change. This decision was taken, as Speaker Denison informed the House on 13th July 1871, 'in the hope that discretion would be ever used and great forbearance practised.'[54] Yet between 20th July and 11th August motions for the adjournment were made, and debates followed, on six separate occasions in the course of questions.

One of these motions was made by Disraeli following an announcement which was clearly of major importance. In answer to a question about the purchasing of commissions in the Army put by Sir George Grey, the former Liberal Home Secretary, Gladstone had announced: 'The Government have resolved to advise Her Majesty to take the decisive step of cancelling the Royal Warrant under which purchase is legal. That advice has been accepted and acted on by Her Majesty. A new warrant has been framed in terms conformable with the law, and it is my duty on the part of the Government to state that at the present moment purchase in the Army no longer exists.'

This announcement was sensational enough to justify Disraeli's action. He declared indignantly: 'I must protest, Sir, against the First Minister making an important communication—one of the most important I have ever heard in Parliament—in answer to a question—I will not say a pre-arranged question.'[55] But the answers given to the other five questions which led to motions for the adjournment were in no way sensational.

When Henry Brand was chosen Speaker in 1872 in succession to Evelyn Denison, the Member who seconded the motion for his election, Peter Locke King, M.P. for East Surrey, expressed the hope that 'an alteration may be effected in the system of moving incessantly the adjournment of the debate and the adjournment of the House.'[56]

The next year, when Baillie Cochrane moved the adjournment after asking a question about concessions granted by the Shah of Persia to Baron de Reuter, he said that he had asked the Speaker if he 'might be allowed to take an exceptional course in doing so,' and that the Speaker 'with his usual courtesy assented.'[57]

Greater discrimination was in fact being shown by the bulk of Members, and the House remained reluctant to alter the rules. But on 27th March 1877 Speaker Brand did suggest that a change in the rules might be considered.

George Anderson, M.P. for Glasgow, had asked a question about the sale by the Egyptian Government of three hundred female slaves. These slaves had belonged to Ismail Sadyk Pasha, the Finance Minister, who had been banished to the Upper Nile region and had had his property, including his slaves, confiscated. The Egyptian Government shortly afterwards informed Her Majesty's

Government that Ismail Sadyk Pasha had died in exile, his death having been 'occasioned by congestion of the brain and accelerated by intemperance.'

Anderson moved the adjournment in order to have the opportunity of pointing out that the transaction had taken place at a time when 'the infamous Turco-Egyptian Government' was 'pretending to negotiate for the suppression of the slave trade.' The Speaker, in reluctantly agreeing to the motion, said: 'I am bound to admit that it is open to an honourable Member to move the adjournment of the House on putting his question. . . . The practice of putting questions to Members of the Government and receiving their answers to questions is highly convenient to the public service, and if motions for adjournment of the House are frequently put, this practice will have to be reconsidered by the House.'[58]

The Select Committee on Public Business which issued its report in 1878 considered this problem in detail and examined Erskine May on it. The answer he gave was: 'I remember the time ten or twelve years ago when it was a very common practice indeed to move the adjournment during the hour of questions, and certainly it is a very rare thing now, and it is much discountenanced by the Speaker and by the House. If it were thought fit, it could be altogether prohibited and on very sound principles. But certainly the evil is not so great as it used to be.'

Erskine May was speaking before the Irish assault on parliamentary practice had gained its full momentum. In June 1877 the adjournment had been moved during questions three times in ten days, twice for the discussion of Irish affairs. These motions had been accepted with only minor protests, but the next year, on 17th June, Frank O'Donnell gave some indication of how far, and for what trivial purposes, he might be prepared to take advantage of his privilege.

He put a question to Colonel Frederick Stanley, Secretary of State for War, in which he alleged that 'an officer of the Royal Tyrone Fusiliers at Omagh, who is also a grazier and dealer in livestock, having failed to sell in open market as fit for food a huge old sow no longer suitable for breeding purposes, succeeded in disposing of it to the meat contractor of his regiment.' The answer he got was sceptical and discouraging, and he thereupon moved the adjournment of the House.[59]

13

The Irish were not alone in making adjournment motions against the wishes of the majority of the House. Alexander Macdonald, M.P. for Stafford, did so in March 1878 in order to discuss the subject of accidents in mines, having first admitted that he had been unable, through the accident of the ballot, to raise the subject on an ordinary motion. He was reminded by Speaker Brand that the course he had taken was 'inconvenient.'[60]

The next year Edward Jenkins, M.P. for Dundee, was interrupted almost continuously when he moved the adjournment. He had done so after asking whether the Government intended to remove Lord Chelmsford from his command following the disaster which had occurred at the hands of the Zulus at Isandhlwana.[61]

But it was the action of an Irish Member in moving the adjournment in 1880 which caused the greatest indignation and convinced most Members of the need for some change in the rules. Once again the Member was Frank O'Donnell, M.P. for Dungarvan.

He had put on the paper a question containing an implied attack on Challemel Lacour, the newly appointed French Ambassador. When he rose to put the question on 14th June 1880 Charles Monk, M.P. for Gloucester, intervened to ask the Speaker whether the question was in order.

The Speaker, Henry Brand, seemed a little undecided. He agreed that O'Donnell would have been wise to consult him before giving public notice of the question, but added: 'I am not prepared to say that the question is irregular.'

O'Donnell then proceeded to ask whether Lacour was the man who in his capacity of prefect of the provisional Government in 1870 had ordered the massacre of a French battalion with the words 'fusillez-moi ces gens-là'; and who had been ordered to pay some £3,000 by a French court as compensation for his part in the plunder of a convent.

The question was answered by Sir Charles Dilke, who was then Under-Secretary of State for Foreign Affairs. He said there had been no such massacre, that Lacour denied ever using the words attributed to him, and that the convent had been plundered by some soldiers quartered there, Lacour himself having had no part in the affair.

O'Donnell replied that he could not accept this explanation, and said he would put himself in order by moving the adjournment of the House. This time the Speaker did not accept the motion, as he had so often done in the past, but made an appeal to the feeling of the House.

'I must put it to the House,' he said, 'whether the appointment of a foreign ambassador at the Court can properly be debated on a motion without notice for the adjournment of the House.' He suggested the proper course might be for O'Donnell to give notice of his intention of moving an address to the Crown.

O'Donnell began to speak again, whereupon Gladstone rose on a point of order. He ended with the remarkable motion that O'Donnell 'be not now heard.'

This immediately provoked Parnell, who, nevertheless, made a most temperate speech. He said he had no sympathy with O'Donnell's question, but pointed out to the Speaker that O'Donnell was 'only doing that which a Select Committee of this House on Public Business ... distinctly refused to interfere with, and you, Sir, in your evidence before that committee refused to recommend an interference with.'

As for Gladstone's motion, he suggested that on reflection Gladstone might realize that he was 'founding a dangerous precedent and one which at some time or other may be fatal to freedom of speech in this House.' Rather than let Gladstone's motion be put to the vote, he himself moved the adjournment.

Gladstone at this stage became rather muddled in his interpretation of the House's rules. 'I affirm,' he said, 'subject to the correction of you, Sir, that so far from being according to the rules of the House it is a breach of the rules of the House that any Member, after receiving an answer to a question, should rise and, except through the courtesy of the House and the belief that he is about to ask for further explanations, should proceed to discuss the subject matter of the question.'

A number of Members were ready to correct Gladstone on this point and even to remind him that motions for the adjournment had been made by Members of his own Government when they had been in opposition. One Member even asked whether Gladstone's own motion that O'Donnell be not heard had been in order. To this the Speaker replied that no such motion had been made for two hundred years, but that there had been precedents in the seventeenth century.

As the debate became more heated, W. E. Forster, Chief Secretary for Ireland, whom Gladstone once described as 'a very impracticable man placed in a position of great responsibility,' added some highly combustible fuel by describing O'Donnell's original question as 'contrary to the decencies of society.' To this O'Donnell replied by saying, not unreasonably, of Forster: 'He has not hitherto been a success in the domestic legislation of Ireland.'

Most speakers ignored entirely the matter of the appointment of the French Ambassador and concentrated on the procedural issue, which was becoming more and more entangled. One motion for the adjournment was defeated after another, Alexander Sullivan pointing out with delight that when the motion for the punishment of the printers of parliamentary debates had been made in 1771, the minority had divided the House twenty-three times.

In the end a compromise of a kind was reached. O'Donnell withdrew his motion and Gladstone withdrew his, and the reputation of the French Ambassador was left as it was.[62] But the outcome on the procedural issue was not altogether difficult to forecast. On 17th January 1881 Gladstone stated, in answer to a question about possible amendments of the rules, that the practice of moving the adjournment had 'undoubtedly attracted the attention of the Government as well as, I believe, the attention of every Member of this House.'

He went on: 'There is a great and, I fear, a growing inconvenience in the abuse of this practice. . . . It may be the duty of the Government to take rather a wide view of the whole subject.'[63] The way was open for the modern practice of conferring on the Speaker the power to decide, on grounds of urgency and public interest, whether a motion for the adjournment was acceptable.

The understanding of what constituted, in the words of Erskine May, a question 'regular and fit to be put,' was also gradually modified between 1867 and 1881. Under the direction of Henry Brand, in particular, less and less laxity in the framing of questions was permitted, and the Commons on the whole seemed to welcome the firmness he showed.

Even before Brand had been elected Speaker and before irritation with the irregularities of certain Members had become general, the

Commons were ready to show their disapproval of what were held to be improper questions.

On 22nd March 1870, for instance, H. A. Bruce protested against being asked, as Home Secretary, to explain his reasons for recommending reprieves for three convicts sentenced to death, but said he was ready to answer the question in that particular case. There were cries of 'No! No!,' whereupon he said: 'If that is the opinion of the House, I will not answer the question, and I confess I am thankful to the House in having supported me in my resistance to it.'[64]

Two questions asked on issues connected with the Franco-Prussian War also gave rise to rulings which could serve as precedents. On 10th March 1871 Hugh Birley, M.P. for Manchester, asked Gladstone whether he considered it 'desirable to prohibit by express enactment the exportation of arms and destructive munitions of war to belligerent states.' Before Gladstone could answer Edward Pleydell Bouverie, M.P. for Kilmarnock, asked Speaker Denison whether it was 'consistent with the rules and practice of the House to ask questions such as this.' He suggested the subject would more properly be one for a debate.

The Speaker agreed that Birley had 'passed the prescribed rule relating to questions in asking the opinion of the Minister upon a point of so great importance.' Nevertheless, Gladstone did answer the question to the extent of saying the Government did not contemplate any legislation.[65]

Some two months later Sir Robert Peel, who, like his more distinguished father, represented the constituency of Tamworth, put a question jointly to Gladstone as Prime Minister and Disraeli as Leader of the Opposition. The question was in fact an invitation to the House to consider 'whether this would not be a fitting moment to express its sympathy with France.' In explaining his intention Peel spoke of 'appalling events occurring,' and when he began a new sentence with the words: 'The finest moments of France are—' he was loudly interrupted. He tried to repeat his original question, but was told by Speaker Denison that he was 'transgressing the rules prescribed.'[66]

Another topic which seemed to invite irregularities was the extraordinary affair of personation known as the Tichborne case. The Tichborne claimant, Arthur Orton, had two outspoken champions in the House of Commons. One was George Whalley, M.P. for Peterborough, who was imprisoned for contempt of court for his activities in the affair. The other was Dr. Edward Kenealy, M.P. for Stoke. Whalley on one occasion summarized his views on the case by describing it as 'an instance of Jesuit intrigue or conspiracy.'

On 1st July 1875 Whalley was ruled to be out of order in trying to put the same question twice on the subject of the Tichborne case, Speaker Brand curtly stating: 'The question having been put and answered cannot be put a second time.'[67]

A little more than a month later Kenealy, by putting a series of questions designed to show the unreliability and criminal backgrounds of the witnesses whose testimony had helped to ensure Orton's conviction, incited even the moderate Assheton Cross to observe: 'I think the time has almost come when questions of this kind might be stopped, for the privilege of interrogating Ministers is liable, like every other privilege, to be abused.'[68]

Kenealy was not to be put off. On 5th April 1878 he asked Assheton Cross on whose authority he had stated a year earlier that 'Mina Jury, a witness against the defendant in the Tichborne case and who is now in penal servitude for several robberies, was not the same person as Mercevina Caulfield, who was sentenced to seven years' transportation for robbery in Dublin in 1847; and whether the person who gave him the information is still in the Government or receiving a pension.' He also put a number of related questions.

Speaker Brand informed the House that Kenealy had already been told that according to the rules his questions could not be put, and that his correct course was, if he chose, to raise the matter by a specific motion. Kenealy protested strongly, and announced that if he did not get an answer to his question he would invite the House to consider the communication he had had from the Speaker as a breach of privilege.

'I contend,' he said, 'that no one has a right to interfere with the freedom and independence of Members of the House, who upon their own responsibility put questions of an important nature upon the paper.'[69]

Kenealy carried out his threat. On 13th May he moved that it was 'a high breach of the privileges of this House to obstruct the freedom and independence of Members of Parliament in putting questions to Ministers.'

The Commons chose the simplest and most effective way of upholding the authority of their Speaker. When Kenealy made his motion, less than forty members were present, and the House was counted out.[70]

By 1881 questions were regularly put to Ministers in the House of Commons according to prescribed rules and at a prescribed time; desultory conversations arising out of questions had come to an end; there was already an appreciable volume of rulings to show what did and what did not constitute a proper question; and it had become clear that the House would not tolerate a motion for the adjournment in the course of questions except for the most compelling reasons.

Nearly all these regulations had come into being because questions had grown so greatly in number that steps had had to be taken to ensure that too much time was not devoted to them. Yet the system in force before 1881 caused in one respect a great and unnecessary wastage of time.

Before 1880 the words of virtually all questions put in either the House of Commons or the House of Lords were spoken. Although there was no official record, Hansard's reports of the proceedings, which served as such, were reports of words actually said. Occasionally Members suggested that time might be saved if the words of a question, which had already appeared on the notice paper, were not read aloud, but these suggestions were seldom encouraged.

On 30th July 1874 Mitchell Henry, M.P. for Galway, who had given notice of a question about the Irish judicial system, said he would not 'at this period of the session waste the time of the House by reading the question.' Disraeli described his forbearance as 'very considerate.'[71]

But a year later when George Whalley announced that his friend, Dr. Kenealy, could not be present to ask a question which was down in his name, and that he himself would ask the question without reading it, he was greeted with loud cries of 'Read! Read!'[72]

On 9th August 1875 an Irish Member who wanted to ask a question about prosecutions in Belfast without reading it aloud was treated in the same way;[73] and in May 1877 Whalley, who had put on the paper one of his questions directed against the Jesuits, was told by Sir Stafford Northcote that he must 'trouble the House by reading it.'[74]

Then on 8th July 1880, towards the close of a troubled session, Joseph Cowen, M.P. for Newcastle-on-Tyne, suddenly said: 'We have now been employed close on two hours in asking questions, and having been able to minute the time I can say that the reading of the questions has occupied above an hour. I wish to ask Mr. Speaker if it is absolutely incumbent on honourable Members to read their questions; because, if not, it would be a considerable saving of the time of the House.'

Speaker Brand replied: 'In answer to the enquiry of the honourable Member I have to state that there is no absolute rule on the matter to which he refers. It has been the general practice for many years for honourable Members in putting questions to read those questions, and it has been generally found to be a convenient course. There is, however, as I have said, no rule on the subject.'[75]

Less than a month later the Speaker said in answer to a number of questions from Parnell and others: 'It was formerly the practice for Members to read their questions and that practice has generally prevailed down to the present day. But I am bound to say that latterly the practice has prevailed of putting questions at such extraordinary length that I am inclined to think the House would do well to depart from it.'[76]

As casually and as accidentally as the first question in Parliament had been asked, the last stage in the passage towards the modern form of the parliamentary question was reached. The history of parliamentary questions since 1881 must be the subject of another study.

References

Quotations and references to debates are taken from the *Parliamentary History* and the *Parliamentary Debates*.

PREFACE and CHAPTER I

1. *Introduction to the Procedure of the House of Commons.*
2, 3. *P.H.*, vol. 7, c. 646–7.
4. *P.H.*, vol. 7, c. 687.
5. *P.H.*, vol. 7, c. 769.
6. *P.H.*, vol. 7, c. 713.
7. *P.H.*, vol. 7, c. 706–7.
8. *P.H.*, vol. 7, c. 711–2.
9, 10. *P.H.*, vol. 7, c. 707–8.
11, 12. *P.H.*, vol. 7, c. 709.
13. *P.H* , vol. 9, c. 189.
14. *P.H.*, vol. 11, c. 630.
15. *P.H.*, vol. 15, c. 371.
16. *P.H.*, vol. 18, c. 461.
17. *P.H.*, vol. 11, c. 753.
18. *P.H.*, vol. 10, c. 978–9.
19. *P.H.*, vol. 10, c. 980.
20. *P.H.*, vol. 10, c. 1008.
21. *P.H.*, vol. 14, c. 1318–26.
22. *P.H.*, vol. 13, c. 1155.
23. *P.H.*, vol. 8, c. 54–5.
24. *P.H.*, vol. 8, c. 501–2.
25. *P.H.*, vol. 8, c. 548.
26. *P.H.*, vol. 8, c. 550–1.
27. *P.H.*, vol. 10, c. 1013–9.
28. *P.H.*, vol. 10, c. 1091–1241.
29. *P.H.*, vol. 10, c. 1258.
30. *P.H.*, vol. 10, c. 1413.
31. *P.H.*, vol. 13, c. 486–504.

32. *P.H*, vol 13, c. 1197.
33. *P.H.*, vol. 14, c. 359–383.

CHAPTER II
1. *P.H.*, vol. 16, c. 720.
2. *P.H.*, vol. 21, c. 338.
3. *P.H.*, vol. 21, c. 319–20.
4. *P.H.*, vol. 19, c. 210.
5. *P.H.*, vol. 21, c. 616.
6. *P.H.*, vol. 17, c. 529–30.
7. *P.H.*, vol. 19, c. 326.
8, 9. *P.H.*, vol. 16, c. 476–85
10. *P.H.*, vol. 16, c. 487.
11. *P.H.*, vol. 16, c. 511.
12. *P.H.*, vol. 16, c. 606–7.
13. *P.H.*, vol. 16, c. 131–2.
14. *P.H.*, vol. 18, c. 837–41.
15. *P.H.*, vol. 18, c. 1431–46.
16. *P.H.*, vol. 19, c. 775.
17. *P.H.*, vol. 19, c. 834–5.
18. *P.H.*, vol. 19, c. 907–12.
19. *P.H.*, vol. 20, c. 25–28.
20. *P.H.*, vol. 20, c. 28–30.
21. *P.H.*, vol. 21, c. 469–82.
22. *P.H.*, vol. 21, c. 669.
23. *P.H.*, vol. 22, c. 963–6.
24. *P.H.*, vol. 23, c. 264–5.
25. *P.H.*, vol. 23, c. 687–8.
26. *P.H.*, vol. 23, c. 915–23.
27. *P.H.*, vol. 23, c. 923–5.

CHAPTER III
1. *P.H.*, vol. 24, c. 420–6.
2. *P.H.*, vol. 24, c. 426–8.
3. *P.H.*, vol. 24, c. 429–34.
4. *P.H.*, vol. 24, c. 595.
5. *P.H.*, vol. 24, c. 744.
6. *P.H.*, vol. 26, c. 1009–10.
7. *P.H.*, vol. 26, c. 1064–74.
8. *P.H.*, vol. 26, c. 1207–10.
9. *P.H.*, vol. 36, c. 1197–1202.
10. *P.H.*, vol. 28, c. 133–40.

11. *P.H.*, vol. 25, c. 1002–28.
12. *P.H.*, vol. 29, c. 33–55.
13. *P.H.*, vol. 29, c. 55–79.
14. *P.H.*, vol. 29, c. 217–8.
15. *P.H.*, vol. 29, c. 750–87.
16. *P.H.*, vol. 29, c. 849–66.
17. *P.H.*, vol. 28, c. 226–7.
18. *P.H.*, vol. 30, c. 1–60.
19. *P.H.*, vol. 31, c. 879–86.
20. *P.H.*, vol. 33, c. 464.
21. *P.H.*, vol. 33, c. 477–83.
22. *P.H.*, vol. 33, c. 483–9.
23. *P.H.*, vol. 33, c. 489–93.
24. *P.H.*, vol. 32, c. 1062.
25. *P.H.*, vol. 31, c. 206.
26. *P.H.*, vol. 32, c. 922–9.
27. *P.H.*, vol. 33, c. 1458–60.
28. *P.D.*, 1st series, vol. 1, c. 1565.

CHAPTER IV

1. *P.D.*, 1st series, vol. 1, c. 504–6.
2. *P.D.*, 1st series, vol. 15, c. 212–3.
3. *P.D.*, 1st series, vol. 15, c. 437–40.
4. *P.D.*, 1st series, vol. 14, c. 29–31.
5. *P.D.*, 1st series, vol. 22, c. 23–9.
6. *P.D.*, 1st series, vol. 28, c. 131.
7. *P.D.*, 1st series, vol. 28, c. 261–4.
8. *P.D.*, 1st series, vol. 15, c. 424–6.
9. *P.D.*, 1st series, vol. 16, c. 426–49.
10. *P.D.*, 1st series, vol. 6, c. 350–1.
11. *P.D.*, 1st series, vol. 2, c. 1146–7.
12. *P.D.*, 1st series, vol. 5, c. 808–35.
13. *P.D.*, 1st series, vol. 4, c. 29, 225–53.
14. *P.D.*, 1st series, vol. 16, c. 451.
15. *P.D.*, 1st series, vol. 14, c. 1021–8.
16. *P.D.*, 1st series, vol. 27, c. 462.
17. *P.D.*, 1st series, vol. 30, c. 113–5.
18. *P.D.*, 1st series, vol. 30, c. 545–83.
19. *P.D.*, 1st series, vol. 18, c. 193–240.
20. *P.D.*, 1st series, vol. 6, c. 178–9.
21. *P.D.*, 1st series, vol. 6, c. 253–84.
22. *P.D.*, 1st series, vol. 6, c. 286–342.

23. *P.D.*, 1st series, vol. 10, c. 685–8, 1173–8.
24. *P.D.*, 1st series, vol. 14, c. 392–400.
25. *P.D.*, 1st series, vol. 12, c. 655.
26. *P.D.*, 1st series, vol. 27, c. 430.
27. *P.D.*, 1st series, vol. 2, c. 325.
28. *P.D.*, 1st series, vol. 21, c. 1201.
29. *P.D.*, 1st series, vol. 23, c. 11–27.
30. *P.D.*, 1st series, vol. 23, c. 330.
31. *P.D.*, 1st series, vol. 5, c. 566–7.
32. *P.D.*, 1st series, vol. 9, c. 496–7.
33. *P.D.*, 1st series, vol. 22, c. 192–5.
34. *P.D.*, 1st series, vol. 27, c. 649.
35. *P.D.*, 1st series, vol. 29, c. 638–40.
36. *P.D.*, 1st series, vol. 3, c. 478–80.
37. *P.D.*, 1st series, vol. 9, c. 171–4.
38. *P.D.*, 1st series, vol. 6, c. 128.
39. *P.D.*, 1st series, vol. 6, c. 173–4.
40. *P.D.*, 1st series, vol. 20, c. 746–7.
41. *P.D.*, 1st series, vol. 16, c. 437–48.
42. *P.D.*, 1st series, vol. 6, c. 137–43.
43. *P.D.*, 1st series, vol. 10, c. 1159–60.
44. *P.D.*, 1st series, vol. 10, c. 1170–2.

CHAPTER V

1. *P.D.*, 1st series, vol. 21, c. 1166–88.
2. *P.D*, 2nd series, vol. 12, c. 1.
3. *P.D.*, 1st series, vol. 33, c. 1177–8.
4. *P.D.*, 1st series, vol. 34, c. 878–903.
5. *P.D.*, 1st series, vol. 35, c. 506–29.
6. *P.D.*, 1st series, vol. 37, c. 150–5.
7. *P.D.*, 1st series, vol. 40, c. 465–73.
8. *P.D.*, 3rd series, vol. 1, c. 334–5.
9. *P.D.*, 3rd series, vol. 7, c. 1144.
10. *P.D.*, 2nd series, vol. 7, c. 141.
11. *P.D.*, 2nd series, vol. 7, c. 146–50.
12. *P.D.*, 2nd series, vol. 7, c. 1123–6.
13. *P.D.*, 2nd series, vol. 7, c. 470–5.
14. *P.D.*, 2nd series, vol. 17, c. 393–5.
15. *P.D.*, 2nd series, vol. 17, c. 17–18.
16. *P.D.*, 2nd series, vol. 18, c. 69.
17. *P.D.*, 2nd series, vol. 18, c. 259.
18. *P.D.*, 2nd series, vol. 20, c. 4.

19. *P.D.*, 2nd series, vol. 20, c. 13.
20. *P.D.*, 2nd series, vol. 20, c. 727–892.
21. *P.D.*, 2nd series, vol. 20, c. 646.
22. *P.D.*, 1st series, vol. 36, c. 1205.
23. *P.D.*, 1st series, vol. 36, c. 1282–93.
24. *P.D.*, 1st series, vol. 33, c. 417–8.
25. *P.D.*, 1st series, vol. 35, c. 404–8
26. *P.D.*, 1st series, vol. 35, c. 503–5.
27. *P.D.*, 2nd series, vol. 10, c. 927–30.
28. *P.D.*, 2nd series, vol. 22, c. 1264–5.
29. *P.D.*, 3rd series, vol. 13, c. 618–9.
30. *P.D.*, 3rd series, vol. 13, c. 731–3.
31. *P.D.*, 1st series, vol. 41, c. 1621–8.
32. *P.D.*, 2nd series, vol. 2, c. 166–7.
33. *P.D.*, 2nd series, vol. 3, c. 1746.
34. *P.D.*, 2nd series, vol. 23, c. 713.
35. *P.D.*, 3rd series, vol. 1, c. 606.
36. *P.D.*, 3rd series, vol. 3, c. 1741–2.
37. *P.D.*, 3rd series, vol. 3, c. 1807–10.
38. *P.D.*, 3rd series, vol. 12, c. 1071–2.
39. *P.D.*, 3rd series, vol. 12, c. 1096.
40. *P.D.*, 1st series, vol. 37, c. 1780–1880.
41. *P.D.*, 1st series, vol. 40, c. 866–7.
42. *P.D.*, 1st series, vol. 40, c. 1177–82.
43. *P.D.*, 2nd series, vol. 15, c. 384–5.
44. *P.D.*, 2nd series, vol. 15, c. 1271–5.
45 *P.D.*, 2nd series, vol. 7, c. 1511–2, vol. 8, c. 377–8.
46. *P.D.*, 2nd series, vol. 22, c. 799–800.
47. *P.D.*, 2nd series, vol. 22, c. 902.
48. *P.D.*, 2nd series, vol. 22, c. 430.
49. *P.D.*, 1st series, vol. 41, c. 699.
50. *P.D.*, 1st series, vol. 41, c. 1391–2.
51. *P.D.*, 3rd series, vol. 10, c. 265–71.
52. *P.D.*, 3rd series, vol. 10, c. 443–5.
53. *P.D.*, 3rd series, vol. 2, c. 642–3.
54. *P.D.*, 3rd series, vol. 4, c. 356.
55. *P.D.*, 3rd series, vol. 1, c. 130–43
56. *P.D.*, 2nd series, vol. 8, c. 435.
57. *P.D.*, 2nd series, vol. 8, c. 439–41.
58. *P.D.*, 3rd series, vol. 5, c. 1274.
59. *P.D.*, 3rd series, vol. 5, c. 1212.
60. *P.D.*, 3rd series, vol. 2, c. 554.

61. *P.D.*, 3rd series, vol. 7, c. 263–5.
62. *P.D.*, 3rd series, vol. 10, c. 1065.
63. *P.D.*, 3rd series, vol. 11, c. 112–21.
64. *P.D.*, 3rd series, vol. 14, c. 505–18.
65. *P.D.*, 2nd series, vol. 10, c. 165–6.
66. *P.D.*, 3rd series, vol. 14, c. 935.

CHAPTER VI

1. *P.D.*, 3rd series, vol. 29, c. 3–5.
2. *P.D.*, 3rd series, vol. 23, c. 1228–48.
3. *P.D.*, 3rd series, vol. 73, c. 726–7.
4. *P.D.*, 3rd series, vol. 94, c. 215–6.
5. *P.D.*, 3rd series, vol. 33, c. 527–31.
6. *P.D.*, 3rd series, vol. 29, c. 679–80.
7. *P.D.*, 3rd series, vol. 35, c. 1336.
8. *P.D.*, 3rd series, vol. 15, c. 1012–3.
9. *P.D.*, 3rd series, vol. 24, c. 1294–9.
10. *P.D.*, 3rd series, vol. 36, c. 205.
11. *P.D.*, 3rd series, vol. 70, c. 1213–23.
12. *P.D.*, 3rd series, vol. 70, c. 1281–3.
13. *P.D.*, 3rd series, vol. 98, c. 329–40.
14. *P.D.*, 3rd series, vol. 19, c. 383–469.
15. *P.D.*, 3rd series, vol. 39, c. 979–82.
16. *P.D.*, 3rd series, vol. 45, c. 129–30.
17. *P.D.*, 3rd series, vol. 45, c. 197–9.
18. *P.D.*, 3rd series, vol. 60, c. 105–20.
19. *P.D.*, 3rd series, vol. 65, c. 7–17.
20. *P.D.*, 3rd series, vol. 65, c. 495–6.
21. *P.D.*, 3rd series, vol. 65, c. 588–9.
22. *P.D.*, 3rd series, vol. 60, c. 105–20.
23. *P.D.*, 3rd series, vol. 17, c. 383–4.
24. *P.D.*, 3rd series, vol. 17, c. 1101–4.
25. *P.D.*, 3rd series, vol. 44, c. 574–5.
26. *P.D.*, 3rd series, vol. 44, c. 720–1.
27. *P.D.*, 3rd series, vol. 52, c. 1155–7.
28. *P.D.*, 3rd series, vol. 53, c. 1208–9.
29. *P.D.*, 3rd series, vol. 58, c. 6–7.
30. *P.D.*, 3rd series, vol. 82, c. 1320–1.
31. *P.D.*, 3rd series, vol. 82, c. 1450.
32. *P.D.*, 3rd series, vol. 83, c. 454–8.
33. *P.D.*, 3rd series, vol. 84, c. 625–77.
34. *P.D.*, 3rd series, vol. 32, c. 846–54.

35. *P.D.*, 3rd series, vol. 33, c. 533–80.
36. *P.D.*, 3rd series, vol. 42, c. 623–4.
37. *P.D.*, 3rd series, vol. 42, c. 671–3.
38. *P.D.*, 3rd series, vol. 43, c. 1165–70.
39. *P.D.*, 3rd series, vol. 45, c. 588–600.
40. *P.D.*, 3rd series, vol. 21, c. 999–1002.
41. *P.D.*, 3rd series, vol 22, c. 192–3.
42. *P.D.*, 3rd series, vol. 94, c. 330–1.
43. *P.D.*, 3rd series, vol. 18, c. 825–7.
44. *P.D.*, 3rd series, vol. 18, c. 1263–81.
45. *P.D.*, 3rd series, vol. 51, c. 237–8.
46. *P.D.*, 3rd series, vol. 51, c. 1176–1217
47, 48. *P.D.*, 3rd series, vol. 101, c. 669–721
49. *P.D.*, 3rd series, vol. 33, c. 634.
50. *P.D.*, 3rd series, vol. 36, c. 635.
51. *P.D.*, 3rd series, vol. 54, c. 487–8.
52. *P.D.*, 3rd series, vol. 54, c. 779–81.
53. *P.D.*, 3rd series, vol. 55, c. 1156–7.
54. *P.D.*, 3rd series, vol. 81, c. 1348.
55. *P.D.*, 3rd series, vol. 26, c. 525–6.
56. *P.D.*, 3rd series, vol. 30, c. 310, 559
57. *P.D.*, 3rd series, vol. 31, c. 779–861.
58. *P.D.*, 3rd series, vol. 31, c. 930–9.
59. *P.D.*, 3rd series, vol. 40, c. 774.
60. *P.D.*, 3rd series, vol. 95, c. 527–30.
61. *P.D.*, 3rd series, vol. 80, c. 1232.
62. *P.D.*, 3rd series, vol. 56, c. 181.
63. *P.D.*, 3rd series, vol. 62, c. 376.
64. *P.D.*, 3rd series, vol. 74, c. 106–7.
65. *P.D.*, 3rd series, vol. 82, c. 1369–70.
66. *P.D.*, 3rd series, vol. 66, c. 197–8.
67. *P.D.*, 3rd series, vol. 95, c. 927–8.
68. *P.D.*, 3rd series, vol. 77, c. 530–42.
69. *P.D.*, 3rd series, vol. 77, c. 529–30.
70. *P.D.*, 3rd series, vol. 75, c. 1210–12.
71. *P.D.*, 3rd series, vol. 64, c. 789.
72. *P.D.*, 3rd series, vol. 86, c. 329–30.
73. *P.D.*, 3rd series, vol. 86, c. 811–15.
74. *P.D.*, 3rd series, vol. 86, c. 958–60.
75. *P.D.*, 3rd series, vol. 87, c. 123–9.
76. *P.D.*, 3rd series, vol. 34, c. 1268–9.
77. *P.D.*, 3rd series, vol. 34, c. 1269.

78. *P.D.*, 3rd series, vol. 35, c. 96–105.
79. *P.D.*, 3rd series, vol. 94, c. 189–90.
80. *P.D.*, 3rd series, vol. 25, c. 21–3.
81. *P.D.*, 3rd series, vol. 25, c. 464–9.
82. *P.D.*, 3rd series, vol. 28, c. 202.
83. *P.D.*, 3rd series, vol. 41, c. 189–93.
84. *P.D.*, 3rd series, vol. 73, c. 798–800.
85. *P.D.*, 3rd series, vol. 83, c. 164–83.

CHAPTER VII
1. *P.D.*, 3rd series, vol. 129, c. 644–7.
2. *P.D.*, 3rd series, vol. 147, c. 1225.
3. *P.D.*, 3rd series, vol. 111, c. 430.
4. *P.D.*, 3rd series, vol. 122, c. 126–7.
5. *P.D.*, 3rd series, vol. 180, c. 45.
6. *P.D.*, 3rd series, vol. 183, c. 172–7.
7. *P.D.*, 3rd series, vol. 102, c. 1327–8.
8. *P.D.*, 3rd series, vol. 142, c. 979.
9. *P.D.*, 3rd series, vol. 142, c. 1163.
10. *P.D.*, 3rd series, vol. 142, c. 1403–6.
11. *P.D.*, 3rd series, vol. 142, c. 1499–1513.
12. *P.D.*, 3rd series, vol. 129, c. 1425.
13. *P.D.*, 3rd series, vol. 131, c. 674–88.
14. *P.D.*, 3rd series, vol. 132, c. 993–4.
15. *P.D.*, 3rd series, vol. 133, c. 38–9.
16. *P.D.*, 3rd series, vol. 132, c. 999–1003.
17. *P.D.*, 3rd series, vol. 132, c. 1226–7.
18. *P.D.*, 3rd series, vol. 136, c. 1119–21.
19. *P.D.*, 3rd series, vol. 136, c. 736–46.
20. *P.D.*, 3rd series, vol. 136, c. 947–9.
21. *P.D.*, 3rd series, vol. 136, c. 1118–9.
22. *P.D.*, 3rd series, vol. 133, c. 589–93.
23. *P.D.*, 3rd series, vol. 136, c. 295.
24. *P.D.*, 3rd series, vol. 138, c. 403.
25. *P.D.*, 3rd series, vol. 140, c. 1725–6.
26. *P.D.*, 3rd series, vol. 146, c. 1043–4.
27. *P.D.*, 3rd series, vol. 149, c. 847–50.
28. *P.D.*, 3rd series, vol. 173, c. 1627.
29. *P.D.*, 3rd series, vol. 176, c. 337–55.
30. *P.D.*, 3rd series, vol. 119, c. 333.
31. *P.D.*, 3rd series, vol. 122, c. 792–7.
32. *P.D.*, 3rd series, vol. 148, c. 272–3.

33. *P.D.*, 3rd series, vol. 148, c. 748–52.
34. *P.D.*, 3rd series, vol. 149, c. 177–81.
35. *P.D.*, 3rd series, vol. 149, c. 463–4.
36. *P.D.*, 3rd series, vol. 150, c. 1915–8.
37. *P.D.*, 3rd series, vol. 150, c. 277–8.
38. *P.D.*, 3rd series, vol. 125, c. 429–33.
39. *P.D.*, 3rd series, vol. 124, c. 1045–6.
40. *P.D.*, 3rd series, vol. 125, c. 37–70.
41. *P.D.*, 3rd series, vol. 128, c. 604–5.
42. *P.D.*, 3rd series, vol. 150, c. 180–1.
43. *P.D.*, 3rd series, vol. 150, c. 147.
44. *P.D.*, 3rd series, vol. 150, c. 324–6.
45. *P.D.*, 3rd series, vol. 150, c. 404–12.
46. *P.D.*, 3rd series, vol. 150, c. 524–5.
47. *P.D.*, 3rd series, vol. 150, c. 693–1060.
48. *P.D.*, 3rd series, vol. 150, c. 1921–4.
49. *P.D.*, 3rd series, vol. 117, c. 343–4.
50. *P.D.*, 3rd series, vol. 123, c. 979.
51. *P.D.*, 3rd series, vol. 151, c. 10.
52. *P.D.*, 3rd series, vol. 176, c. 1388–90.
53. *P.D.*, 3rd series, vol. 176, c. 1468–9.
54. *P.D.*, 3rd series, vol. 179, c. 1342–7.
55. *P.D.*, 3rd series, vol. 181, c. 969.
56. *P.D.*, 3rd series, vol. 175, c. 779.
57. *P.D.*, 3rd series, vol. 171, c. 1315–6.
58. *P.D.*, 3rd series, vol. 171, c. 1432–4.
59. *P.D.*, 3rd series, vol. 184, c. 1384–5.
60. *P.D.*, 3rd series, vol. 184, c. 2140.
61. *P.D.*, 3rd series, vol. 186, c. 904–7.
62. *P.D.*, 3rd series, vol. 186, c. 1203–28.
63. *P.D.*, 3rd series, vol. 187, c. 398.
64. *P.D.*, 3rd series, vol. 105, c. 194.
65. *P.D.*, 3rd series, vol. 126, c. 1142–67.
66. *P.D.*, 3rd series, vol. 116, c. 1328–9.
67. *P.D.*, 3rd series, vol. 161, c. 2066.
68. *P.D.*, 3rd series, vol. 153, c. 817–21.
69. *P.D.*, 3rd series, vol. 156, c. 768–71.
70. *P.D.*, 3rd series, vol. 160, c. 1783–9.
71. *P.D.*, 3rd series, vol. 162, c. 1490–1528.
72. *P.D.*, 3rd series, vol. 170, c. 1303–15.
73. *P.D.*, 3rd series, vol. 139, c. 18–19.
74. *P.D.*, 3rd series, vol. 160, c. 1827–31.

75. *P.D.*, 3rd series, vol. 161, c. 342–4.
76. *P.D.*, 3rd series, vol. 188, c. 1065–7.
77. *P.D.*, 3rd series, vol. 143, c. 1035–7.
78. *P.D.*, 3rd series, vol. 147, c. 1819–20.
79. *P.D.*, 3rd series, vol. 148, c. 1083–4.
80. *P.D.*, 3rd series, vol. 147, c. 1291.
81. *P.D.*, 3rd series, vol. 102, c. 1097–1100.
82. *P.D.*, 3rd series, vol. 173, c. 1255–60.
83. *P.D.*, 3rd series, vol. 174, c. 250–86.
84. *P.D.*, 3rd series, vol. 174, c. 322–43.
85. *P.D.*, 3rd series, vol. 174, c. 396–402.
86. *P.D.*, 3rd series, vol. 150, c. 1438–9.
87. *P.D.*, 3rd series, vol. 150, c. 1596–1600.

CHAPTER VIII
1. *P.D.*, 3rd series, vol. 216, c. 1413.
2. *P.D.*, 3rd series, vol. 233, c. 499–500.
3. *P.D.*, 3rd series, vol. 233, c. 1542–3.
4. *P.D.*, 3rd series, vol. 205, c. 1582.
5 *P.D.*, 3rd series, vol. 204, c. 1770–1.
6. *P.D.*, 3rd series, vol. 221, c. 1036–8.
7. *P.D.*, 3rd series, vol. 241, c. 1843–4
8. *P.D.*, 3rd series, vol. 199, c. 1736–7.
9. *P.D.*, 3rd series, vol. 216, c. 834–5.
10. *P.D.*, 3rd series, vol. 216, c. 1163–4.
11. *P.D.*, 3rd series, vol. 196, c. 745.
12. *P.D.*, 3rd series, vol. 209, c. 141.
13. *P.D.*, 3rd series, vol. 192, c. 711.
14. *P.D.*, 3rd series, vol. 202, c. 1089–90.
15. *P.D.*, 3rd series, vol. 207, c. 1340.
16. *P.D.*, 3rd series, vol. 210, c. 594–6.
17. *P.D.*, 3rd series, vol. 225, c. 1379–80.
18. *P.D.*, 3rd series, vol. 226, c. 777–8.
19. *P.D.*, 3rd series, vol. 229, c. 667.
20. *P.D.*, 3rd series, vol. 252, c. 1608
21. *P.D.*, 3rd series, vol. 253, c. 428–9.
22. *P.D.*, 3rd series, vol. 234, c. 1571–5.
23. *P.D.*, 3rd series, vol. 215, c. 1871.
24. *P.D.*, 3rd series, vol. 245, c. 1587–8.
25. *P.D.*, 3rd series, vol. 223, c. 718–9.
26. *P.D.*, 3rd series, vol. 233, c. 107–9.
27. *P.D.*, 3rd series, vol. 232, c. 825.

28. *P.D.*, 3rd series, vol. 232, c. 1089–90.
29. *P.D.*, 3rd series, vol. 233, c. 551.
30. *P.D.*, 3rd series, vol. 238, c. 758–9.
31. *P.D.*, 3rd series, vol. 233, c. 323–4.
32. *P.D.*, 3rd series, vol. 218, c. 110–73.
33. *P.D.*, 3rd series, vol. 222, c. 269–70.
34. *P.D.*, 3rd series, vol. 222, c. 334.
35. *P.D.*, 3rd series, vol. 235, c. 684–5.
36. *P.D.*, 3rd series, vol. 242, c. 1380–93.
37. *P.D.*, 3rd series, vol. 190, c. 153–7.
38. *P.D.*, 3rd series, vol. 190, c. 180.
39. *P.D.*, 3rd series, vol. 190, c. 620–1.
40. *P.D.*, 3rd series, vol. 191, c. 1337–8.
41. *P.D.*, 3rd series, vol. 209, c. 1643–6.
42. *P.D.*, 3rd series, vol. 190, c. 153–7.
43. *P.D.*, 3rd series, vol. 191, c. 690–4.
44. *P.D.*, 3rd series, vol. 201, c. 1462–8.
45. *P.D.*, 3rd series, vol. 203, c. 317–8.
46. *P.D.*, 3rd series, vol. 230, c. 14.
47. *P.D.*, 3rd series, vol. 236, c. 27–82.
48. *P.D.*, 3rd series, vol. 252, c. 12.
49. *P.D.*, 3rd series, vol. 257, c. 2032–3
50. *P.D.*, 3rd series, vol. 191, c. 832.
51. *P.D.*, 3rd series, vol. 200, c. 1706.
52. *P.D.*, 3rd series, vol. 204, c. 182–92.
53. *P.D.*, 3rd series, vol. 196, c. 17–20.
54. *P.D.*, 3rd series, vol. 207, c. 1636–7.
55. *P.D.*, 3rd series, vol. 208, c. 16–48.
56. *P.D.*, 3rd series, vol. 209, c. 181–91.
57. *P.D.*, 3rd series, vol. 217, c. 803–4.
58. *P.D.*, 3rd series, vol. 233, c. 978–83.
59. *P.D.*, 3rd series, vol. 240, c. 1610–2.
60. *P.D.*, 3rd series, vol. 238, c. 1491–4.
61. *P.D.*, 3rd series, vol. 244, c. 907–24.
62. *P.D.*, 3rd series, vol. 252, c. 1902–91.
63. *P.D.*, 3rd series, vol. 257, c. 843–4.
64. *P.D.*, 3rd series, vol. 200, c. 420–2.
65. *P.D.*, 3rd series, vol. 204, c. 1764.
66. *P.D.*, 3rd series, vol. 206, c. 1264.
67. *P.D.*, 3rd series, vol. 225, c. 791–2.
68. *P.D.*, 3rd series, vol. 226, c. 554–5.
69. *P.D.*, 3rd series, vol. 239, c. 669–71.

70. *P.D.*, 3rd series, vol. 239, c. 1712–6.
71. *P.D.*, 3rd series, vol. 221, c. 966–7.
72. *P.D.*, 3rd series, vol. 223, c. 222.
73. *P.D.*, 3rd series, vol. 226, c. 771–2.
74. *P.D.*, 3rd series, vol. 234, c. 495–6.
75. *P.D.*, 3rd series, vol. 253, c. 1920.
76. *P.D.*, 3rd series, vol. 255, c. 309–11.

Index

Abbot, Charles, 69, 70, 71
Abercromby, James, 104, 126
Aberdeen, Earls of, 95, 117, 136, 139, 162
Abyssinian expedition, 184, 185, 186
Accounts, improved form of, 67
Addington, Henry, 31, 48, 56, 57, 62
Adjournment, motion for, 155–9, 187, 191–5
Administration: enquiries into, 55–9, 63, 132; faults in, 96, 114, 133, 176; reforms in, 67; of Army, 111. *See* Civil Service
Aggravated Assaults Act, 150
Aislabie, Sir John, 12
Althorp, Lord, 85, 86, 91, 99, 107, 115, 127
America, 35, 38, 39, 42, 44, 62, 135, 136
Anderson, George, 192–3
Anglesea, Earl of, 24
Anstey, Chisholm, 142–3
Answers: delayed, 58; effect on public of, 89–91; impromptu, 58, 114; Ministers to answer only once, 146–8; publication of, 54; supply of information for, 66, 131, 170. *See* Information
Appeals, 16
Appointments, 58, 112, 163
Arguments, 126, 160, 161, 163
Ashburton, Lord, 109
Ashley, Lord, 102
Assault, criminal, 176–7
Attwood, Thomas, 83, 107

Bagehot, Walter, 129
Bagwell, John, 152
Baillie, H. J., 145, 148
Ballot, secret, 21, 104, 178, 181
Barran, Alderman John, 169
Barré, Colonel Isaac, 30, 36, 37, 38
Barrington, Lord, 37, 38
Bass, Michael, 170
Bastard, John, 61
Baxter, W. E., 174
Bedford, Duke of, 53, 54
Bennet, Henry, 59–60, 79, 80
Berkeley, Craven, 139
Berkeley, Francis, 141
Berkeley, Grantley, 125
Bethell, Sir Richard, 136
Biggar, Joseph, 182–3
Birley, Hugh, 197
Blandford, Marquis of, 84
Boswell, James, 32
Bowring, Dr., 118
Bowyer, Sir George, 178
Bragge, Charles, 57
Brand, Henry, 175, 188, 189, 192, 194, 196, 198, 200
Bright, John, 122, 131, 137, 144, 145, 148, 149, 156
Bristol, Earl of, 64
British nationals, treatment of, 142–4
Brooke, Rajah, 165, 166
Brougham, Henry, 75, 76, 82, 85, 93, 94, 99, 100, 113, 128
Broughton, Lord, 108, 145
Bruce, Henry Austin, 172, 175, 197
Brudenell, Lord. *See* Cardigan, Earl of

213